200

A-level Study Guide

Religious Studies

Sarah K. Tyler

Gordon Reid

Series Consultants: Geoff Black and Stuart Wall

Pearson Education Limited

Edinburgh Gate, Harlow

Essex CM20 2JE, England

and Associated Companies throughout the world

© Pearson Education Limited 2005

British Library Cataloguing in Publication Data

A catalogue entry for this title is available from the British Library.

ISBN 1405-81051-3

Set by 35 in Univers, Cheltenham

Printed by Ashford Colour Press, Hants

Christianity

In this chapter, Christian teachings on the nature of God and Jesus Christ are examined, beginning with the qualities of God – an omnipotent being who creates, suffers and offers a personal relationship to believers. It then moves to the person of Christ – including the notion of the Trinity and Christological themes of sonship, messiahship and the nature of Christ's sacrifice and concluding with an examination of the many efforts to establish what Christ was actually like, through the quest for the historical Jesus. The chapter then covers the most important aspects of Christian doctrine and practice, beginning with the nature of worship, the sacraments and the significance of prayer, Eucharist and baptism. It moves on into matters of quite complex doctrine, such as atonement, sin, grace and spirituality, and examines the controversial notion of justification by faith before moving on to examime different movements within Christianity in the modern world: liberation theology, black theology, feminist theology and the poor. Finally, this chapter examines the nature of the Church itself and the people within it.

Exam themes

→ God the creator
→ Omnipotence
→ A personal God
→ The God who suffers
→ The Trinity
→ Christology
→ The person of Jesus
→ The quest for the historical Jesus
→ The nature of worship
→ The significance of the sacraments
→ Baptism
→ The Eucharist
→ The nature of atonement
→ Sin and grace
→ Justification through faith
→ Liberation and black theology
→ Feminist theology
→ Ordination and laity
→ Saints, orthodoxy and spirituality
→ The views of scholars

Topic checklist

AS ○ A2 ●	OCR	AQA	EDEXCEL
Christian beliefs about God			○ ●
Christian beliefs about Jesus Christ			●
The quest for the historical Jesus			●
Christian practice		○	
Christian doctrine	●	○ ●	●
Christianity and the wider world	○ ●		●
The Christian Church	○ ●	○ ●	○ ●

Christian beliefs about God

The Christian view of God comes from the Bible. He is the creator of all things and humanity's redeemer. He is shown as the all-powerful, all-knowing, eternal God of love, grace, providence, morality and truth.

Terminology

In the Nicene Creed the Christian view states that God created the universe 'ex nihilo' ('out of nothing').

Checkpoint 1

What does redeemer mean?

Useful quotations

'So God created man in his own image, in the image of God he created him; male and female he created them' (Genesis 1 v. 27).

Terminology

Humanity is said to hold the world in stewardship for God – that is, humanity must look after the world thoughtfully. Humanity does not own the world.

Useful quotations

'On account of divine omnipotence, God is not now able to do everything. By exercising the divine power, God has limited options' (A. McGrath (ed.) The Blackwell Companion to Modern Christian Thought (2000)).

God the creator

The theme of God as creator is an important one throughout the Old Testament, not only in Genesis, but also in the Prophets and in the books of wisdom such as Job and the Psalms. The important concepts are:

→ God is the creator and sustainer of the universe.
→ God created order out of formless chaos. It is not creation that is holy, but God the creator.
→ God has authority over his creation.
→ Humans having stewardship over creation.
→ Humans are required to look after the world in a responsible manner.
→ God's creation is good.
→ Creation is no longer perfect, due to human sin.
→ Human beings are made in the image of God.

There are several different viewpoints as to how God made the universe:

→ *Emanation* – creation was an overflowing of God's creative energy. Creation comes ('emanates') from God and shows his divine nature.
→ *Construction* – God is the craftsman who constructs the world with planning and purpose.
→ *Artistic expression* – creation is the 'handiwork of God' – a work of art and beauty which expresses the love of God.

The omnipotence of God

Christians believe in an omnipotent or almighty God. Within the realms of logic, omnipotence means that God can do anything. However, there are problems, for God cannot act against his own nature. Thus:

→ If God decides to always act in a loving way, then he cannot do evil. God cannot sin.
→ Once God established the order of creation, he had to act within those boundaries.
→ This is the notion of divine self-limitation. The supreme example of divine self-limitation was when God chose to become human as Jesus Christ.

The personal God

God is said to be loving and trustworthy and to offer a personal relationship, rather like a parent and a child, with those who love him. The concept of a personal God is an *analogy*. To say that God is like a person does not mean that he is human, but instead it shows that God has the ability and willingness to relate to his people. Scholars are divided over this issue:

→ **Spinoza** argued that there could not be a personal two-way relationship between humans and God because such a relationship would require God to change in his being. He cannot do this, since he is perfect and this perfection could not be altered.

→ **Buber** disagreed, saying a person is able to become aware of and to 'know' God, just as God knows and is aware of them.

A suffering God

The biblical teaching is of a God who is both personal and loving and he feels the pain of human suffering. In the Old Testament God shares in the suffering of the people of Israel, and in the New Testament Christ suffered and died on the Cross. This causes controversy among scholars:

→ **Philo** argued that God was perfect and unchangeable and therefore could not suffer.

→ **Aquinas** believed that love implied being vulnerable and that God could therefore never be truly affected by human sorrow.

→ **Spinoza** said that if God was truly perfect then he could never change or experience suffering.

→ **Martin Luther** argued that God did suffer in the humiliation of the Cross – what he called '*a crucified God*'.

→ **Moltmann** said that a truly perfect God must be able to experience suffering. He chooses suffering because that is the nature of his love.

Terminology

The word person comes from the Latin 'persona', which means 'a mask'.

Useful quotations

'God, strictly speaking, loves no one nor hates anyone. For God is affected with no emotion of joy or sadness, and consequently loves no one nor hates anyone' (Benedict Spinoza, *Ethics* (2001)).
'A God who cannot suffer is poorer than any human. For a God who is incapable of suffering is a being who cannot be involved . . . the one who cannot suffer cannot love either. So he is also a loveless being' (Jurgun Moltmann, *The Crucified God* (2001)).

Checkpoint 2

What is divine self-limitation?

Examiner's secrets

Don't retell the creation story and make sure you can refer to the text and the views of scholars with accuracy.

Exam question   answer: page 18

Consider what is meant by the concept of a personal God.   (30 mins)

Christian beliefs about Jesus Christ

Christians believe that Jesus Christ is the Son of God. The study of the nature of Christ is crucial to understanding the importance of this notion.

Christ and the Trinity

The doctrine of the Trinity is the notion of one God in three persons – God the Father, God the Son and God the Holy Spirit.

→ Human redemption is achieved when the three persons of the Godhead perform their distinct tasks yet act together in one unity. Father, Son and Spirit are all equal within the Trinity.
→ Augustine identified the Son (Christ) with the wisdom of God (*sapientia*) and the Spirit with the love of God (*caritas*).
→ The Spirit binds humanity to God and also binds together the persons of the Trinity.

Christology

Christology is the study of the person of Jesus Christ. It is concerned with the spiritual and theological aspects, rather than the historical facts of the life of Jesus – who exactly was Jesus? The most important issues are:

→ Jesus Christ makes God known.
→ Jesus Christ is God in human form.
→ Jesus reveals God to humanity.
→ Jesus brings salvation.
→ Salvation comes from the life, death and resurrection of Christ.
→ Jesus is the Messiah.
→ Jesus is the Son of God.
→ Jesus is the Son of Man, whose coming will bring divine judgement upon humanity.
→ Jesus is God.
→ He performs the tasks that God performs.
→ He saves people from their sins.
→ He is the Saviour.
→ To have seen Jesus is to have seen God the Father.

The debate over the person of Christ

Scholars are divided as to the true nature of the person of Christ. It centres on the question of just how 'human' Christ really was. The main views were:

→ **Docetists** argued that Christ was totally divine and that his humanity was just appearance.
→ **Justin Martyr** said Christ was the wisdom (logos) of God in human form.

→ **Origen** said that the human soul of Christ was united with the logos.
→ **Arius** argued that God was the only source of created things and that Christ was created by God with superior status to the rest of creation, but not the same status as God.
→ **Athanasius** highlighted the unity of the Father and Son. He said that only God saves and that, since Jesus saves, Jesus must be God.

The debate boiled down to two points – either Jesus was:

→ 'of like substance' with the Father (**homoiousios**); or
→ 'of the same substance' (**homoousios**).

The Nicene Creed of 381 CE settled on the term 'of the same substance' as the Father. Jesus Christ is God incarnate. The Council of Chalcedon in 451 CE declared that Jesus Christ was both truly human and truly divine. However, there are differing views on how the two natures relate:

→ Christ is an example – he acts as a living example of how to live the godly life.
→ Christ is a moral teacher and, in his death, shows self-giving love.
→ He has a deep inner or spiritual relationship with God that the believer should seek to have as well.
→ Christ is a symbolic presence – he is a symbol of how humanity can truly achieve salvation.
→ Christ as mediator – he acts between God and humanity.
→ **Brunner** said that faith was a personal encounter with God, who meets his people in Christ.
→ Christ was a unique channel through which God's redeeming work could be made available to humanity.
→ **Calvin** said that true knowledge of God and salvation comes from Christ.
→ Christ had to become human in order to offer himself as a ransom for sin – through his sacrifice, he broke the power of sin and death over the human race.
→ God could become incarnate as the Son, yet also remain, as Father, in heaven.
→ Christ was a prophet, a king and a priest who offered himself as a ransom for humanity's sin.

Terminology

Logos means wisdom and refers to the wisdom or word of God. Christ is sometimes seen as the word of God in human form.

Terminology

The argument between Arius and Athanasius was known as the Arian Controversy.

Checkpoint 2

What is a mediator?

Useful quotations

'The Word became flesh and made his dwelling among us. We have seen his glory, the glory of the One and Only, who came from the Father, full of grace and truth'. (John 1:14).

Examiner's secrets

These concepts have deep theological meaning. Practise writing them so that you know exactly what they mean and why they are significant. You can't bluff this one!

Exam question   answer: page 18

Examine and comment on the views of scholars concerning the nature of Christ.   (45 mins)

The quest for the historical Jesus

The quest for the historical Jesus is a scholarly movement that seeks to understand the historical figure of Jesus, rather than the Christ of faith that the Gospels proclaim. The view is that the early Church had an unreal picture of Jesus – the reality was that he was a Jewish peasant leader, concerned with the overthrow of Israel's enemies.

Background

The quest for the historical Jesus was centred on the idea that there was a difference between the historical figure of Jesus, who was a religious teacher, and the 'Christ of Faith' figure that had been developed by the Christian Church. It was thought that by going back to the historical Jesus and taking away the dogmas added by the church, a more credible version of Christ would result.

The quest was inspired by the work of **Hermann Samuel Reimarus**. He argued that:

→ The early Christians may have tampered with the Gospel accounts of Jesus.
→ There was a real difference between the beliefs of Jesus and those of the early Church.
→ Jesus was a political figure who led a popular rising against Rome and was shattered by his failure.
→ The disciples invented the concept of 'spiritual redemption' in place of what he said was Jesus' message of a liberated Israel.
→ They invented the idea of the resurrection to cover up Jesus' death.

At the beginning of the twentieth century, new ideas arose. Three differing critiques appeared in the thinking of scholars:

→ *Apocalyptic critique*, associated with **Weiss** and **Schweitzer**. It is the belief that Jesus' ministry was determined by his apocalyptic outlook. Christ is a remote figure, whose hopes and expectations came to nothing.
→ *Sceptical critique*, associated with **Wrede**. He suggested that, in the Gospel of Mark, theology had been imposed on history, creating an unreal picture.
→ *Dogmatic critique* was highlighted by **Kahler**, who said that what was important was not who Christ was, but what he presently does for believers. What is important is the Christ of faith, rather than the Jesus of history.

Terminology

The 'Christ of Faith' is the view of Jesus as Son of God and Saviour.

Background

The Gospels do make reference to the human side of Jesus. For instance, he ate and drank, he wept and experienced pain and doubt.

Background

The early Church may have tampered with the original Gospels in order to present a picture of Jesus that suited the difficult times the believers were facing, particularly Roman persecution.

Checkpoint 1

What is spiritual redemption?

The new quests

Many scholars felt that the quest for a historical reconstruction of the life of Jesus was a waste of time, and developed new approaches to the study of the person of Jesus:

→ **Bultmann** argued that the Cross and resurrection were historical actions, but had to be understood by faith – they are divine acts of judgement and salvation. He said that all that could be known about the historical Jesus was the fact that he lived.

→ **Kasemann** claimed that the Gospel writers did give historical information alongside theological truths. He said that the important thing was to see the links between the preaching of Jesus and the later preaching about Jesus.

→ **Jeremias** and **Bornkamm** stressed the continuity between the historical Jesus and the Christ of faith and the ongoing link between the preaching of Jesus himself, and the preaching about Jesus in the Church.

→ **Crossan** argued that Jesus was a poor Jewish peasant who broke down social conventions.

→ **E.P. Sanders** claimed that Jesus was a prophet who was concerned with the final restoration of Israel.

Useful quotations

'The Jesus of the "life of Jesus" movement is merely the modern brainchild of the human imagination' (Martin Kahler, *The So-Called Historical Jesus and the Historical Biblical Christ* (1988)).

Checkpoint 2

What does apocalyptic mean?

Examiner's secrets

This is a difficult area, and you can't use guesswork. You must know the scholars as well as the biblical material. Don't take shortcuts!

Exam question   answer: page 18

To what extent was the quest for the historical Jesus a failure?   (40 mins)

Christian practice

God is at the heart of the Christian faith and worship is humanity's response to God. God reveals himself to humanity, and humanity responds.

Worship

God makes himself known in a number of ways:

→ through creation;
→ through scripture;
→ through Jesus Christ and the Holy Spirit.

Worship depends on knowledge of God, which helps the worshipper to know how to worship God.

There are different aspects of worship, but the central message is the same:

→ God alone is to be worshipped.
→ He is to be worshipped and served with the believer's whole being.
→ Worship requires fellowship and evangelism.
→ Worship can be corporate or personal.
→ The Holy Spirit fills the hearts and minds of believers.

Liturgical worship takes place in the church. Its characteristics include:

→ The reading of the Scriptures.
→ The preaching of a sermon.
→ Prayers.
→ The confession of faith through the recital of the creeds.
→ A formal structure of music, prayer and preaching.

Sacraments

A sacrament is a rite or ceremony that acts as an outward sign of an inner, spiritual truth. Sacraments express the way believers understand the fundamental relationship between God, Christ, the Church, humanity and creation. The Roman Catholic Church has seven sacraments organised by Peter Lombard and pronounced orthodox by the Fourth Lateran Council. They were confirmed by Aquinas in his *Summa Theoloigca*.

→ Baptism.
→ Eucharist.

These two are the most important, and are applicable to all Catholics. Some believe that salvation is dependent on receiving these sacraments.

→ Confirmation (after first Communion for Catholics).
→ Marriage (for those not called to celibacy, or who choose not to marry).
→ Penance for sins (confession and repentance).
→ Unction for the sick and dying (if applicable).
→ Ordination (for those called to full-time ministry).

The Christian churches have emphasised the importance of the sacraments as an aid to faith, because they help believers to feel closer to God and to experience the presence of Christ.

Other denominations accept some, but not all, of these practices as sacraments. Although Protestant denominations encourage confession, it is a matter of personal choice if a Church member chooses to confess to their minister, rather than a formal sacrament. Marriage is not seen by all Christians as an indissoluble spiritual bond and thus not necessarily a sacrament with the same spiritual implications.

Baptism ●●●

Baptism is a symbolic washing away of spiritual uncleanliness. Jesus commissioned his disciples to go out and baptise all believers. For Christians, baptism is a rite that signifies:

→ their union with Christ;
→ that they are at one with all who are united in him;
→ that they have been spiritually renewed by the Holy Spirit;
→ that they may enter into the kingdom of God;
→ that they will lead a life of obedience to God.

Eucharist ●●●

Eucharist refers to the Lord's Supper, Holy Communion or Mass. It is based on the Last Supper in which Christ told his disciples to eat the bread as his body and drink the wine as his blood to symbolise the making of the new covenant. There has been controversy among scholars as to the nature of the Eucharist:

→ **Aquinas** argued that the bread and wine were actually transformed into the body and blood of Christ (*transubstantiation*).
→ **Luther** said that the body and blood of Christ were present in the bread and wine (the *real presence*) but the substances did not actually become Christ's body and blood (*consubstantiation*).

Prayer ●●●

Prayer is communicating with God in worship. God is personal and seeks a loving relationship with humanity. There are different kinds of prayer:

→ prayers of *praise* and adoration, thanksgiving for God's goodness;
→ prayers of *confession* and repentance for sins;
→ prayers of *petition* for personal needs and for the needs of the world.

Useful quotations

'And he took the bread, gave thanks and broke it, and gave it to them, saying, "This is my body given for you, do this in remembrance of me". In the same way, after the supper he took the cup, saying, "This cup is the new covenant in my blood which is poured out for you . . ."' (Luke 22:19–20).

'Baptism signifies grace and call for lifelong growth in Christ, with a view to the resurrection at the last day' (Beasley-Murray, George, *John* (1999)).

Checkpoint 2

What is the difference between transubstantiation (really there) and consubstantiation (symbolic)?

Background

In the early Church, the Eucharist was part of a larger feast called the **agape** or 'love feast' (Jude 12), which was provided by wealthy Christians for the benefit of the poorer ones.

The Bible teaches that God hears prayers and, by faith, will fulfil the needs of believers: *'If you believe, you will receive whatever you ask for in prayer'* (Matthew 21:22).

Exam question   answer: page 18

Explain the importance of prayer and the sacraments in Christianity.

(45 mins)

Christian doctrine

Terminology

The new covenant is based on love, not strict obedience to the Law of Moses.

Useful quotations

'For even the Son of Man did not come to be served, but to serve, and to give his life as a ransom for many' (Mark 10:45).
'God presented him as a sacrifice of atonement, through faith in his blood' (Romans 3:25).

Terminology

The elect are those chosen by God to receive eternal life.
Sin is that which keeps people apart from God.

Checkpoint 1

What is the difference between limited and universal atonement?

The Christian doctrines of atonement, sin, grace and justification through faith are central themes in Christianity and lay out the foundation for salvation.

Atonement

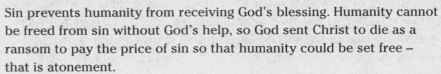

Sin prevents humanity from receiving God's blessing. Humanity cannot be freed from sin without God's help, so God sent Christ to die as a ransom to pay the price of sin so that humanity could be set free – that is atonement.

Atonement brings reconciliation and peace between God and humanity, and the beginning of a new covenant. There has been much theological debate concerning atonement and whom Christ actually died for as an act of atonement:

→ Some theologians have argued that he died only for the 'elect'. This is called **limited atonement**.
→ Others argue that Christ died for all humanity. His atoning death makes salvation possible for all people who choose to believe in him. This is called **universal atonement**.

Sin and grace

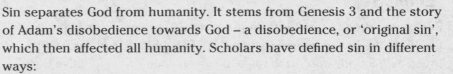

Sin separates God from humanity. It stems from Genesis 3 and the story of Adam's disobedience towards God – a disobedience, or 'original sin', which then affected all humanity. Scholars have defined sin in different ways:

→ **St Augustine** said it was the going wrong of something that is inherently good.
→ **Calvin** called it the total corruption of humanity.
→ **Barth** defined it as *nothingness*.

Grace is God's love that is given to humanity, even though it is undeserved. This love is shown through Jesus Christ.

Justification through faith

Justification by faith is the way in which humanity is freed from the guilt and condemnation of sin. The doctrine was first put forward by St Paul, who said:

→ The death of Jesus meant that sin had been overcome.
→ The resurrection was God's judgement and all who accept and believe in Jesus are not condemned.
→ Justification is based on faith in Jesus and is available to all who believe (Galatians 2:21).
→ It has nothing to do with being good or doing good works.
→ It requires belief in Christ and his atoning sacrifice.

Kung and **Hooker** have argued that it is possible to be saved by believing in Christ even if a believer has never heard of justification by faith. **Wright** notes:

> What the doctrine provides is the assurance that, though Christian doctrine is still imperfect, the believer is already a full member of God's people. It establishes, in consequence, the basis and motive for love towards God. The teaching of present justification is thus a central means whereby the fruits of the spirit – love, joy, peace and the rest – may be produced. (*The New Testament and the People of God*, (1999))

Useful quotations

'The reason why some people do not understand why faith alone justifies is that they do not know what faith is' (Martin Luther).

'. . . for all have sinned and fall short of the glory of God, and are justified freely by his grace through the redemption that came by Christ Jesus' (Romans 3:24).

'He was delivered over to death for our sins and was raised to life for our justification' (Romans 4:25).

Examiner's secrets

These doctrines are very technical. Don't attempt a question on these unless you really know and understand the material.

Checkpoint 2

What does justification mean?

Exam questions

answers: page 18

(a) Why is 'justification by faith' such a controversial doctrine?

(b) What is meant by the terms 'sin' and 'grace'? (30 mins)

Christianity and the wider world

Christianity faces the task of adapting to the changing circumstances of the modern world. This involves reviewing attitudes and approaches to the problems of the world and keeping the Gospel of Christ alive and relevant to all people. This has not been easy.

The poor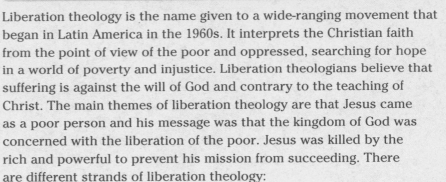

The 'poor' in the Bible are not just those who have no money. They are the 'poor in spirit' – those who know the weakness of the human condition and understand their complete dependence on the love of God. There are many differing groups who understand this through their own suffering and exploitation.

Jesus taught a great deal about the poor:

→ He was from a poor background.
→ His ministry was to the outcasts, sinners and the poor.
→ His message to the poor was that forgiveness and salvation were near.
→ Jesus taught that those who are rich in worldly terms will not be the automatic inheritors of spiritual wealth.
→ Jesus taught that those who followed him should give to the poor.

Liberation theology

Liberation theology is the name given to a wide-ranging movement that began in Latin America in the 1960s. It interprets the Christian faith from the point of view of the poor and oppressed, searching for hope in a world of poverty and injustice. Liberation theologians believe that suffering is against the will of God and contrary to the teaching of Christ. The main themes of liberation theology are that Jesus came as a poor person and his message was that the kingdom of God was concerned with the liberation of the poor. Jesus was killed by the rich and powerful to prevent his mission from succeeding. There are different strands of liberation theology:

→ Pastoral, which seeks to care for the poor and is supported by writers such as **Gutierrez**.
→ Academic, emphasising the teachings of the Scriptures, supported by **Segundo**.
→ Populist, seeking to establish old-style Catholicism.
→ Liberation theologians argue that the poor and oppressed are not to be pitied.
→ The concept of 'praxis' requires Christians to seek to change society on behalf of the poor.
→ Critics say that liberation theology is too simplistic. It has reduced religion to a worldly affair and neglected the spiritual dimension.

Black theology

Black theology originated as a response by black church leaders to the civil rights movements of the 1960s. It is linked to black history and racism and it represents a growing feeling among black people that their past is theologically important. There are differing views as to what this means:

→ **Cone** said that the Gospel of Christ was brought to black people by their 'white oppressors'.
→ **Wilmore** argued that black people have accepted the Gospel in a unique way, through the experience of their suffering.
→ To call Jesus 'black' is to speak of the freedom black people can find in the Jesus of the black gospel.
→ Salvation is for everyone, black and white, who can enter the black experience of oppression, with Jesus as their liberator.

Feminist theology

Women's liberation created a feminist consciousness that challenged many Christian theological traditions. Feminist theologians argue that Christianity, as a faith, treats women as second-rate humans in terms of their role and in the way in which they are understood in the image of God. There are three different viewpoints:

→ **The rejectionist view** – the Bible promoted a male-dominated structure, with a male view of God at the summit. **Daly** and **Hampson** argued that Christianity is biased against women and they urged women to leave the faith.
→ **The reformist view** – the Bible was written and interpreted by men and should be re-defined so that women occupy a place of greater importance. **Ruether** and **Johnson** suggested that the maleness of Jesus has been used to put forward the idea that only males are truly in the image of God.
→ **The loyalist view** – there is no oppressive sexism in the Bible and the woman's place in God's creation is fulfilled in her role of submission and dependence on Church and family.

Feminist theology suggests that the Bible is not about male dominance, but about God's relationship with all humanity.

Useful quotations

'. . . it emerges from a Black reading of the Scriptures, from a Black hearing of Jesus and a Black appreciation of him as the liberator of Black people, Jesus himself being the Black Messiah' (Bediako, *The New Dictionary of Theology*, ed. Fergusen and Wright (1988)).

'. . . the religious explication of the need for black people to define the scope and meaning of black experience in a white racist society. While Black Power focuses on the political, social and economic condition of black people, Black Theology puts black identity in a theological context, showing that Black Power is not only consistent with the Gospel of Jesus Christ, but that it is the Gospel of Jesus Christ' (James H. Cone, *Alach Theology and Black Power* (1997)).

Background

In the creation story, Eve is Adam's equal partner and she has the same unique qualities as he does. Both men and women are created in the image of God.

Useful quotations

'There is neither Jew nor Greek, slave nor free, male nor female, for you are all one in Christ Jesus' (Galatians 3:28).

'. . . women should remain silent in the churches. They are not allowed to speak, but must be in submission, as the Law says' (I Corinthians 14:34).

Checkpoint 2

What word (beginning with P) is used by scholars to refer to the male-dominated society of biblical times?

Exam question   answer: page 19

Examine and comment on the main teachings of liberation and feminist theology.   (45 mins)

The Christian Church

The Christian Church is the worldwide community of Christians. It is through the Church that Christ's work on Earth is said to continue.

Useful quotations

'The sacramental ministry of the ordained is to manifest in life and action the ways of Jesus Christ' (Fink, *The New Dictionary of Theology*, ed. Fergusen and Wright (1988)).

Terminology

The original Church of Christ is called the Apostolic Church.
The word laity comes from the Greek 'laos', meaning people.

Terminology

Canonised is the term given to the process of making someone into a saint.

Checkpoint 1

Who is the head of (a) the Roman Catholic Church and (b) the Church of England?

Terminology

In the Church calendar, many days commemorate particular saints and churches have been named after them. Asking the saints to intercede with Christ is called the 'invocation of the saints'.

Background

Throughout the ages Christians have made pilgrimages to the shrines of the saints and have venerated the bodies or other relics of the saints themselves.

Checkpoint 2

What does intercession mean?

Ordination

Ordination generally means becoming a priest. Those who are ordained have a practical and symbolic function in the church:

→ They are a link to the original Church of Christ.
→ This is symbolically expressed when a bishop enacts the laying on of hands on the newly ordained in order that they may carry out Christ's work.
→ The representation of Christ is present in the priestly ministries of preaching, teaching and prayer.
→ Ordination is a sacrament, so the church can see its own nature and mission in the work of its clergy.
→ In the Roman Catholic Church, priests may not marry and women cannot be ordained.
→ In the Anglican Church, marriage is permitted and women can be ordained.

Laity

The term 'laity' refers to those people who are members of the Church but are not ordained clergy, and it is the task of the laity not only to learn from the clergy, but also to help the clergy to carry out the work of the Church. There are different types of ministry that lay people can offer:

→ **Sunday ministry** in which the laity help within the Church itself.
→ **Personal ministry** of friendship and family.
→ **Monday ministry** in the workplace.
→ **Saturday ministry** in places of sport and entertainment.

Some churches, including the Roman Catholic and high Anglican, have experienced difficulties with priests and lay people trying to work together as equals. The problems include:

→ Many lay people do not want authority.
→ They are happy to accept a lower standard of Christian commitment and behaviour than the clergy.
→ The laity prefers to be led by the clergy in matters of liturgy and worship, rather than take it upon themselves to lead.

Saints

A saint is someone who lived such a holy life that, after they died, they were canonised. They must have lived their lives so close to the image of God and in the imitation of Christ that it is possible to say that they are with Christ in heaven.

The requirements of canonisation are:

→ an exemplary life;
→ miracles have actually been performed, either by the person, or in response to their prayers of intercession.

In the Roman Catholic Church, believers may pray to the saints to ask them to intercede with Christ on behalf of humanity.

Many Roman Catholics venerate the saints for their Christ-like example. The communion of saints is the title given to the fellowship of the saints in heaven. Today, the term is also used to mean the fellowship of all Christians – past, present and future.

Orthodoxy

Orthodoxy means a belief in the fundamental truths of the faith. Orthodoxy requires the following:

→ Belief in confessional truths such as 'Jesus is Lord', and 'Jesus is the Son of God'.
→ Acceptance of the creeds, such as the Apostles' Creed, and the Nicene Creed.

Spirituality

Spirituality enables believers to reach out of themselves and towards God. It involves the relationship between the believer and God, who reveals himself in the person of Jesus Christ. Christian spirituality is shown by:

→ Living in accordance with the example of Christ.
→ Accepting the presence and power of the Holy Spirit in the life of the believer.
→ Obedience to God's will
→ Spirituality enables the understanding of the believer to be lifted beyond themselves.
→ Spirituality requires practice, involving thought, prayer and meditation.

Evangelicals and charismatics

The fastest growing churches of the Christian church in the twenty-first century are evangelical and charismatic churches. Both are invariably found within Protestant denominations, or they may be independent, non-denominational churches. Evangelical churches based their teaching on a conservative view of the Bible and are often characterised by their rejection of liberal Christian attitudes towards society, sexual relationships and medical ethics. Evangelical churches may also be charismatic – that is, their worship is based on the manifestation of the gifts of the Holy Spirit, and is usually spontaneous and contemporary. Some evangelical churches, however, are strongly anti-charismatic, while most charismatic churches will also teach from a largely evangelical perspective. Charismatic churches have a powerful appeal to young Christians and to those coming to Christianity without any traditional Church background. The Alpha course is associated with the move of evangelicalism in modern culture.

Exam question   answer: page 19

Explain the religious and theological significance of (a) ordination and (b) the communion of saints. (30 mins)

Terminology

Orthodoxy is an ambiguous term since it can refer to either 'right worship' or 'right belief'.
The most famous Christian text on the subject of spirituality is Thomas à Kempis: *The Imitation of Christ.*

Useful quotations

'A new commandment I give you: Love one another. As I have loved you, so you must love one another. By this all men will know that you are my disciples, if you love one another' (John 13:34–35).

Examiner's secrets

This is a straightforward topic, but make sure you know about the different denominations of the Church. Also avoid generalisations like 'All Roman Catholics are against women priests . . .'

Answers
Christianity

Christian beliefs about God

Checkpoints

1 A redeemer is someone who saves another from danger or harm.
2 Divine self-limitation means that God, although omnipotent, chooses to limit what he does, e.g. by giving humans freewill, God limits himself from interfering in their lives.

Exam question

Begin by defining what personal means and then apply the notion to God. Make use of biblical and other references, together with the views of scholars and critics. Consider a range of viewpoints. Make reference to God's love, the notion of God as Father, the power of God and the message of the Scriptures. Give a couple of brief examples. Don't forget to quote.

Examiner's secrets

It is especially important to make sure that answers to questions on Christianity do not become preachy or suggest that there is only one correct view. This can actively reduce the marks the examiner can award you.

Christian beliefs about Jesus Christ

Checkpoints

1 Resurrection means rebuilding or to stand up again.
2 A mediator is someone who aids communication between two opposing parties.

Exam question

A good answer requires discussion of the views of scholars, backed up by detailed examination of the evidence and textual narrative. Remember to consider a range of ideas and include technical terms. Reference to the Old Testament will also help, and ensure you have considered the views of critics. Don't forget to quote.

The quest for the historical Jesus

Checkpoints

1 Spiritual redemption means that it is a person's spirit that is saved and will receive eternal life, rather than their physical body.
2 Apocalyptic means the end or the final judgement/battle.

Exam question

Start by defining what the various quests were. The important aspect of this question is to discuss the differing views of scholars and critics. You must make extensive use of technical terms and consider a range of views and give evidence to support the different ideas. There is no right or wrong conclusion, but balance up the evidence and try to offer some sort of judgement concerning the quests at the end.

Christian practice

Checkpoints

1 Evangelism means spreading the message of the Scriptures.
2 Transubstantiation means that Christ is actually present in the bread and wine. Consubstantiation means that Christ is symbolically present.

Exam question

Begin by defining what prayer and the sacraments are. Then examine their meaning and significance. Make reference to such notions as worship, sin, forgiveness, love and salvation. You will need to define and use technical terms and look at the different views of the church and believers – particularly contrasting the difference in viewpoints of the Roman Catholic and the Protestant churches. Don't forget the views of scholars.

Christian doctrine

Checkpoints

1 Limited atonement is only for the chosen people (the elect); universal atonement is for everyone.
2 Justification means found innocent – someone is proved to be in the right.

Exam questions

(a) Begin by defining the term and remember to include the biblical support for and against it and the views of scholars and the Church – particularly Martin Luther. Then consider the controversy – faith over good works. You will need to refer to the teachings of St Paul and others.
(b) Careful here – you will need to define the terms carefully and precisely. Back this up with evidence – including the teachings of Christ and St Paul and make extensive reference to the biblical text.

Examiner's secrets

Remember that this is a Religious Studies exam, and be sure that your essay does not run into the danger of becoming a historical survey only.

Christianity and the wider world

Checkpoints

1 Liberation means freedom from imprisonment or oppression.
2 Patriarchal.

Exam question

You will need to explain what these two notions are, what they mean and why they are important. This will require reference to the Bible and to the views of scholars and the Church. You need to include the notions of poverty, feminism, righteousness, equality and how the Scriptures are perceived. Don't forget to consider alternative viewpoints and the views of critics.

The Christian Church

Checkpoints

1 The Pope is the head of the Roman Catholic Church and the Queen is the head of the Church of England.
2 Intercession means speaking on behalf of, or acting for, another person.

Exam question

Define carefully what these terms mean and why they are significant. You will need to make use of technical terms and consider the history and background. Most important are the views of scholars, believers and the Church itself – not forgetting the biblical teachings, particularly those of Christ and St Paul.

Revision checklist
Christianity

1 Know and understand Christian beliefs about God.	Confident	Not confident. **Revise** pages 4–5
2 Be aware of the key Christian beliefs about Jesus.	Confident	Not confident. **Revise** pages 6–7
3 Be informed about the quest for the historical Jesus.	Confident	Not confident. **Revise** pages 8–9
4 Have knowledge of the important aspects of Christian practice.	Confident	Not confident. **Revise** pages 10–11
5 Be able to demonstrate an understanding of Christian doctrine.	Confident	Not confident. **Revise** pages 12–13
6 Have gained a solid foundation on issues concerning Christianity and the world.	Confident	Not confident. **Revise** pages 14–15
7 Know and understand the key features of the Christian Church.	Confident	Not confident. **Revise** pages 16–17

Old Testament

The Old Testament or, as it is known in Judaism, the Hebrew Bible, consists of 39 books written over many centuries. These books cover the origins and history of the Jewish people, the law, wisdom and the prophets. It contains the sagas of the patriarchs – Abraham, Isaac and Jacob, the exodus and the leadership of Moses and the famous lives of the kings, such as David and Solomon, together with the stories of the exile and the prophecies of the coming of the Messiah. The most famous books are the first five, known as the Pentateuch, together with the Psalms and the books of wisdom. With the golden age of Israel over, the prophets entered the scene. These were people whom God had chosen and given a vision and a message to take to the people. In particular, prophets such as Amos and Hosea came to warn the people of God's anger and righteous judgement upon his people, while others, such as Isaiah, spoke of the coming of God's redeemer and Jeremiah called for a new covenant. With the prophets came the growth of wisdom literature – writings that reflected the innermost fears and feelings of the people concerning the very meaning of life and death and the nature of God himself.

Exam themes

→ The Covenant
→ The Law of Moses
→ The development of the monarchy
→ The life and example of Abraham
→ The life and example of Moses
→ Samuel and King Saul
→ The early life of David
→ The reign of King Solomon
→ Understanding the background to the Old Testament
→ The religious, social and cultural setting
→ The nature and development of prophecy
→ The messages of judgement – Amos and Hosea
→ The coming of the Saviour – Isaiah and Micah
→ Future hope – Ezekiel, Jeremiah and Jonah
→ The Psalms
→ The Book of Job and the nature of suffering
→ The views of scholars

Topic checklist

AS ○ A2 ●	OCR	AQA	EDEXCEL
Introducing the Old Testament	○●	○●	○●
Old Testament concepts	○●	○●	○●
Abraham			○
Moses	○●	○	○
The monarchy			○
Saul and David			○
King Solomon			●
The development of prophecy		○●	●
Amos and Hosea		○	●
Micah and Isaiah	○	○●	●
Jonah, Jeremiah and Ezekiel	○●	○●	
Wisdom literature	○●		

Introducing the Old Testament

The Old Testament, or Jewish Bible, is not a single book, but 39 books – a combination of history, poetry, law, ethics, politics and stories of human courage and intrigue. It is also full of theological and philosophical enquiries about the meaning and mystery of life.

What is the Old Testament about?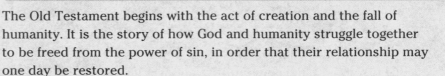

The Old Testament begins with the act of creation and the fall of humanity. It is the story of how God and humanity struggle together to be freed from the power of sin, in order that their relationship may one day be restored.

The process starts with the saga of Abraham, a man selected by God to be the father of a special race of people – God's chosen people, who would:

→ be holy;
→ have a close relationship with God;
→ spread the word of God to all peoples.

Abraham makes an agreement or Covenant with God, under which he and his descendants would:

→ worship God;
→ live in the promised land;
→ become God's chosen people.

Abraham is the first of the patriarchs or fathers, followed by his son Isaac and his grandson, Jacob, who has 12 sons.

Centuries later, under the leadership of Moses, God's people are saved from slavery by God, who leads them out of Egypt and leads them to the promised land of Canaan (Israel). During this period, known as the Exodus, the Israelites are given the Law of Moses – guidance given by God for his people, to enable them to lead holy lives.

The Israelites settle into Israel. Later, in the reigns of King David and King Solomon, they enjoy a golden age of prosperity. However, the people turn their backs on God. God sends prophets – holy people with a message to the people to change their ways – but the people do not heed the warnings and the lands are conquered and God's people are sent into exile.

How God is portrayed in the Old Testament

God is one

For the Israelites, the God of Israel was the only God (this is called monotheism).

God is portrayed as a personal force in his own right, who offers a relationship to all who believe in him.

God is personal

God is encountered through the history of Israel's national life and he is in control of history – all that happens is part of his plan for his people. God is seen to have a personal relationship with his people. He chooses certain individuals, such as Abraham and Moses, to play a special part in his plan, but he also interacts with the people as a whole through his saving actions (his grace).

God also has a personality that is recognisably human, in order to highlight the sense of personal relationship. He is therefore depicted as a loving parent and the guide and protector of his people.

God as king

God is the ruler of his people. He is their king. Even when the people of Israel have a human king, God is Israel's true ruler.

God as lawgiver

God is depicted as the lawgiver who gives his law (Torah) to his people. They had to live their lives in accordance with the requirements of justice and righteousness.

Useful quotations

'Hear, O Israel: the Lord our God, the Lord is one' (Deuteronomy 6:4).

Useful quotations

'Life is not just a meaningless cycle of empty existence. It has a beginning and end, and events happen not in a haphazard sequence, but as part of a great design that in turn is based on the character of God himself. And this God is encountered by his people in the ordinary events of everyday life' (John Drane, Introducing the Old Testament (2001)).

Useful quotations

'But let justice roll on like a river, righteousness like a never-failing stream!' (Amos 6:24).

Checkpoint 2

What does it mean to say God is personal?

Exam question   answer: page 46

Discuss the meaning and importance of the following terms: (i) original sin (ii) Exodus.   (20 mins)

Old Testament concepts

To understand the Old Testament fully, it is important to grasp the meaning of four significant concepts.

Election

Throughout the Old Testament, God chooses ('election') certain people, such as Abraham and Moses and, of course, the 'chosen' people themselves, to carry out his will. The notion of 'election' is an important one because it gives Israel a strong awareness that it has a unique status among the nations of the world. Election brings responsibility – Israel is called to be 'holy' and the people must behave in a way that befits their calling.

Exodus

The Exodus is the pivotal point in the history of the people of Israel. In the Exodus, God saves his people from slavery and leads them to the promised land.

Covenant

A covenant was a legal agreement that set out the terms of a relationship between two parties. The Covenant was the basis of Israel's relationship with God. There was not one covenant, but several, made with individuals – Noah, Abraham and David, and with the people of Israel as a whole in the Sinai covenant.

The Covenant set out the basis of the relationship between God and the individual or people – the Covenant was God's initiative and the people accepted the terms of the Covenant and attempted to be obedient to them. The Old Testament is an account of how well, and how badly, the people followed the covenants.

The Covenant relationship

The Covenant relationship in the Old Testament had five crucial elements:

1 Promise – made by God to Abraham (that he would have a son).
2 Commitment – of obedience, faithfulness and worship, made by the people.
3 Favour – God places his people in a favoured position – they are 'chosen'.

4 Intimacy – the Covenant allows the people an intimate relationship with God.

5 Setting apart – the people of Israel are set apart from others to be a 'holy nation'.

> I will establish my covenant as an everlasting covenant between me and you and your descendants after you for the generations to come, to be your God and the God of your descendants after you. (Genesis 17:7)

Law

The Law given by God to the people at Mount Sinai was a code that provided a guidance to the people on how to live righteous and holy lives. The people of Israel signified their acceptance of these laws by sprinkling blood on them on the altar and then eating a Covenant meal.

> Then he took the Book of the Covenant and read it to the people. They responded, 'We will do everything the Lord has said; we will obey.'
>
> Moses then took the blood, sprinkled it on the people and said, 'This is the blood of the Covenant that the Lord has made with you in accordance with all these words.' (Exodus 24:8)

The Law rested on the authority of God and had many important features:

→ All of creation is under God's Law.
→ A high value was placed on human life.
→ Punishments are clearly laid out.
→ There were special laws relating to the Sabbath.

The most famous part of the Law was the 'Ten Commandments' (the 'Decalogue'), found in Exodus 20. These were a set of absolute regulations stating in a very precise way God's will and requirements for his people.

Background

To show the importance of the Covenant, it was sealed in blood and circumcision.

Useful quotations

'This is what the Old Testament means by "the covenant": an agreement in which the freed slaves were reminded of what God had done for them, and they were called in return to promise to fulfil his commands and be loyal to him' (John Drane, *Introducing the Old Testament* (2001)).

Terminology

The Hebrew word for law is 'Torah', which means 'guidance' or 'instruction'.

Examples

The majority of Laws were expressed in one of three differing forms: 'vetitive' (you shall not . . .), 'imperative' ('do this . . .') and 'jussive' ('you shall do this . . .').

Checkpoint 2

What did it mean for the people of Israel to be called a 'holy nation'?

Exam questions   answers: page 46

(a) Examine the Hebrew understanding of the term 'covenant'.

(b) Consider the importance of the notion of covenant for the Hebrews' understanding of their relationship with God.   (45 mins)

Abraham

Abraham was the first of the patriarchs and he was considered to be the father of the people of Israel, who saw themselves as his descendants – the 'children of Abraham'. He was seen by the Israelites as one of the greatest of the prophets and the recipient of God's Covenant.

Abraham the patriarch

Abraham was originally named Abram and was born in Ur about 2,000 BCE. At the age of 75, Abram received a call from God:

> Leave your country, your people and your father's household and go to a land I will show you.
> I will make you into a great nation and I will bless you.
> (Genesis 12:1–2)

Abram obeyed God and travelled to the land of Canaan. The important features of the saga are:

→ Abram was forced to divert into Egypt to escape from a famine.
→ His people split up, some going with his nephew Lot into the Plain of Jordan, with the rest going with Abram to Canaan.
→ Abram had to rescue Lot, who became a prisoner of a group of renegade 'kings'.
→ Abraham made the Covenant with God (Genesis 17).
→ Abraham saw God's destruction of the sinful cities of Sodom and Gomorrah (Genesis 19).
→ Believing that his wife Sarai was barren, Abraham had a child, Ishmael, by a maidservant called Hagar.
→ Abraham cast Hagar and Ishmael out when Sarai gave birth to a son, Isaac (Genesis 21).
→ He was prepared to sacrifice Isaac (Genesis 22).
→ Abraham died at the age of 175.

> Abram fell face down, and God said to him, 'As for me, this is my covenant with you: You will be the father of many nations. No longer will you be called Abram, your name will be Abraham, for I will make you the father of many nations.' (Genesis 17:4–5)

Terminology

Abraham was so important that, later on in the Bible, God is referred to as being the 'God of Abraham'.
I am the God of your father, the God of Abraham' (Exodus 3:6).

Useful quotations

'We know nothing of Abraham, Isaac and Jacob save what the Bible tells us' (John Bright, *A History of Israel* (2000)).

Terminology

The title of 'patriarch' was given to Abraham and his immediate descendants – his son Isaac, his grandson Jacob and the 12 sons of Jacob, whose descendants became the 12 tribes of Israel.

Useful quotations

'I swear by myself, declares the Lord, that because you have done this and have not withheld your son, your only son, I will surely bless you and make your descendants as numerous as the stars in the sky' (Genesis 22:16–17).

Checkpoint 1

Why did Abraham cast Hagar and Ishmael out?

The character of Abraham ●●●

Abraham is remembered as a man of great faith. He is shown in Genesis to have a very close relationship with God.

→ Abraham speaks to God (18:31);
→ Abraham meets angels (18:1);
→ he has visions and revelations (17:1).

His faith is shown by:

→ His willingness to obey God's call and leaving his homeland.
→ His willingness to be guided by God throughout his life.
→ He agrees to sacrifice his own son.
→ With God's help, he rescues his family and wages war against superior forces (14:5).

Abraham also has serious flaws in his character and shows a lack of faith in God when:

→ He deceives the Pharaoh by pretending that his wife Sarai is his sister and allows Pharaoh to sleep with her in order to save his own life (Genesis 12).
→ He does not believe God's promise of many descendants and conceives Ishmael through his maidservant.

Life at the time of the patriarchs ●●●

The patriarchs were nomadic, leading tribes or clans from one fertile spot to another with their herds. They had unique social customs, for example, members of families could inter-marry (Abraham's wife was also his half-sister) and the ancient Nuzi texts show that a childless wife could allow her husband to produce a child that would belong to her through the use of a 'substitute' slave-girl – just as Abraham does with Hagar (Genesis 16).

Terminology

The patriarch sagas as religious or theological history: they do not record accurate historical facts, but do show the origins of the people of Israel as part of the actions and plan of God.

Useful quotations

'The Bible's picture of the Patriarchs is deeply rooted in history. Abraham, Isaac and Jacob stand in the truest sense at the beginning of Israel's history and faith' (John Bright, *A History of Israel* (2000)).

Terminology

These tribes may have been called 'Apiru' or 'Hapiru' by the town-dwellers, a term which meant a group, maybe of mixed races, who lived on the fringes of society. It is possible that this term evolved into the word 'Hebrew', which was the name given to the first of Abraham's descendants, the people of Israel.

Examiner's secrets

Abraham is a major topic in the examination, but try to avoid spending too long in your answer just 'telling the story'.

Checkpoint 2

Why does Abraham agree to sacrifice his own son?

Exam question   answer: page 46

With reference to two separate incidents, examine the importance of trust in God in the life of Abraham.   (45 mins)

Moses

Moses is, arguably, the greatest figure in the Old Testament. He was the leader and lawgiver of the people of Israel, who led them out of slavery in Egypt and made them into a 'holy nation'.

The life of Moses

→ Moses dates from 1350 to 1230 BCE.
→ He was born when the Israelites were slaves in Egypt and raised in the Pharaoh's court.
→ He killed an Egyptian officer and fled to the Land of Midea, where he lived as a shepherd.
→ God spoke through a Burning Bush, telling Moses that he was to lead the Israelites out of slavery.

God said to Moses, 'I AM WHO I AM. This is what you are to say to the Israelites: I AM has sent me to you.' (Exodus 3:14)

→ God sent down a series of plagues to ravage Egypt and the Pharaoh lets the Israelites go free.
→ The Egyptian army is destroyed when God parts the waters of the Red Sea.
→ Moses leads the Israelites in the wilderness for a period of 40 years, known as the 'Exodus'.
→ On Mount Sinai, God gives Moses the Law, including the Ten Commandments (Exodus 20).
→ Moses dies on Mount Nebo, just before the people enter the promised land.

The character of Moses

He was a strong, caring leader and when the people failed to obey God during the Exodus, he constantly pleaded with God on their behalf. Moses had a deep, personal relationship with God. He became the model for all the later prophets and the forerunner of the Messiah (Deuteronomy 18:18).

Background

The story of the plagues and the escape from Egypt is a mixture of factual truth (they do have plagues of frogs and grasshoppers in Egypt) and folklore. It is a story to be understood as an illustration of the power and majesty of God.

Background

The final plague is remembered in the Feast of the Passover as the time when the Angel of Death spared the Israelites by 'passing over' their homes and entering the unprotected houses of the Egyptians to kill the first-born (Exodus 12:29).

Useful quotations

'This is the land I promised to Abraham, Isaac and Jacob . . . I have let you see it with your own eyes, but you will not cross over into it . . . And Moses, the servant of the Lord died there in Moab' (Deuteronomy 34:4–5).

Terminology

Moses gave the people God's law, which became known as the 'Law of Moses'.

Checkpoint 1

Why was it important for Moses to know the name of God?

The Exodus

This was one of the most crucial events in the history of the people of Israel because it showed that God was with his people and that he had freed them from slavery and taken them to a promised land. A great many Israelites left Egypt with Moses – apparently 600,000 men and an unknown number of women and children, together with their herds and flocks.

The Law

Moses received the Law from God at the top of a mountain. This was then followed by the ceremony of the making of the Covenant – and confirms the agreement that was earlier made with Noah and Abraham.

> Now if you obey me fully and keep my covenant, then out of all nations you will be my treasured possession. Although the whole earth is mine, you will be for me a kingdom of priests and a holy nation. (Exodus 19:5–6)

There are two versions:

➜ In the first (Exodus 24:1–2, 9–11) the Covenant was made at a sacred meal held on top of the mountain with God and the elders of Israel.
➜ In the second version, (Exodus 24:4–8) the whole community of Israel takes part in a ceremony at the foot of the mountain.

The stone tablets of the Law were carried in a sacred box known as the 'Ark of the Covenant'. This was, symbolically, the dwelling place of God. The Ark went everywhere with the people, highlighting God's actual presence with his people.

Useful quotations

In *History of Pentateuchal Traditions* (1981), Martin Noth said the Exodus was an event:
'. . . so unique and extraordinary that it came to constitute the essence of the primary Israelite confession and was regarded as the real beginning of Israel's history and the act of God fundamental for Israel.'

Terminology

The people of Israel spent 40 years wandering in the wilderness. This may not be an accurate figure since the number 40 was often used to mean 'a long time'.

Terminology

The people see thunder, lightning and dense cloud on the mountain, accompanied by a loud trumpet blast. This is the divine appearance of God (called a 'theophany'), showing them God's divine holiness and majesty.

Checkpoint 2

Why was the Ark of the Covenant so important?

Exam questions   answers: page 46

(a) Examine the main religious features of Moses' encounter with God at the Burning Bush.

(b) To what extent was Moses a successful leader of the people?   (45 mins)

The monarchy

The establishment of a Hebrew monarchy was highly controversial – the Covenant had established that God was the ruler of Israel. However, the people were not satisfied and wanted to have a king, so that they could be like the other nations.

The development of the monarchy

The story moved on two centuries. The Israelites settled in the promised land, with each of the 12 tribes living in their own area under a series of leaders called 'judges'. This was an inefficient system because:

→ The areas were small and the nation was weak and divided.
→ The Philistines were an enemy with superior weapons of iron.
→ The Israelites were facing defeat and total conquest.
→ The system of judges prevented the people properly uniting against the Philistines.

The people's request for a king was based on a number of factors:

→ The Philistine threat.
→ Need for unity under one leader.
→ Need for a leader of the Israelite army.
→ A desire to be more like the other nations, who had kings.
→ Failure of the system of judges.

Samuel and the establishment of the monarchy

Samuel was a judge in Israel. He had a unique relationship with God, having been dedicated to God from birth. He had led his people for many years but, in his old age, wanted to hand over power to his two sons, Koel and Abijah. However, these were an unworthy pair and the elders of Israel would not accept them. The elders of the tribes met together and asked Samuel to appoint a king to rule over all the 12 tribes of Israel (1 Samuel 8:4).

Samuel initially refused to anoint a king because:

→ God was the true ruler.
→ A king would make Israel like the pagan nations.
→ It would be a rejection of Samuel and the end of the era of the judges.
→ Having a king will be costly in financial and social ways (1 Samuel 8).

The Old Testament contains two conflicting accounts of the development of the monarchy:

→ In the first account, which comes from an early source, the monarchy is seen as a very positive thing. Samuel is seen as little more than a local leader of limited influence. A king is seen as the real hope for Israel's future. This account is found in 1 Samuel 9:1–10 and 16 and 1 Samuel 11.
→ In the second, later account, the monarchy is seen in a very negative way. The monarchy upsets the relationship between God and his people. Samuel is depicted as a figure of national importance – a priest, prophet and judge (1 Samuel 8 and 10:7–27).

The anointing of Saul as king

Saul is a member of the tribe of Benjamin and meets Samuel while he is looking for some donkeys belonging to his father. God had earlier told Samuel that he would meet a man from the tribe of Benjamin whom he should anoint as king. Saul is anointed by Samuel (1 Samuel 9–10).

Saul is touched by the Spirit of God and soon leads the Israelite army to victory over the Ammonites at Jabesh Gilead and is confirmed by the people as their king (1 Samuel 11).

Useful quotations

'This is what a king who will reign over you will do: He will take your sons and make them serve in his chariots and horses . . . He will take your daughters to be perfumers and cooks and bakers . . . He will take the best of your fields . . . a tenth of your grain . . . your menservants and maidservants and the best of your cattle . . . and you yourselves will become his slaves' (1 Samuel 8:11–27).

Background

The story takes place around 1050 BCE and can be found in 1 Samuel.

Checkpoint 2

Why did the establishment of a monarchy upset the relationship between God and the people?

Exam questions   answers: page 46

(a) For what reasons did the Hebrews want a king?

(b) Why did Samuel resist the call to anoint a king?   (30 mins)

Saul and David

Saul was the first King of Israel and his reign was controversial and tragic.

The kingship of Saul

Saul's reign started promisingly and he was seen to have the Spirit of God within him. His reign had many positive aspects:

→ He fulfilled the people's demands for a king
→ He raised an efficient army.
→ He was a good military leader.
→ He was a charismatic leader.
→ He led the Israelite army to victory over the Ammonites at Jabesh Gilead and the Philistines.

However, his kingship was filled with difficulties and his relationship with Samuel deteriorated rapidly. Saul clashed with Samuel in a number of ways:

→ Saul refused to wait for Samuel before a battle and offered the burnt sacrifice himself.
→ Saul spared the life of his enemy, King Agag, in apparent disobedience of God's will.
→ Samuel himself killed Agag and told Saul that God had rejected his kingship.
→ Samuel secretly anointed David as the next king.
→ The people resented having to pay taxes to Saul for the upkeep of the army.

Saul and David

One of the most puzzling aspects of the story of Saul is his relationship with David. The Old Testament writers give two conflicting accounts of how they met.

→ In the first, 1 Samuel 16, David is a shepherd who is called by Saul to come and play music to soothe his troubled mind.
→ In the second, 1 Samuel 17, David arrives on the scene as a boy who helps Saul's army to defeat the Philistine giant Goliath.

Whichever story is true, Saul seems unaware that David has been anointed as his successor. Saul treats David well:

→ David is given a place of honour in the court.
→ He is given high rank in the army.
→ He marries Saul's daughter Michal.
→ He becomes good friends with Saul's son Jonathan.

Background

Saul's main problem was that Samuel remained on the scene and was a constant critic of the king – even going so far as to anoint David as his successor.

Background

Saul was about 30 years old when he became king and reigned for 40 years.

Useful quotations

'You have rejected the word of the Lord, and the Lord has rejected you as king over Israel!' (1 Samuel 15:26).

Terminology

At the start of his reign, Saul has the Spirit of God (1 Samuel 10:10), which gives him inner strength. When God rejects Saul (1 Samuel 15), he loses that Spirit and, with that, his strength. He spends the rest of his kingship in a mood of depression.

Examiner's secrets

A popular area of study. Most questions require you to have an understanding of the relationship between Saul and Samuel and why Samuel anointed David as Saul's successor.

Checkpoint 1

Why did Samuel kill King Agag?

Yet the relationship became strained and Saul grew jealous of David's great military prowess. Saul tried to kill David, who fled and became a rebel leader. Saul's reign was regarded as a failure for several reasons:

→ He was disobedient to God and incurred the displeasure of both God and Samuel.
→ He failed to preserve the link with Samuel and the old order of judges.
→ He became jealous and depressed.
→ He ruthlessly slew the priests of Nob.
→ The anti-monarchy writers portray him in a negative way.
→ He lost the support of the people.
→ Saul was badly affected by mental instability.
→ Saul committed suicide after his forces were defeated by the Philistines.

The reign of King David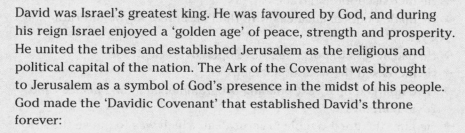

David was Israel's greatest king. He was favoured by God, and during his reign Israel enjoyed a 'golden age' of peace, strength and prosperity. He united the tribes and established Jerusalem as the religious and political capital of the nation. The Ark of the Covenant was brought to Jerusalem as a symbol of God's presence in the midst of his people. God made the 'Davidic Covenant' that established David's throne forever:

> Your throne and your kingdom shall endure for ever before me; your throne will be established forever. (2 Samuel 7:16)

Useful quotations

'Saul has slain his thousands, and David his tens of thousands' (1 Samuel 18:7).

Background

Saul is, perhaps unfairly, depicted by the anti-monarchy writers in the Bible as being a selfish man who put his own will before that of God and who turned his back on the religious ideals of his people.

Useful quotations

'The complexity of Saul's personality eludes us, but he emerges as a tragic figure. He had great potential as the recognised successor to the judges, but the nature of the conflict in which he was involved more or less forced him to go against the old tribal ideals of his people and led to his downfall' (John Drane, Introducing the Old Testament (2001)).

Checkpoint 2

Why do you think Saul committed suicide?

Exam questions   answers: page 47

(a) How good or bad a king was Saul?

(b) Did Samuel help or hinder him?   (45 mins)

King Solomon

Useful quotations

'Solomon's position as king was founded on court intrigues and military strength . . . in Solomon, Israel certainly got a king like the kings of other nations around them . . . for the first time, Israel was a state, rather than a nation, and this led to far-reaching changes in Israelite society' (John Drane, *Introducing the Old Testament* (2001)).

Useful quotations

'I will give you a wise and discerning heart, so that there will never have been anyone like you, nor will there ever be. Moreover, I will give you what you have not asked for – both riches and honour – so that in your lifetime you will have no equal among kings' (1 Kings 3:12–13).

Terminology

The Ark of the Covenant was an ornate chest in which the tablets of the Law were kept. It was a sacred object and was seen as a unique point of contact between God and his people (see Exodus 25).

Examiner's secrets

Solomon is a very popular area of study. Make sure you know about his reign in detail and are able to assess his good and bad points fully.

Checkpoint 1

Why was the Ark of the Covenant housed in the temple?

David chose his son Solomon as his successor, even though Solomon's brother Adonijah had the stronger claim. He dates from approximately 971 to 931 BCE.

The reign of Solomon

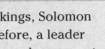

Solomon's reign was controversial. Unlike the earlier kings, Solomon had been born into the royal family. He was not, therefore, a leader among equals, but a figurehead. He did not need the popular support of the tribes because he had royal birth.

Solomon's reign began with God blessing him with great wisdom. He was a fortunate leader; he inherited a large and stable kingdom and his enemies were all weak. Solomon concentrated on establishing his own position. He did this in a number of ways:

→ He increased the size of the army and established a series of powerful chariot stations.
→ He increased foreign trade.
→ He made political alliances with the Pharaoh of Egypt and Hiram of Tyre.
→ He had access to ports and developed overseas trade.
→ He increased the wealth of Israel.
→ He embarked on a vast building programme, including palaces and royal buildings.
→ He built the great temple in Jerusalem, which was to house the Ark of the Covenant.

However, Solomon was not a popular king for a number reasons:

→ The people paid heavy taxes to cover the cost of Solomon's extravagant lifestyle.
→ He established a central administrative system, with tax districts under the control of an officer.
→ The people felt that they were being ruled by an elite group, which went against the notion that all were equal before God.

→ Solomon introduced a programme of forced labour to complete his building programme.

→ Solomon had 700 wives and 300 concubines, many of them foreign and he permitted them to worship pagan gods.

Solomon's reign ended in discontent, with plots against his life and rebellions among the northern tribes. When Solomon died, these tribes refused to accept his son Rehoboam as king and broke away and the land was divided.

Was Solomon a success or a failure? ●●●

In a number of ways, Solomon was a very successful king:

→ Israel was militarily strong.

→ It had strong alliances and trading routes.

→ There was great wealth.

→ There was an efficient central administration.

However, Solomon had his weaknesses:

→ He was 'born to the purple' and always lived in luxury.

→ He found it difficult to relate to the ordinary people.

→ He failed to understand the importance of the old tribal loyalties.

→ He allowed the worship of foreign gods.

→ The people resented the high taxes and forced labour.

→ The northern tribes disliked Solomon and believed he was breaking the old traditions.

Background

When Solomon allowed his foreign wives to worship their own gods, he was in direct violation of the Law of Moses. He also allowed certain pagan ornamentation in the temple itself. This made him very unpopular as he was seen to be defying God.

Terminology

After Solomon's death, the northern land of ten tribes was called 'Israel' and the two tribes in the south, with Jerusalem, called themselves the land of 'Judah'.

Useful quotations

'Judged by the standards of world powers, Solomon was outstandingly successful, the greatest of all Israel's rulers. But judged by the moral and spiritual standards of the covenant, he was a miserable failure' (John Drane, *Introducing the Old Testament* (2001)).

Checkpoint 2

What is meant by the term tribal loyalties?

Exam question   answer: page 47

To what extent is it fair to say that Solomon's reign was a mixture of early success and later failure?   (45 mins)

The development of prophecy

The prophets were among the greatest of the religious teachers. A prophet was a person who had been called by God to deliver his message to a particular people at a particular time.

Links

There were several types of prophet:
(i)   Diviners/seers (1 Samuel 9:1–35)
(ii) Royal court prophets (1 Samuel 22:5)
(iii) Ecstatic prophets (1 Samuel 10:5–8)
(iv) War prophets (Judges 4:4)
(v)   Cultic prophets (1 Samuel 10:5–8)
(vi) 'False prophets' (Jeremiah 23:16)

Mainstream prophecy

There were three Hebrew words for 'prophet':

→ 'Nabi' – the earliest groups of prophets.
→ 'Roeh' and 'Hozeh'. These were 'seers', individual prophets with close personal contact with God, who were regarded as more important than the 'nabi'.

There were certain features that characterised a true prophet:

→ A personal call from God.
→ A message of ethical and social concern.
→ Acting as a messenger between God and humanity.

There were two titles given to the prophets:

→ 'Man of God', to highlight the difference between the prophet and the ordinary people.
→ 'Servant', which illustrated the relationship between God and his prophet.

The prophets spoke God's message ('oracles') in a particular way:

→ Demanding that the people change their sinful ways.
→ Addressing the situation before them.
→ Using warnings and encouragements concerning the future.
→ Sometimes using parables, allegories or acting out their message, e.g. Isaiah 20.
→ Calling the people to repent and follow the path of righteousness.
→ Warning of the coming of God's judgement.

Background

The first person to be called a prophet was Abraham (Genesis 20:7), but the prophet who set the standard for all the others was Moses.

Background

Some prophets received God's word directly, others received it through dreams and visions or through divine inspiration. A few found God's word through the use of the sacred dice, Urim and Thummin.

Checkpoint 1

In the message of the prophets, what did righteousness mean?

Other types of prophet

→ Ecstatic prophets – some prophets felt ecstacy, an experience of being so overcome with emotions as to lose self-control or reason as a result of the work of the Spirit of God within them.
→ Cultic prophets – dwelt in the great holy places and sanctuaries. They were experts in worship.
→ Royal court and war prophets – often worked within the power structure and the royal court, influencing the decisions of the rulers.
→ 'False prophets' – the true prophet would call the people to holiness and righteousness, with a message of judgement upon sin. The false prophet was immoral, preaching peace without regard to moral and social conditions.

The prophetic literature

The prophetic literature in the Old Testament is divided into two types:

1 ***The former prophets*** These are the historical books Joshua–2 Kings. They show Israel's history as God's hand working through his people. The prophets are Samuel, Elijah and Elisha.
2 ***The latter prophets*** These are the books named after the prophets themselves and containing the word of God and a warning for the future. There are three 'major' prophets – Isaiah, Jeremiah and Ezekiel and twelve 'minor' prophets, the most famous being Amos and Hosea.

Prophetic literature had several aspects:

→ The divine call – the prophet is called by God.
→ Obedience – the main warning was for Israel to be obedient to God.
→ The message – the messages usually beginning with phrases such as 'The Lord says . . .' or 'The word of the Lord came to . . .'.
→ The situation – the prophets spoke of the present situation and warnings for the future.

Background

The royal prophets included Nathan in King David's court, and Isaiah of Jerusalem. These prophets had a lasting effect on the history of Israel.

Useful quotations

'Do not listen to what the prophets are prophesying to you, they speak to you. They speak visions from their own minds, not from the Lord' (Jeremiah 23:16).

Background

There were usually three parts to the prophet's message. First, that God was the source of true authority. Second, that a person's relationship with God affects his/her relationship with other people. Third, that there will be a time of judgement and future hope.

Checkpoint 2

What was a false prophet?

Examiner's secrets

This is a difficult area, and not very popular. It is vital you know all the different technical terms and have a clear understanding of the message of the prophets.

Exam question   answer: page 47

Examine the various ways in which scholars have attempted to explain the forms and functions of Hebrew prophecy.   (45 mins)

Amos and Hosea

Useful quotations

'They trample on the heads of the poor as upon the dust of the ground and deny justice to the oppressed' (Amos 2:7).

Useful quotations

'But let justice roll on like a river, righteousness like a never-failing stream!' (Amos 5:23).

Background

Amos told the people they were too complacent – they believed that all was well simply because they were God's chosen people.

Terminology

The 'Day of the Lord' was celebrated every year during the Covenant festival in anticipation of the final great 'Day of the Lord' when God would fulfil the promises of the Covenant and crown Israel with glory and honour. Amos warned the people that judgement would come on this day.

Useful quotations

'Amos interpreted Israel's crisis in the light of a shared memory of the events which had made Israel Yahweh's people with a special task and destiny' (Bernhard W. Anderson, *The Living World of the Old Testament* (1988)).

Checkpoint 1

What did Amos mean by 'empty rituals'?

Amos and Hosea lived in the eighth century BCE and the historical background to their times can be found in 2 Kings 14–15.

The prophet Amos

Amos' message was for the people of the northern kingdom. At that time, the rich would not share their wealth with the poor; instead they squandered it on immorality and high living. The poor were oppressed and exploited. This led to moral and social decay in the land, and religion was perverted with godlessness, immorality, empty rituals and the worship of foreign gods. Amos was called to deliver God's message of judgement. The essence of the message was:

→ They were God's people and that they had a Covenant relationship with God.
→ This gave them great privileges, but also imposed a responsibility to lead holy and righteous lives.
→ The people must return to the ways of the Covenant and restore their personal relationship with God.
→ God would not forgive them simply because they performed empty rituals and sacrifices.
→ The people had to uphold standards of justice and righteousness.
→ Without a return to the ways of righteousness, Israel would be destroyed and the people would be taken away in exile.
→ The 'Day of the Lord' would be one of judgement and despair.

Amos illustrated his message with a series of visions: a plague of locusts consuming the crops, fire destroying the soil and a plumb-line showing the end of Israel and the destruction of the temple.

The message of future hope

Amos ends with a message of hope for the future. The exile will eventually be over and Israel will be restored through God's grace and love for his people:

> I will plant Israel in their own land, never again to be uprooted from the land I have given them' says the Lord. (Amos 9:15)

The prophet Hosea

● ● ●

The political situation at that time was turbulent. The Assyrians were waging a campaign of conquest and in Israel King Manahem was forced to pay them heavy tribute. The people did not trust in God and were worshipping pagan 'gods'. They had abandoned the Covenant relationship. Hosea's message was a 'real-life' story – he used his own personal life to symbolise his message of God's love for Israel:

→ His wife Gomer was unfaithful, just as Israel was unfaithful to God.
→ They had three children, whom Hosea gave symbolic names.
→ 'Jezreel', named after a battle.
→ 'Lo-Ruhamah' meaning 'not pitied', highlighting that God's patience with Israel had run out.
→ 'Lo-Ammi', meaning 'not my people', showing that God had rejected the Israelites.

The essence of Hosea's message was:

→ The people of Israel no longer knew God.
→ The Covenant relationship with God was over.
→ The people must remember the Covenant tradition and what God had done for them.
→ The priests had failed to give the people proper guidance in the ways of God.
→ Israel would be punished by their enemies.

Yet Hosea offered a message of hope:

→ The people will not be destroyed by the Assyrians and, through their suffering, God will heal them.
→ The suffering of the people – punishment – is an act of loving discipline.
→ After the time of discipline, Israel will repent and return to a new beginning.

Hosea's words come true. In 721 BCE the Assyrians conquered the land of Israel and the Israelites were taken away in exile.

Background

Hosea used the symbolism of husband and wife to illustrate the relationship between God and Israel, with God as the bridegroom and Israel as the unfaithful bride.

Terminology

Hosea taught that 'knowing' God really meant responding personally to God's love.

Terminology

God will change the emphasis of the relationship – from husband and wife to parent and child.

Checkpoint 2

What did Hosea mean by 'pagan gods'?

Examiner's secrets

Amos and Hosea are very popular. The most important thing is to know the meaning and significance of their message, rather than tell the story of their lives.

Exam question   answer: page 47

Explain the message of Amos and Hosea concerning righteousness and God's judgement of Israel.   (45 mins)

Micah and Isaiah

The idea of a 'Messiah' (Hebrew: 'mashiach') or 'Anointed One' became an important feature of Judaism. It was the belief that God would one day send a great Messiah-King who would establish God's everlasting kingdom. Two of the most important prophets who spoke of the future Messiah were Micah and Isaiah.

The prophet Micah

Micah lived in the eighth century BCE. He warned the people that God was going to punish them for their sins. Yet after this punishment would come peace and restoration. One day, a redeemer from God would come and deliver the people from oppression and injustice and restore their relationship with God.

The prophet Isaiah

Isaiah lived at the same time as Micah. His message to the people was that the real danger for them was not the Assyrians but their disobedience and their failure to trust God. He also had a message of hope – a future time when God would send a deliverer for his people.

Second Isaiah

Most theologians believe that chapters 40–66 of Isaiah come from about two hundred years later, when the people were living in exile. These chapters are sometimes called Second Isaiah or Deutero-Isaiah. The setting is at the time when the Jews in exile in Babylon prepared to return to Jerusalem, their punishment over.

God's forgiveness means a new beginning for Israel and the kingdom of God will be established on earth.

The theme of universalism

God is Israel's redeemer, and he is the redeemer for all humanity, not just the Israelites:

> I will keep you and will make you
> to be a covenant for the people
> and a light for the Gentiles. (Isaiah 42:6)

Background

Micah is best known for his prophecy that the Messiah would be born in Bethlehem: 'But you, Bethlehem Ephrathah, though you are small among the clans of Judah, out of you will come for me one who will be ruler over Israel, whose origins are from old, from ancient times' (Micah 5:2).

Useful quotations

'For to us a child is born, to us a son is given, and the government will be on his shoulders. And he will be called Wonderful Counsellor, Mighty God, Everlasting father, Prince of Peace . . .' (Isaiah 9:6).

Background

In 539 BCE, the Babylonian Empire was overthrown by King Cyrus of Persia. He was an enlightened ruler and he soon allowed all the foreign exiles in the empire to return to their homelands, including the Jews.

Terminology

'Gentiles' is the term used to describe the peoples that are non-Jews.

Checkpoint 1

What does the term redeemer mean?

The servant

Isaiah talks of the servant, a mysterious figure who will undertake to do God's future work of redemption. It is not clear who the servant actually is – he may be a symbolic representation of Israel itself, or a person or prophet chosen by God or the Messiah. He is blessed and empowered by God, with a mission to all humanity. The important features of the servant narratives are:

→ He is not a warrior, but comes in humility.
→ It is through his suffering that Israel will enter into a new age and the kingdom of God will be established.
→ The servant is depicted as 'a man of sorrows'.
→ He is despised by the world.
→ His heavenly background is unrecognised.
→ The servant will suffer a great 'punishment' from God.
→ He will not be punished for his own sins, but instead he will take upon himself the sins of humanity.
→ The servant is a 'vicarious sacrifice', that is, through his redemptive act, all those who accept his sacrifice and turn to God will be saved.
→ He is imprisoned and executed as a criminal.
→ The servant willingly goes to his death and does not cry out or blame others.
→ The suffering of the servant is part of God's divine plan of salvation.
→ The sacrifice of the servant was God's way of providing a means by which people could be freed from sin and have a personal relationship of love with God.
→ The servant's mission will end in victory. Through God's love and justice, the servant will be restored.

Useful quotations

'But it is more likely that he was thinking of some future person in whose life the ideals of Israel's covenant faith would become a reality, and through whom God's intentions for his people and the world could be brought to pass' (John Drane *Introducing the Old Testament*, p. 175).

Useful quotations

'He was despised and rejected by men, a man of sorrows, and familiar with suffering' (Isaiah 53:3).

Background

In the days of Moses, the people of Israel would symbolically place their sins on a goat (Leviticus 16) that would then be sacrificed – the goat was a 'guilt offering' and would die for the sins of the people.

Checkpoint 2

What is a vicarious sacrifice?

Examiner's secrets

This is a difficult area. You must be aware of the prophecies concerning the servant and what his mission of redemption was. Don't try this unless you really understand the subject well!

Exam question   answer: page 47

Consider the different views of scholars concerning the possible identity of the servant.   (30 mins)

Jonah, Jeremiah and Ezekiel

The later prophets were concerned with the judgement of God and a message of future hope for the people.

The prophet Jonah

Jonah is commissioned by God to go to the city of Nineveh (the capital of Israel's enemy, Assyria) and warn the citizens that their city would be destroyed if they did not repent and change their wicked ways. Jonah refuses to go and is swallowed by a fish, which spewed him up on land near Nineveh. Jonah preached repentance and the people of Nineveh changed their ways and God forgave them. Jonah was furious with God for not carrying out his threat and sulks in the desert. Jonah is rebuked by God for not accepting that God can show sorrow and pity for the people of Nineveh.

The Book of Jonah had a special message for the people of Israel:

→ God was a being of love, not anger.
→ God showed compassion, justice and mercy.
→ God loved all peoples, not just the Jews.

The prophet Jeremiah

Jeremiah's message was that God was God of all creation, not just the Jews. He worked from about 626 BCE until 587 BCE after the fall of Jerusalem and the destruction of the temple by the Babylonians. His message had the following features:

→ He warned the people to repent or face God's judgement.
→ He urged the people not to resist the invading Babylonians – an invasion that ended in great destruction and the exile of the people.
→ The temple could be a sign not just of salvation, but of God's judgement as well.
→ He warns them that God will reject the people.
→ Empty rituals and sacrifice will not save them.
→ The temple will not act as a guarantee that he will protect them.
→ What God requires are loyal and obedient hearts.

The people did not change their ways, the temple was destroyed and the people were taken to Babylon in exile.

Jeremiah had a message of hope. The exile would last 70 years and then God would restore them to the promised land.

Jeremiah goes on to say that the future holds fresh hope because God will make a new covenant with the people. This covenant will not be like the old one, based on laws and obedience; instead it will be a personal covenant, written on the people's hearts, based on love, faith and trust.

The prophet Ezekiel ●●●

Ezekiel lived in exile in Babylon from around 593–571 BCE. His teaching concerned human destiny. He said that God was concerned with individuals as well as the community. The people complained about their suffering. They felt that God was punishing them for the sins of their forefathers and that they were not to blame.

Ezekiel said that this response was wrong. His message to the people was:

→ The acts of previous generations did not determine the situation of the present generation.
→ Each individual was responsible for their own destiny and would answer personally to God.
→ The present generation were not innocent – they were sinful and had to accept responsibility for their actions.
→ God's justice means that they must take personal responsibility and have faith in God's mercy.

Useful quotations

'I will put my law in their minds and write it on their hearts. I will be their God, and they will be my people' (Jeremiah 31:33).

Background

Ezekiel is difficult to understand. He claimed to receive the word of God through ecstasy and visions and seemed to have psychic abilities. His words were often obscure.

Useful quotations

'The fathers eat sour grapes, and the children's teeth are set on edge . . . The way of the Lord is not just' (Ezekiel 18:2, 25).
'Repent! Turn away from all your offences; then sin will not be your downfall. Rid yourselves of all the offences you have committed and get a new heart and a new spirit' (18:31–32).

Checkpoint 2

What did the Jews mean by the sins of their forefathers?

Exam question   answer: page 48

What was new about Jeremiah's 'new covenant'?   (30 mins)

Wisdom literature

Wisdom is the search for the meaning of life. The wisdom literature books are different from the rest of the Old Testament. They do not speak about worshipping God or the covenant relationship between God and Israel, but instead they focus on human experience and morality.

Background

The literature falls into two categories. The first is advice on how to live a godly life. The second examines the meaning of life and the nature of suffering.

Useful quotations

'Wisdom is not just the key to proper ethical behaviour; it seeks to grasp the secret of the divine plan behind the whole creation' (Bernhard W. Anderson, *The Living World of the Old Testament* (1988)).

Useful quotations

'There is a time for everything, and a season for every activity under heaven . . .
. . . I know that everything God does will endure forever' (Ecclesiastes 3:1,14).
'I despise my life; I would not live forever. Let me alone; my days have no meaning' (Job 7:16)

Background

Job's problem is that he sees everything only from his own viewpoint – he tries to find the meaning of life on his own terms, not God's.

Checkpoint 1

Why does Satan want to torment Job?

The Book of Ecclesiastes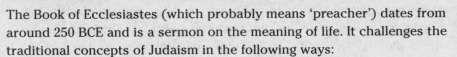

The Book of Ecclesiastes (which probably means 'preacher') dates from around 250 BCE and is a sermon on the meaning of life. It challenges the traditional concepts of Judaism in the following ways:

→ By suggesting that life has little or no meaning.
→ There may be no real way for humanity to ever truly understand God or life.
→ Wisdom would show people how to live righteously and lead them to an understanding of God himself.
→ There is order and there is mystery beyond man's understanding.

The Book of Job

The Book of Job is concerned with the nature of existence and the individual's personal relationship with God. It tells the story of Job, a righteous man whom God allows to be tormented by Satan. Job loses his family and loved ones and is inflicted with severe boils and forced to sit alone outside the city. His friends tell Job that he must have sinned and should ask God for forgiveness and say that Job is too proud and God is rightly punishing him. Job challenges God:

→ He maintains his innocence – he may have sinned, but he does not deserve this punishment.
→ He wishes to die, because he no longer seems to have a meaningful relationship with God.
→ He calls God a tyrant (9:18) and a savage beast (16:7).
→ He wishes that God would leave him alone.
→ Job is frustrated because he cannot meet God as an equal in order to defend himself.

This highlights the great divide between God and humanity.

→ The wisdom of God is completely beyond human thought.
→ God is the absolute ruler and humans are earthly creatures trapped by the power of sin and death.

God speaks to Job in a whirlwind. God does not answer Job's questions. Instead, he tells him at great length that he is a finite creation who cannot begin to comprehend God, the creator of the universe.

Job is wrong to challenge God, who maintains the universe itself by divine power. Job knows he has presumed too much. He has no grounds for being angry with God and repents. Job's fortunes are restored and he enjoys a new and personal relationship with God.

The meaning of the Book ●●●

Job highlights the fact that the mystery of suffering cannot be resolved simply by reference to reward and punishment. It looks deeper, into the very heart of the relationship between God and humanity, a relationship that is based upon God's grace and human faith.

The Psalms ●●●

The Book of Psalms (Hebrew 'Tehillin') consists of 150 pieces of religious poetry and songs that were brought together for use in worship in the second temple after the return from exile, around 520 BCE. Although many were written at that time, several are much older. The Psalms had an important function because Israel was a covenant community, united in worship of God. The people could praise God, question God and complain to him in times of distress.

Psalm 105 is the grandest of the hymns of praise and it speaks of God's goodness and greatness, as shown through his deeds in creation and throughout history. It begins with a call to worship, followed by reasons for praise and the confession of faith in God's actions.

Other Psalms reflect the dark state of human despair and mystery. These are not songs of self-pity, but of praise in the depths of despair, looking forward to the time when God will redeem his people. A good example is Psalm 137.

Useful quotations

'Where were you when I laid the earth's foundation?
Tell me, if you understand. Who marked off its dimensions?
Surely you know!' (Job 38:4–5).

Terminology

The German scholar Hermann Gunkel classified the Psalms into five categories – hymns of praise, individual laments, community laments, individual songs of thanks and the 'Royal Psalms'.

Useful quotations

'Sing to him, sing praise to him, tell of his wonderful acts . . . for he remembered his holy promise given to his servant Abraham.
He brought his people out rejoicing' (Psalm 105:2, 42).
'By the rivers of Babylon we sat and wept when we remembered Zion . . .
How can we sing the songs of the Lord while in a foreign land?' (Psalm 137:1).

Checkpoint 2

What did it mean to say that Israel was a covenant community?

Examiner's secrets

The key to answering Job questions is to concentrate on his conversations with his friends and with God, rather than write about the details of his life.

Exam question   answer: page 48

Explain how the Book of Job tries to answer the question of the relationship between God and suffering.   (45 mins)

Answers
Old Testament

Introducing the Old Testament

Checkpoints

1 Holy means set apart from the physical word or belonging to God.
2 To say God is personal means that he can be related to directly by the individual. He is not remote and distant.

Exam question

For original sin, try to discuss the nature of sin in the story of Adam and Eve. Also, what sin means and why the sin of Adam is said by believers to still be in humanity today. For the Exodus, you need to discuss the journey in the wilderness, the importance of God's guiding and saving actions, the giving of the Law and the bonding together of the people of God into one community in the promised land.

Examiner's secrets

There is a tremendous danger of narrative answers when dealing with Old Testament questions. This can gain you very few marks indeed and is often the sign of a very weak candidate.

Old Testament concepts

Checkpoints

1 Election means chosen – in this case, people who are chosen by God.
2 To be a holy nation meant that the people, having been chosen by God, had to live their lives with God at the centre.

Exam questions

(a) You must discuss how the Covenant was a special agreement between God and his people. Say what the terms of the Covenant were and quote from Scripture. Don't forget, there were covenants with Noah, Abraham, Moses and David.
(b) Try to show how the Covenant meant that the Hebrews were special to God and different from other races. Explain the importance of this – include such terms as holiness, righteousness, faith and obedience. Then consider why they had been chosen – to spread the word of God to all nations and to be a holy nation themselves. Don't forget to include some scholars.

Abraham

Checkpoints

1 Abraham threw them out because he now had a legitimate son, Isaac, to inherit his property.

2 Abraham agreed to sacrifice Isaac because he had faith in God and knew he had to obey his commands – whatever they were.

Exam question

Pick two incidents that give you plenty to say – perhaps the sacrifice of Isaac and the fact that Abraham had left his homeland and obeyed God's calling. Examine these incidents – and the views of scholars – and highlight how trust in God was at the heart of Abraham's life. You might also comment on the fact that Abraham did not always trust God – for example, when he handed his 'sister' over to the Pharaoh.

Moses

Checkpoints

1 Moses had to know the name of God because, in those days, people worshipped many gods and it was important that Moses could verify to his people just who God was.
2 The Ark of the Covenant was the box which not only held the tablets of the Law, but was also, symbolically, the place where God dwelt when he was with his people.

Exam questions

(a) This question requires an understanding of the religious features – such as Moses having to take his shoes off, the fact that God speaks through fire, the bush does not burn, light, obedience and so on. Very important – don't just tell the story of the incident, but look for the meaning and symbolism.
(b) You must assess the good and bad points of Moses' leadership. For instance, he is a strong leader, as shown in the getting of the Law, the Golden Calf incident and firm leadership through 40 years in the wilderness. He has great faith in God. However, he has his weaknesses too – he gives in to some of the people's demands and he is not always faithful to God. Try to get arguments on both sides – and don't forget the views of scholars.

The monarchy

Checkpoints

1 The role of a judge was to govern the tribe in accordance with the Law of Moses.
2 It upset the balance because the relationship between God and the people was based on the notion that God was king of all creation.

Exam questions

(a) You will need to discuss a variety of reasons – such as the failure of the system of judges, the need for unity and the desire of the people to be like the other nations.
(b) Examine carefully Samuel's reasons, which are based on the notion of the Covenant and on the kingship of God. Make use of the textual narrative and the views of scholars to back up your arguments.

Saul and David

Checkpoints

1 Samuel killed Agag because that is what God had commanded.
2 Saul committed suicide because he was mentally disturbed and believed that God had deserted him.

Exam questions

(a) Try to weigh up Saul's reign from both the good and bad sides – he was a skilful warrior who saved his people from their enemies and he didn't burden the people with oppressive taxes. On the bad side, he disobeyed God's express commands.
(b) Look at both sides of the argument – Samuel anointed Saul and helped him in the early stages, but later turned against Saul when he disobeyed God. Try to assess whether Samuel could have done more to help. The views of scholars concerning the varying accounts from the writers of the text could be useful.

Examiner's secrets

Evaluation shouldn't be difficult in these essays about the monarchy. The biblical writers have clearly laid out the different sides of the cases and you can use a good blend of textual analysis, scholarly exegesis and good essay technique to build strong arguments.

King Solomon

Checkpoints

1 The Ark was housed in the temple because the temple was the dwelling place of God among his people.
2 Each tribe had particular traditions and members felt a sense of belonging (loyalty) to their particular tribe and its traditions.

Exam question

You will need to balance both sides. Show how Solomon was successful – he built up strong trade, made the nation secure, built the temple and so on. Then look at the failures – oppressive taxation, end of tribal loyalties, pagan gods, extravagance and failure to unite the nation, leading to a split at his death. The views of scholars are very important.

The development of prophecy

Checkpoints

1 Righteousness is the quality of being right, good or innocent, through obedience to God's laws.
2 A false prophet is someone who claims to bring a message from God but who has received no such message.

Exam question

This is a difficult question. You must know the views of several scholars and understand the forms and functions – this will include extensive use of technical terms such as 'nabi' and an appreciation of what the prophets did – bringing messages from God, calling for repentance, warning of judgement, guiding the people, leading in worship and so on.

Amos and Hosea

Checkpoints

1 Empty rituals were ceremonial actions performed by the people in the hope that God would bless them. They were empty because they were done without real love or feeling for God – they did not come from the heart.
2 Pagan gods were the gods worshipped by other nations and peoples.

Exam question

Amos and Hosea are popular. Make sure you know their message and the meaning behind them. You might include the link between Hosea's message and his own family life and look at Amos' view of moral and social righteousness. When discussing judgement, remember that after judgement came a message of hope for the future. This question requires extensive reference to the text itself and to the views of scholars.

Micah and Isaiah

Checkpoints

1 A redeemer is someone who pays the price for another person's freedom – in this case, freedom from sin.
2 A vicarious sacrifice is one that is made by someone who is innocent on behalf of another, who is guilty.

Exam question

You must be aware of the views of a range of scholars and the controversy surrounding the identity of the servant – ideal man, Messiah, redeemer and so on. Make extensive reference to the detail of the textual narrative and assess the views of scholars. You might conclude by evaluating which view is the most convincing.

Jonah, Jeremiah and Ezekiel

Checkpoints

1 The destruction was a blow because the Jews believed the temple was the dwelling place of God and that God would never allow it to be destroyed.
2 The Jews believed that people could be punished in this generation for the sins committed by their ancestors (forefathers).

Exam question

This question requires detailed knowledge of Jeremiah, particularly chapters 29–31. Keep close to the textual narrative and explain how the covenant Jeremiah was talking about was different – based on love, written on the hearts of the people and so on. Be prepared to quote from the text and the views of scholars. You should also make reference to the previous covenants, e.g. those made with Moses and Abraham, to highlight the difference.

Wisdom literature

Checkpoints

1 Satan wanted to torment Job to prove that Job only worshipped God because God had treated him so well.

2 A covenant community is a community based on everyone being committed to, and leading their lives in accordance with, the Covenant.

Exam question

This question requires a detailed knowledge of the Book of Job, particularly the conversations between Job and his friends and with God. Quote from the textual narrative and the views of scholars and look for the important issues – why does a loving God allow his people to suffer? Can people influence God? Why does God act as he does? The best answers will be those that look at a few major issues in depth, rather than those that simply retell the story.

Revision checklist
Old Testament

1	Have a secure knowledge of Old Testament concepts.	Confident	Not confident. **Revise** pages 24–5
2	Know, understand and evaluate the role of Abraham.	Confident	Not confident. **Revise** pages 26–7
3	Be able to discuss and evaluate the role of Moses.	Confident	Not confident. **Revise** pages 28–9
4	Have a strong foundation of facts and understanding regarding the Israelite monarchy.	Confident	Not confident. **Revise** pages 30–31
5	Be clear as to the roles and contributions of Saul and David.	Confident	Not confident. **Revise** pages 32–3
6	Know and understand the textual information regarding Solomon and evaluate his effectiveness.	Confident	Not confident. **Revise** pages 34–5
7	Have a secure knowledge and understanding of the development of prophecy.	Confident	Not confident. **Revise** pages 36–7
8	Know, understand and evaluate the key ideas associated with Covenant and Law.	Confident	Not confident. **Revise** pages 24–5
9	Be able to convey knowledge and understanding of the work of Amos and Hosea.	Confident	Not confident. **Revise** pages 38–9
10	Have a strong bank of information regarding the prophecies of Isaiah and Micah.	Confident	Not confident. **Revise** pages 40–41
11	Understand the place of Jonah, Jeremiah and Ezekiel in the prophetic tradition.	Confident	Not confident. **Revise** pages 42–3
12	Be able to discuss the nature and purpose of wisdom literature.	Confident	Not confident. **Revise** pages 44–5

The New Testament consists of 27 books written in the decades following the death of Christ. These books cover the life and teachings of Jesus Christ, the development of the early Church and the letters of Paul, which contained the fundamental Christian teachings. It ends with the book of Revelation, which talks about the end of all things. The most famous books, the four Gospels, tell of the life and ministry of Jesus Christ. This chapter looks at the ministry of Jesus, including his controversial teachings and the inevitable conflict with the religious and political authorities. It culminates in the Passion of Christ, his death and, finally, the resurrection, and includes deeper and more complex religious teachings, on the nature of forgiveness, atonement and salvation. The Fourth Gospel is a more symbolic and thematic gospel than the synoptic gospels. It requires a greater understanding of religious and theological issues. The background is therefore key to appreciating the main themes and the signs, wonders and teachings of Christ contained within it.

Exam themes

→ The birth and infancy of Jesus
→ The nature of discipleship
→ The parables
→ The life and example of Jesus Christ
→ The miracles
→ The Sermon on the Mount
→ Women in the Gospels
→ The ethic and social teachings of Jesus
→ The authorship and date of the Gospels
→ The religious, social and cultural setting
→ The purpose of the Gospels
→ Religious and social teachings

→ The nature and person of Jesus Christ
→ Salvation and the kingdom of God
→ The conflict with the authorities
→ The Passion
→ The Last Supper
→ The trial of Jesus
→ The crucifixion narratives
→ The resurrection
→ The Prologue to the Fourth Gospel
→ The Holy Spirit and women in the Fourth Gospel
→ The 'I am' sayings in the Fourth Gospel
→ The views of scholars

Topic checklist

AS ○ A2 ●	OCR	AQA	EDEXCEL
The background to the life of Christ	○●	○●	○●
The birth and infancy narratives			○
Parables in Matthew and Mark	●	●	
Parables in Luke's Gospel			○
Miracles in Matthew and Mark	●	○	
Miracles in Luke's Gospel			○
The Sermon on the Mount	●	○	
Religious themes in Luke's Gospel			○●
Social themes in Luke's Gospel			○●
The Passion in Matthew and Mark	○	●	
The Passion in Luke			●
Death and resurrection in Matthew and Mark	○	●	
Death and resurrection in Luke			●
The authorship of the Fourth Gospel			○
Date, origin and influences			○
The purpose of the Fourth Gospel			●
The Prologue	●	●	●
The Holy Spirit and women in the Fourth Gospel			○
The early ministry of Jesus		○●	○●
Jesus' later ministry		○●	○●
The road to the Cross		○●	○●
The death of Jesus	○	●	●

The background to the life of Christ

Terminology

God's law became known as the 'Law of Moses'. The most famous part was the Ten Commandments.
All Jews saw themselves as 'sons of Abraham'.

Background

The Law of Moses required all Jews to be present at the temple for these festivals at least once per year.
The Sanhedrin was the governing body of the Jews. It governed all the religious aspects of their lives. It was presided over by the High Priest who, at the time of Jesus, was called Caiaphas.

Checkpoint 1

When was the Jewish sabbath?

Take note

The synagogue service followed a pattern – the creed, prayers, readings from the law and the prophets, and a sermon.
Only the High Priest could enter the 'Holy of Holies', and he did so once a year on the Day of Atonement.

The people of Israel, the Jews, believed that they were God's 'Chosen People'.

The historical setting

Abraham, who lived around 2000 BCE, had been chosen by God to be the father of a race of people who would be a holy, chosen people. God and Abraham had made a 'covenant' – an agreement by which the Jews would be God's people and God, in turn, would look after them and be 'their God'. Under the leadership of Moses, the people received God's law. The Jews settled in Israel but, as the centuries passed, ignored the Covenant and failed to live by the law and lapsed into sinful ways. Israel was conquered a number of times. Finally, Israel became part of the Roman Empire.

The social and religious setting

- → Jewish life centred on the home.
- → Most men were farmers, fishermen or shepherds.
- → The women kept house.
- → Everyday issues of justice were resolved by priests.
- → Important cases were decided by the Sanhedrin.
- → The Sanhedrin was made up of 70 priests and elders under the rule of the chief priest at the temple.
- → Religious rules and regulations governed the lives of the Jews.
- → The greatest festival was the Day of Atonement, when the High Priest would enter the innermost shrine of the temple to ask forgiveness for his own sins and the sins of the people.
- → The other great festival was the Passover, which commemorated the escape from slavery in Egypt.
- → The great weekly festival was the sabbath.
- → Regular worship took place in the local synagogue.
- → Only men were permitted to play an active part, under the guidance of the ruler of the synagogue.
- → The temple in Jerusalem was the centre of Judaism. Inside was the 'Holy of Holies', the dwelling place of God.
- → The ordinary people had to pay a 'temple tax' for the upkeep of the temple, which they greatly resented.
- → The temple had its own temple guards, and resembled a fortress and a treasury.

The Jewish authorities had made the religious rules very complex, strict and overbearing, governing the lives of all the Jews. The spirit of God's law had become lost in a mass of regulations.

Religious groups

The Pharisees

→ The Pharisees were the largest of the religious parties.

→ They controlled religious rather than political affairs and worked mostly in the synagogues.

→ Their main concern was to ensure that the people kept the law and traditions in every exact detail.

→ They kept themselves apart from the ordinary people.

→ Their insistence on the letter of the law made them appear dry and legalistic, rather than loving and just.

The Sadducees

→ They were priestly, rich landowners.

→ Their main interest seemed to be in political power.

→ They held half the seats in the Sanhedrin.

→ Most of the chief priests had been Sadducees.

→ They rejected ideas such as immortality and resurrection.

The titles of Jesus

Throughout the Gospels, Jesus is given a variety of titles:

→ **Jesus** – this is a common first name for a Jewish male.

→ **Christ** – from the Greek 'Christos', which means 'anointed one'.

→ **Son of Man** – a title that Jesus used to describe himself when talking about his messiahship and death.

→ **Son of David** – from the Old Testament notion that the Messiah would be a descendant of King David.

→ **Son of God** – highlights Jesus' unique relationship with God.

→ **I am** – the name of God, given to Moses in Exodus (3:14). Jesus uses it to highlight his own divinity.

→ **The Lamb** – Jesus represents the lamb which is sacrificed for the forgiveness of sins.

→ **Messiah** – the anointed one who would one day come from God and save Israel.

Background

The Pharisees had more contact with the ordinary people than the Sadducees. The latter compromised with the Romans and were deeply unpopular.

Terminology

The term 'Messiah' (in Hebrew 'Mashiah' and in Greek, 'Christos') was used to describe anyone entrusted with a divine mission.
Many Jews believed the Messiah would destroy the enemies of Israel and set up a Jewish kingdom, ruled by the line of David. Then, on the Last Day, the Messiah would gather up God's people for Judgement and life in paradise.

Checkpoint 2

What is the significance of the name 'Christ'?

Background

A lamb would be sacrificed as an atonement for sins. Jesus saw his death in the same way. The prophet Isaiah said that the 'servant' (possibly meaning the 'Messiah') would be 'led like a lamb to the slaughter' (53:7).

Examiner's secrets

You are unlikely to be asked specific questions about the background – but you need to know about it in order to put your answers into context.

Exam question   answer: page 96

What was the importance of (a) the temple and (b) the Law of Moses at the time of Jesus?   (30 mins)

The birth and infancy narratives

Many scholars believe that the birth and infancy narratives, even though they tell of Jesus' early life, are actually late additions to the Gospels of Matthew and Luke. The Gospels of Mark and John make no reference to the birth story.

Matthew's account (1:18–2:23)

The theme of Matthew's birth narratives is that the coming of Jesus Christ fulfils the prophesies in the Old Testament.

→ The account traces the ancestry of Jesus back to Abraham.
→ Jesus is referred to as the 'son of David', fulfilling the Old Testament promise that the throne of King David would be established forever (2 Samuel 7:16).
→ Matthew quotes from the prophet Micah that the king will be born in Bethlehem, the city of David.
→ Matthew quotes from Isaiah that a virgin would give birth and the child would be called 'Immanuel'.
→ Herod's order to slaughter the baby boys reflects the prophecy of Jeremiah.

Luke's account (1:8–2:40)

The theme in Luke's account is the continuity between Judaism and Christianity:

→ It begins in Judaism, with the story of John the Baptist. His parents are of Jewish priestly heritage.
→ The angel later visits Mary and tells her that she has been chosen to be the mother of God's son.
→ The child will be from the line of David and his kingdom will never end (v. 33).
→ He will be conceived by the power of the Holy Spirit.
→ Mary visits Elizabeth, the mother of John the Baptist. She refers to Mary as 'the mother of my Lord' (v. 43).
→ Mary sings a hymn full of Old Testament language and imagery.
→ Zechariah, John's father, sings a hymn of praise, thanking God for the salvation that is to come.

Scholars' views

Some scholars have suggested that the narratives were put in by the early Church to provide answers to some of the problems concerning the nature of Jesus ('Christology').

Terminology

'Immanuel' means 'God with us'.

Useful quotations

'A voice is heard in Ramah, weeping and great mourning, Rachel weeps for her children and refusing to be comforted, because they were no more' (Jeremiah 31:15).

Terminology

The visit of the angel to Mary is called the Annunciation.
Mary's hymn is called the Magnificat.
Zechariah's hymn is called the Benedictus.
Simeon's hymn is called the Nunc Dimittis.

Checkpoint 1

Why was it important that Jesus was born in Bethlehem?

Examiner's secrets

Questions on the birth of Jesus are often badly done because candidates just tell the Christmas story, rather than look at the detail and religious significance.

Luke's account of the birth of Jesus is well known:

→ Joseph and Mary go to Bethlehem for a census.
→ Jesus is born there in humble surroundings.
→ Angels sing songs of praise.
→ He is visited by shepherds.
→ He is circumcised, like John, after eight days.
→ At the temple, Simeon, a righteous man who had been told that he would not die until he had seen the Messiah, sings a hymn when he sees Jesus.
→ Anna, a prophetess, meets the holy family. She too was awaiting the coming of the Messiah.
→ He has come for all people, Jews and Gentiles (2:32).

Luke's narrative includes a further piece:

→ At the age of 12, Jesus is taken to Jerusalem for the Passover.
→ He is missing when his family leave Jerusalem.
→ They find him three days later talking with the teachers in the temple.
→ His words to his parents show that Jesus knew of his unique relationship with God: 'Didn't you know I had to be in my Father's house?' (2:49).

Luke's account emphasises the humble circumstances of Jesus' birth:

→ He has come for the poor and needy.
→ He was placed in a manger.
→ His first visitors are shepherds.

Background

Jesus' circumcision is known as the time he was 'presented at the temple'.

Background

Anna represents the view that some Jews were looking ahead to their salvation.

Background

In accordance with tradition (Exodus 23:14–17) Jewish boys aged 12 were taken to Jerusalem for the Passover. They would then become a 'son of the commandment' – in effect, an adult male.

Examiner's secrets

Beware – the Three Wise Men do *not* appear in Luke's account of the birth of Jesus.

Background

There is considerable reference in the Old Testament to the notion of God being a shepherd for his people – for instance, Psalm 23. However, in Jewish society, shepherds had a very low status and, because of their job, were unable to take part in religious ceremonies.

Checkpoint 2

What does the term 'Gentiles' mean?

Exam question   answer: page 96

Outline and examine the main features of the birth narratives presented in Luke's Gospel.   (30 mins)

Parables in Matthew and Mark

Much of Jesus' teaching was done in parables – short stories that Jesus used to teach religious truths. He tried to make his listeners think, so the meanings are not always clear at first – people had to discover the meaning for themselves.

Parables of the kingdom

Many of Jesus' parables were about the kingdom of God, and usually began with the words 'the kingdom of God is like . . .' He taught that the kingdom was present in him and would arrive for all people now and in the future. This has caused debate among scholars. The two most famous parables of the kingdom are the sower, (Matthew 13:1–23, Mark 4:1–20) and the banquet (Matthew 22:1–14).

The parable of the sower

This parable deals with the reasons why those who hear the message of the kingdom of God do not always act upon it. This parable shows that:

→ God's word is not heard in the same way by everyone.
→ It can only grow if the hearer has faith and a responsive heart.
→ The Word of God is represented by the seeds – falling on deaf ears, or on people who are too busy to listen.
→ Those who do hear it and accept it will benefit.

The parable of the banquet

The message of the kingdom is a symbolic one:

→ God, as the King, invites the Jews first.
→ They reject his invitation so he invites others – the Gentiles.
→ The invitation to the feast is made through God's grace to all – the deserving and the undeserving.
→ It will be an occasion of great joy, but those who refuse the invitation will miss out.
→ The meaning of the parable is that people must repent and change their lives.

Terminology

In the Old Testament, God's kingdom was shown through his mighty power. At the time of Jesus, the people believed that God would rid the land of the Romans and, under the Messiah, establish his kingdom on earth.

Scholars' views

The kingdom of God has caused debate among scholars:

Schweitzer said that Jesus was preparing the people for the immediate coming of the kingdom.

Dodd spoke of 'realised eschatology', that is, the kingdom of God was already present in the person and ministry of Jesus.

Sanders argued that the kingdom was coming in the distant future, after a Day of Judgement.

Background

In the parable of the banquet the guest who is thrown out represents a warning that God's gift is not to be taken lightly – if a person accepts the offer of the kingdom of God he/she must change their ways accordingly.

Checkpoint 1

What does the word 'parable' mean?

Parables of judgement: Matthew 25

Parables of judgement teach about the need to be prepared for the coming of the Messiah and the need for salvation.

The parable of the ten virgins: Matthew 25:1–13

The meaning of the parable is that the Jews, as God's chosen people, should have been prepared for the coming of the Messiah, but they were not and miss the Messianic Banquet.

The Parable of the talents: Matthew 25:14–30

Jesus is not talking about making lots of money. His teaching is concerned with how people see their relationship with God.

→ The first two servants represent the people who have used God's gifts wisely.
→ They will receive even greater gifts.
→ The third servant represents the Jewish religious authorities.
→ They were entrusted with God's law and failed to act wisely – they did not allow God's law to grow or his people to develop in righteousness.
→ The gift will be taken away from them.

The parable of the sheep and the goats: Matthew 25:31–46

Jesus' clearest teaching on judgement:

→ Those who help the needy with an open heart and not seeking reward for themselves will escape judgement.
→ By helping someone in such a way, people are actually loving God.

For I was hungry and you gave me something to eat. I was thirsty and you gave me something to drink . . . whatever you did for one of the least of these brothers of mine, you did for me. (35:40)

Background

One of the customs at a Jewish wedding was that the time of the ceremony would be kept secret and the guests would have to keep alert, waiting for it to happen.

Terminology

A talent was not a coin but a weight. Its value depended on whether it was made of gold, silver or copper.

Examiner's secrets

Remember – it is more important to explain the meaning of a parable than simply to tell it.

Useful quotations

'For everyone who has will be given more, and he will have an abundance. Whoever does not have, even what he has will be taken from him' (Matthew 25:29).

Checkpoint 2

What is the 'Messianic Banquet'?

Exam question   answer: page 96

Examine the message of judgement contained in the parable of the talents.

(30 mins)

Parables in Luke's Gospel

Jesus often taught in parables – short stories using real-life situations in which he taught religious truths. Such teaching was very popular among Jewish teachers. The parables were designed to make the listeners think, and they had to discover the meaning for themselves.

Parables of the kingdom

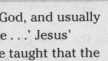

Many of Jesus' parables were about the kingdom of God, and usually began with words such as 'the kingdom of God is like . . .' Jesus' teaching on the kingdom is difficult to grasp since he taught that the kingdom was, on the one hand, 'present' and, on the other hand, would arrive at some time in the future.

The parable of the sower: 8:1–15

This parable deals with the reasons why not everyone who hears the message of the kingdom of God acts upon it. This parable shows that:

→ God's word is not heard in the same way by everyone.
→ It can only grow if the hearer has faith.
→ God's word is represented by the seeds – sometimes it falls on deaf ears, or on people who are too busy to listen.
→ Those who do hear it and accept it will benefit.

The parable of the banquet: 14:15–23

This is an image of the 'Messianic Banquet', where the righteous will eat with the Messiah. The parable addresses important religious issues:

→ Places at the banquet will not be given first to those who are important by human standards.
→ It is the humble who will receive the seats of honour.
→ Those who share the feast will not just be the Jews, who were first invited.
→ If they refuse then new guests, the Gentiles, will take their place.

Parables of the 'lost': Luke 15

The parables of the lost emphasise Luke's theme of seeking God and finding salvation. They add a fresh dimension – God does not simply wait for people to find him, he actively helps them to find him.

The parable of the lost sheep

Jesus shows God as a shepherd with 99 safe sheep and one lost sheep. He seeks the lost one and rejoices when he finds it. This highlights the joy of God over the return of one sinner who has repented.

The parable of the lost coin

A woman with ten silver coins loses one and she sweeps the whole house until she finds it – just as God will seek out the repentant sinner, and then rejoices.

The parable of the lost son

This parable shows the nature of God's forgiving love and highlights the contrast between the repentant sinner and those who feel they are righteous. The key features are:

→ The younger of two brothers asks his father for his share of the estate.
→ The father agrees and the son goes off to another country and spends it on riotous living.
→ When the money is spent, the son is forced to feed pigs in order to live.
→ He decides to return home and ask his father to give him a job as a servant.
→ His father overwhelms him with welcome.
→ He gives him the finest robe, a ring on his finger and shoes on his feet. He orders a feast of celebration.
→ The eldest brother complains to his father that he has worked hard for him, yet never been given a feast.

The parable is symbolic:

→ The father represents God.
→ The eldest son represents the 'righteous' Jews.
→ The youngest son represents repentant sinners.
→ God welcomes the sinner back and does not accept the complaint of the Jews who believe they are righteous.

Useful quotations

'. . . there will be more rejoicing in heaven over one sinner who repents than over ninety-nine righteous persons who do not need to repent' (v. 7).

Background

Feeding pigs was a distasteful job for a Jew, since the pig was regarded as an unclean creature (Leviticus 11:7).

Terminology

The ring given to the son symbolises authority, and he has shoes because only slaves went barefoot.

Background

The message to the Jews was that showing love to repentant sinners is not a threat to those who are already within the kingdom of God.

Checkpoint 2

What is 'sin'?

Examiner's secrets

Don't just retell the parables. Make sure you can discuss their meaning and significance.

Exam question   answer: page 96

Examine the meaning of the parable of the lost son.   (30 mins)

Miracles in Matthew and Mark

The miracles of Jesus play an important part in his mission. They show he has the authority and power of God over both the natural and the spiritual world. The miracles are of three main types – healings, exorcisms and nature miracles.

Exorcisms

The evil spirit: Mark 1:21–27

Jesus casts out a spirit from a man, to the astonishment of the onlookers. This story shows the authority of Jesus over the spiritual world – he speaks the word of command and, such is his authority, the spirit must leave.

The demon-possessed man: Matthew 8:28–34; Mark 5:1–20

Jesus cast the demons into a flock of swine, which then rushed into the lake and died. The man (men in Matthew) healed and the onlookers were amazed. The people were frightened and wanted Jesus to leave. In Mark, the man wanted to go with him. Jesus told him to stay where he was and to tell the people what had happened.

Healing miracles

The man with leprosy: Matthew 8:1–4; Mark 1:40–45

Jesus healed a leper with the command 'Be clean'. This miracle story contains symbolic elements:

→ Leprosy, as well as being a fatal disease, also made the sufferer ritually unclean.
→ They were often cast out of the community and the religious life of Israel.
→ The Law of Moses could do little for the sufferers.
→ Jesus healed the man and restored his ritual cleanliness so that he could rejoin his faith.
→ Jesus can fulfil the needs of the people far more than the Jewish leaders can.

The paralysed man: Matthew 9:1–8; Mark 2:1–13

Jesus heals the man by forgiving his sins. This miracle is a sign of Jesus' Messiahship:

→ Jesus acts in response to the faith of the man.
→ He cures him by forgiving his sins.
→ The Jewish leaders are outraged, believing that only God himself can forgive sins.
→ Jesus shows he has the power and authority of God.

Terminology

An exorcism is the casting out of an evil spirit.

Scholars' views

D. Nineham suggested that Jesus was actually commissioning the man to begin preaching to the Gentiles – the first step towards taking Jesus' message worldwide.

Background

The story ended with Jesus telling the man not to tell anyone, and to go and make the appropriate sacrifices in the temple (which were outlined in Deuteronomy. 24:8). This is a reference to Jewish practices and, in a sense, allows the man to show his gratitude to God for what has happened.

Background

In those days, it was believed that certain kinds of suffering, such as paralysis, were a punishment from God for the sins of either the person themselves or the sins of their parents.

Checkpoint 1

What did Jesus mean by having faith?

The sick woman: Mark 5:25–34

Jesus met a woman who had been bleeding for 12 years. She touched his cloak and was cured. Jesus said to her, 'Daughter, your faith has healed you. Go in peace and be freed from your suffering' (v. 34). Jesus emphasises the importance of faith. He asks the woman to declare her faith aloud, rather than keeping it secret in order that she can truly understand and accept what has happened.

The dead girl: Mark 5:21–24; 35–43

Jairus was a prominent Jew and the ruler of the local synagogue. He showed remarkable faith by asking Jesus to lay his hands upon his dying daughter. Jesus told Jairus to have faith, and raised the girl from death. The miracle showed:

→ Jesus' authority over death itself.
→ God is the creator of life and rules over death.
→ The miracle is a prelude to Christ's own resurrection.
→ God requires his people to have faith and to acknowledge the limits of human helplessness.

The centurion's servant: Matthew 8:5–13

This miracle highlights the importance of faith and the fact that the message of Jesus is for everyone, Jews and Gentiles. The Jews believed that when the Messiah came, there would be a great feast – the 'Messianic Banquet'. Jesus suggests here that Gentiles that have faith will be invited too.

Miracles over nature ●●●

Calming of the storm: Matthew 8:23–27; Mark 4:35–41

In this miracle, Jesus shows his divine power and control over the forces of nature. Jesus and his disciples were caught in a storm on the lake. Jesus calmed the storm by stern words – Jesus had complete control. There is a good deal of Old Testament symbolism here:

→ God has control over the waters (Isaiah 40:12).
→ He calms the storm (Psalm 107:29).
→ The storm shows the power of evil forces in the world (Psalm 69).
→ The righteous person is said to sleep peacefully in the faith that God will keep them safe.

Background

This illness caused the woman to suffer physically, and made her ritually unclean.

Background

Jesus held the dead girl's hand. This made him ritually unclean.

Useful quotations

'I say to you that many will come from the east and west and will take their places at the feast with Abraham, Isaac and Jacob in the kingdom of heaven' (Matthew 8:11).
'I will lie down and sleep in peace, for you alone, O Lord, make me dwell in safety' (Psalm 4:8)

Examiner's secrets

Don't just retell the story of the miracle – make sure you understand the meaning and significance of it.

Checkpoint 2

Why does Jesus make the bleeding woman declare what she has done?

Exam question   answer: page 96

What can be learned about the person of Jesus from the calming of the storm?   (20 mins)

Miracles in Luke's Gospel

The miracles of Jesus play a vital part in his mission. They emphasise the fact that he had the authority and power of God over both the natural and the spiritual world. They reflect the words spoken by Jesus himself when he quotes from the prophet Isaiah: 'He has sent me to proclaim freedom for the prisoners and recovery of sight for the blind' (Luke 4:18–19).

Exorcisms

The evil spirit: 4:31–37

Jesus was in the synagogue, confronted by a man who was possessed by an evil spirit. Jesus cast the spirit out of the man, to the astonishment of the onlookers. This story illustrates the authority of Jesus over the spiritual world – he speaks the word of command and the spirit must obey.

The demon-possessed man: 8:26–3

Jesus is in the Gentile region called Gerasenes. He casts out demons from the man and into a flock of swine, which then rushed into the lake and died. The man was healed and the onlookers were amazed. The people were frightened and wanted Jesus to leave, but the man wanted to go with him. Jesus told him to stay where he was and to tell the people 'how much God has done for you' (v. 39).

Healings

The paralytic: 5:17–26

Jesus was preaching at a house. A paralysed man was lowered through the roof of the house by his friends. They believed that Jesus could cure him. Jesus healed the man with the words 'Friend, your sins are forgiven' (v. 20).

→ This miracle is a sign of Jesus' Messiahship.
→ Jesus acts in response to the faith of the man. Jesus cures the man by forgiving his sins.
→ The Jewish leaders are angry, believing that only God himself can forgive sins.
→ Jesus' healing the man in this way shows he has the power and authority of God.

The sick woman: 8:40–48

Jesus was surrounded by a large crowd. A woman suffering from an illness that had left her bleeding for 12 years was healed when she touched Jesus' cloak. This highlights the importance of faith. Miracles cannot be performed without it.

Background

In Luke's accounts of exorcisms, the evil spirits always know exactly who Jesus is: *'What do you want with me, Jesus, Son of the Most High God? I beg you, don't torture me!'* (v. 28).

Take note

Some scholars have suggested that the healed man was the first person to preach the message of Jesus to the Gentiles.

Background

In those days, it was believed that certain kinds of suffering, such as paralysis, were a punishment from God for the sins of either the person themselves or the sins of their parents.

Background

This kind of illness also meant that the woman, as well as suffering physically, would be religiously 'unclean'.

Checkpoint 1

Why was the healing of the paralytic so difficult for the Jewish leaders to accept?

Examiner's secrets

Don't just tell the story of the miracles – explain their significance.

The dead girl: 8:49–56

Jairus was the ruler of the local synagogue. He asked Jesus to come to his house to lay his hands upon his dying daughter – quite a remarkable act of faith for a Jewish leader. However, by the time they reached the house, the girl had died. The key features of the miracle are:

→ Jesus tells Jairus to believe.
→ God requires his people to have faith.
→ Jesus takes the dead girl by the hand, even though touching a corpse was an act of ritual uncleanliness.
→ Jesus restores her to life.
→ Jesus tells the parents to keep the matter secret.

The centurion's servant: 7:1–10

This miracle highlights the importance of faith and the fact that Jesus came for both Jews and Gentiles. A Roman centurion asks Jesus to heal his servant. His faith was so great that he did not need Jesus to come to his house, just to say the word. The servant was healed and Jesus commended the centurion's faith: 'I have not found such great faith even in Israel' (v. 9).

Miracles over nature

The calming of the storm: 8:22–25

In this miracle Jesus gives clear evidence to his disciples of his divine power and control over the forces of nature.

Jesus and his disciples were caught in a storm on the lake. Jesus calmed the raging storm by stern words – Jesus had complete control. There is much Old Testament symbolism:

→ God has control over the waters (Isaiah 40:12).
→ God calms the storm (Psalm 107:29).
→ The storm shows the power of evil forces in the world (Psalm 69).
→ The righteous person is said to sleep peacefully in the faith that God will keep them safe.

Background

This miracle shows Jesus' ultimate authority over death itself – God is the creator of life and rules over death. The miracle was also a prelude to Christ's own resurrection.

Terminology

The reason why Jesus does not want people to know that he raised the girl from death is because of the 'Messianic Secret'. This is the view that Jesus did not want everyone to know who he was as this would interfere with his mission.

Useful quotations

'Who is this? He commands even the winds and the water, and they obey him' (8:25).

Checkpoint 2

What is ritual uncleanliness?

Exam question   answer: page 96

Examine the importance of the miracles in the ministry of Jesus.   (45 mins)

The Sermon on the Mount

The Sermon can be broken down into six sections:

1 The Beatitudes (5:1–6)
2 Jesus and the law (5:17–48)
3 True discipleship (6:1–18)
4 True righteousness (6:19–7:12)
5 The narrow gateway (7:13–23)
6 Building on secure foundations (7:24–29)

The Beatitudes

The Beatitudes are a collection of statements and prophecies. They highlight how life will be in the kingdom of God where the qualities of meekness, mercy and peace will be paramount; Jesus is teaching about spiritual qualities – those who mourn at the godlessness of the world and those who seek the will of God will be blessed. Such people face great persecution and Jesus urges them to have faith because in the end they will make a difference to the world.

Jesus and the law

Jesus teaches that the Law of Moses needs to be based upon love. Obedience to God's law must come from the believer's heart. Jesus addressed his teaching against emotions such as anger and lust, which lead to murder and ill-feeling.

True discipleship

Jesus taught that those who wish to follow him must love one another. They should give to the poor and worship God as part of a personal, living relationship. Worship should be done in secret and with a view to seeking and obeying God's will: 'So when you give to the needy, do not announce it with trumpets as the hypocrits do in the synagagues and in the streets to be honoured by men' (6:2).

Useful quotations

'Do not think that I have come to abolish the Law or the Prophets; I have not come to abolish them but to fulfil them' (5:17).

Terminology

The word beatitudes means 'blessings'.

Useful quotations

'Love your enemies and pray for those who persecute you' (5:44).

Examiner's secrets

Don't fall into the trap of thinking that Jesus came to change or abolish the Law of Moses. He came to ensure that the Law was interpreted in the right way – with a spirit of love and mercy, not harsh and judgemental.

Terminology

The most famous Christian prayer, 'The Lord's Prayer', is found in Matthew 6:9–13.

Checkpoint 1

What is the 'kingdom of God'?

True righteousness

Jesus said that disciples should take very seriously their commitment to the kingdom of God and the demands that are made of them. He encouraged his followers not to build up earthly treasure or to worry about earthly needs. He told them to have faith that God will provide for them: 'But seek first his kingdom and his righteousness, and all these things will be given to you as well' (6:33).

The narrow gateway

Jesus said that the path of discipleship was difficult and he warned that there would be trouble ahead. Discipleship requires serious commitment: 'Not everyone who says to me "Lord, Lord" will enter the kingdom of heaven, but only he who does the will of my Father who is in heaven' (7:21).

Building on secure foundations

Jesus emphasised the importance for his followers of three qualities:

→ Humility
→ Love
→ Righteousness.

Useful quotations

'Therefore everyone who hears these words of mine and puts them into practice is like a man who builds his house on the rock' (7:24).

Scholars' views

Barclay suggested that the Sermon on the Mount could be summed up in what he thought were the most famous words which Jesus spoke, namely 7:12: 'So in everything, do to others what you would have them do to you'.

Checkpoint 2

What is righteousness?

Exam question   answer: page 97

What did Jesus teach concerning the nature of discipleship?   (30 mins)

Religious themes in Luke's Gospel

Luke's Gospel contains unique features and teachings not found in the other Gospels.

Background

John is the fulfilment of the prophecy of Isaiah 40:3:
'A voice of one calling in the desert. "Prepare the way for the Lord".'.

John the Baptist

The role of John the Baptist is important. Luke highlights the important aspects of his life:

→ He was born a few months before Jesus and was a relative of Jesus.
→ His birth was unique because the parents were old and Elizabeth was barren. He is chosen by God to be the one who prepares the way for the Messiah.
→ As a man, John baptised the people and preaches a message of repentance and forgiveness.
→ He baptised with water, but told the people that one was coming who was much greater than he and who would baptise with the Holy Spirit and fire.
→ John was imprisoned by Herod and executed.

Scholars are undecided about the role of John:

→ **Conzelmann** argued John is the last of the Old Testament prophets.
→ **Marshall** sees John as a link between the old and new ages.
→ Marshall suggests that, for Luke, the era of salvation begins with John and Jesus.

Useful quotations

'John is the bridge between the old and new eras. He belongs to both, but essentially to the new one since he is the immediate forerunner of the Messiah. He is portrayed both as a prophet and as the first preacher of the gospel' (I. Howard Marshall, *Luke: Historian and Theologian* (1988)).

Terminology

The word 'salvation' comes from the Greek verb 'sozo', which means to 'make safe or well'.

Checkpoint 1

What does the word 'Gospel' mean?

Useful quotations

'This cup is the new covenant in my blood, which is poured out for you' (22:20).
'. . . the idea of salvation supplies the key to the theology of Luke' (Marshall).

Salvation

Luke teaches that humanity needs to be saved from the power of sin, which has separated humanity from God. This is achieved through the saving power of Jesus on the Cross. Luke highlights important issues:

→ Salvation is available to all people, not just the Jews.
→ Salvation is also for the Samaritans (9:51) and Gentiles (2:32).
→ Jesus gave the 'great commission' to his disciples to preach to all nations (24:47).
→ Not all will be saved; people must choose for themselves whether or not to accept it.
→ People must repent in preparation for salvation and the coming of the kingdom.
→ Jesus' death will mean the forgiveness of sins and will lead to reconciliation with God.
→ Salvation results in eternal life and freedom from sin.
→ Jesus as the culmination of God's history of salvation for his people.

Eschatology ●●●

Luke offers two differing views about the end of things:

→ The end is near – Jesus will return quickly and unexpectedly and believers must be ready.
→ The end is in the future – Jesus will come in great glory at a future date.

Luke emphasises the notion that the coming of the last days will be a time of joy and salvation.

Prayer and praise ●●●

Luke emphasises the importance to believers of prayer and praise:

→ He records the prayers of Jesus in detail.
→ In times of crisis, Jesus is shown praying for Peter (22:31), his enemies (23:34) and for himself (22:41).
→ Jesus uses parables to teach the need for meaningful and consistent prayer.
→ Jesus teaches the disciples to pray (6:28, 11:2 and 22:40). Jesus links prayer and praise together.
→ Through salvation and forgiveness humanity is reconciled to God, producing joy and praise.

Luke records several instances of praise, in particular:

→ The Magnificat – Mary's hymn after being told she will be having God's son.
→ The Benedictus – Zechariah's hymn.
→ The Nunc Dimittis – the hymn of Simeon.
→ Luke shows people who have received God's help praising him (2:20, 5:25, 7:16).
→ The Gospel ends on a note of praise: 'And they stayed continually at the temple, praising God' (24:53).

Terminology

Eschatology is the study of the 'end of things'.

Useful quotations

'You must also be ready, because the Son of Man will come at an hour when you do not expect him' (12:40).

Terminology

The word 'rejoice' occurs more times in Luke than in any other book in the New Testament.

Checkpoint 2

What did it mean for a person to repent?

Scholars' views

Leon Morris notes:
'Luke has written with a profoundly theological purpose. He sees God at work bringing salvation and he enjoys bringing out a variety of aspects of this saving work'. (Luke (1988)).

Examiner's secrets

Examiners look for technical terms – try to include words like eschatology and salvation in your answers, where relevant.

Exam question   answer: page 97

Discuss the teaching of Jesus concerning (a) prayer and (b) salvation.

(45 mins)

Social themes in Luke's Gospel

In Luke's Gospel, Jesus teaches much concerning social issues and, in particular, the treatment of others.

Useful quotations

'"Why do you eat and drink with tax collectors and sinners?"
Jesus answered them, "It is not the healthy that need a doctor, but the sick. I have not come to call the righteous, but sinners to repentance"' (5:31–32).
'The status of women was markedly inferior to that of men throughout the ancient world, including Judaism' (Graham Stanton, The Gospels and Jesus (1989)).
'In both pagan and Jewish society women were considered to be less intelligent than men . . . in the wider arena of social life, in politics and religious affairs, women had almost no role at all' (Peter Vardy and Mary Mills, The Puzzle of God (1999)).

Useful quotations

'Blessed are you who are poor, for yours is the kingdom of God' (6:20).

Checkpoint 1

Why did the Jews despise tax collectors?

Examiner's secrets

Women are a very important topic. Make sure you know about their social status as this information will be crucial in your answer.

Outcasts ●●●

Within Judaism, certain people were considered to be outcasts or 'sinners', including tax collectors, prostitutes and lepers. Jesus is seen closely associating with such people:

→ He calls Levi, a tax collector, to be one of his disciples (5:27).
→ He dines with sinners.
→ Jesus is the guest of Zacchaeus, a tax collector who receives salvation (19:1–10).
→ Jesus teaches of God's concern for outcasts in the parables of the lost son (15:11–32) and the great banquet (14:15–24).

Women ●●●

Women had an inferior role in Jewish society. The Law of Moses required them to be obedient and submissive, raising children and keeping house. However, Jesus emphasised the importance of women and they appear in important roles throughout the Gospel. Jesus' relationship with women is characterised in several ways:

→ Jesus allowed certain women to accompany his group.
→ He allowed women to listen to his teaching, as a pupil would to a rabbi – a privilege usually given to men.
→ Jesus breaks social conventions concerning women. For example, he allows a sinful woman to anoint his feet – an action usually seen as defilement.
→ Jesus performs miracles for the benefit of women – the woman with the haemorrhage (8:42), the widow of Nain, Jairus' daughter (8:49) and the crippled woman (13:10).
→ He refers to their great faith in the parables of the lost coin (15:8) and the unjust judge (18:1).
→ Women are always shown as faithful and obedient.
→ It is women who are the first to see the risen Christ.

Rich and poor ●●●

Luke stresses the importance of Jesus' preaching of the Gospel to the poor (4:18) and the preaching of the word of God to the poor seems to be very significant:

→ Jesus was born into humble circumstances.
→ His first visitors were poor shepherds.
→ Jesus spoke of the importance of caring for the poor.

Jesus warns of the dangers of wealth, because it can keep people from having a proper relationship with God. He does not just mean money, but also power and arrogance. The most important teachings are contained in:

→ The parables of the rich fool (12:16), the shrewd manager (16:1) and the rich man and Lazarus (16:19).
→ His conversation with the rich young ruler (18:18–27).
→ His encounter with Zacchaeus, who gives back his property to the poor and receives salvation (19:9).

Discipleship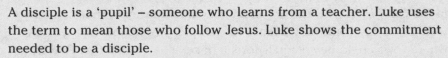

A disciple is a 'pupil' – someone who learns from a teacher. Luke uses the term to mean those who follow Jesus. Luke shows the commitment needed to be a disciple.

→ Repentance.
→ Giving up everything to follow Jesus.
→ Being prepared to accept persecution and death.

Luke also emphasises the positive benefits of discipleship:

→ The Holy Spirit would help in times of trouble.
→ Disciples would have the authority of Jesus to act in his name.
→ They would be filled with joy at their work.
→ They would be blessed by God.
→ The disciples would have a unique relationship with God, which would last forever.
→ They would achieve great things.
→ Their prayers would be answered.

The disciples would bring in the new age.

Exam question   answer: page 97

Examine Jesus' teaching on the problems of wealth.   (30 mins)

The Passion in Matthew and Mark

The last days before Jesus' death are known as 'The Passion' and the accounts of these times are of great religious significance.

The triumphal entry: Matthew 21, Mark 11 ●●●

In the Old Testament, the prophet Zechariah said that the King of the Jews would enter into Jerusalem riding on a donkey's colt. Jesus deliberately entered Jerusalem in this way, and was greeted by cheering crowds.

Cleansing the temple: Matthew 21, Mark 11 ●●●

In the Old Testament, the prophet Malachi had foretold that the Lord would one day come and cleanse his temple. The temple market was where Jews could buy animals for sacrifice, in the belief that God would forgive their sins. Jesus is angry and breaks up the market because God's message in the Old Testament was that he does not want sacrifices, but worship from the heart (Psalm 51:16).

For the next few days, Jesus preaches in the city, not only to Jews, but Gentiles as well. His message was for all people. He told them of the time of judgement to come and a time of darkness when only those who follow him will be saved.

The Lord's Supper: Matthew 26, Mark 14 ●●●

On the day upon which the Passover lamb is sacrificed, Jesus and his disciples eat the meal that is known as the 'Lord's Supper'. Important incidents occur at the meal:

→ Jesus says that one of his disciples will betray him.
→ Jesus breaks the bread and shares it with his disciples.
→ Jesus refers to the bread as his body.
→ He shares a cup of wine with the disciples. He says the wine is his blood, symbolising the new covenant.

The garden of Gethsemane: Matthew 26, Mark 14 ●●●

After the meal, Jesus and the disciples go to the garden of Gethsemane. Jesus tells the disciples that soon they will desert him, as predicted by the prophet Zechariah. Peter boasts that he will never desert Jesus, only to be told that he will betray Jesus three times before the cock crows.

Background

The triumphal entry put the Jewish authorities in a difficult position – if they did nothing, they would be seen to be admitting that Jesus was the Messiah. If they had Jesus arrested, they risked causing trouble among the people.

Checkpoint 1

What was Jesus' message in the market incident?

Background

All this time, the Jewish authorities are looking for a way to arrest and kill Jesus. It is the Passover, and they are anxious not to act during the feast itself in case they cause a riot.

Terminology

The eating of bread without yeast (called 'matzoth') was a requirement of the Law of Moses (Exodus 12:8).

Background

In the Old Testament, the blood of the first Passover lambs was used to protect the people of God from death. The blood from young bulls was used to seal the agreement between God and his people at the making of the Covenant.

In Gethsemane, Jesus asks the disciples to keep watch while he goes to pray. His words are full of intense emotion:

→ Jesus prays by falling to the ground – a sign of great spiritual anguish.
→ He addresses God with the Aramaic expression 'Abba' which is a formal use of the word 'Father'.
→ He asks that 'the cup' of suffering might be taken from him.
→ Jesus says he will carry out God's will.
→ Jesus returns to the disciples and finds them sleeping.

The arrest: Matthew 26, Mark 14 ●●●

The arrest of Jesus is filled with symbolic meaning:

→ Judas appears with an armed crowd.
→ Judas greets Jesus with a kiss and the word 'Rabbi' .
→ A disciple, probably Peter, draws a sword and cuts off the ear of a servant.
→ Jesus orders violence to cease.
→ He rebukes the Jewish authorities for arresting him at night.

Before the Sanhedrin: Matthew 26, Mark 14 ●●●

Jesus is taken before the Sanhedrin for a hearing, which soon becomes a trial. The proceedings are completely irregular and the Gospel writers make it clear that justice is not being done:

→ It takes place at night.
→ Jesus is not allowed to call witnesses on his own behalf.
→ Proper trial procedures are not observed. Jesus tells the Council he is the Christ.
→ He is found guilty of blasphemy under the Law of Moses, which is punishable by death.
→ They take Jesus before Pontius Pilate, the Roman Procurator.
→ Pilate asks Jesus if he is the King of the Jews.
→ Pilate reverts to the custom of releasing a prisoner to the people at Passover.
→ The crowd shout for Barabbas.
→ Reluctantly, Pilate condemns Jesus to death, even though he was innocent of any crime.

answer: page 97

Exam question

Discuss the view that it was the religious, rather than the political, authorities who were responsible for Jesus' death.   (45 mins)

Terminology

The cup is a symbol of suffering, referring to the Old Testament notion of the 'cup' of the anger of God (Psalm 75).

Background

Remaining awake and watchful was to be an important aspect of discipleship.

Checkpoint 2

What was the Sanhedrin?

Useful quotations

'The chief priests and the whole Sanhedrin were looking for evidence against Jesus so that they could put him to death' (Mark 14:55).

Examiner's secrets

Remember – the Jewish leaders have no authority to condemn a person to death, only the Roman political authorities could pass the death sentence or 'ius gladii'.

The Passion in Luke

The last days before Jesus' death are known as 'The Passion' and the accounts of these times are of great religious significance.

Background

The triumphal entry put the Jewish authorities in a difficult position – if they did nothing, they would be seen to be admitting that Jesus was the Messiah. If they had Jesus arrested, they risked causing trouble among the people.

The triumphal entry: 19:28–44 ●●●

In the Old Testament, the prophet Zechariah said that the King of the Jews would enter into Jerusalem riding on a donkey's colt. Jesus deliberately entered Jerusalem in this way, and was greeted by cheering crowds.

Terminology

Jesus' message in the market incident is that salvation does not require the sacrifice of animals. What is needed is faith in Jesus.

Cleansing the temple: 19:45–48 ●●●

In the Old Testament, the prophet Malachi had foretold that the Lord would one day come and cleanse his temple. The temple market was where Jews could buy animals for sacrifice, in the belief that God would forgive their sins. Jesus is angry and breaks up the market because God's message in the Old Testament was that he does not want sacrifices, but worship from the heart (Psalm 51:16).

For the next few days, Jesus preaches in the city, not only to Jews, but Gentiles as well. His message was for all people. He told them of the time of judgement to come and a time of darkness when only those who follow him will be saved.

Checkpoint 1

Why were the Jewish authorities anxious not to arrest Jesus during the Passover festival?

The Last Supper: 21:7–38 ●●●

On the Day of Unleavened Bread, upon which the Passover lamb is sacrificed, Jesus and his disciples eat the meal that is known as the 'Last Supper'. Important incidents occur at the meal:

Terminology

By eating the bread that is Christ's body, the disciples are symbolically able to have Jesus 'within' them.

→ Jesus says that one of his disciples will betray him.
→ Jesus breaks the bread and shares it with his disciples.
→ Jesus refers to the bread as his body.
→ He shares a cup of wine with the disciples. He says the wine is his blood, symbolising the new covenant.
→ Peter boasts that he will never desert Jesus, only to be told that he will betray Jesus three times before the cock crows.

Background

In the Old Testament, the blood of the first Passover lambs was used to protect the people of God from death. The blood from young bulls was used to seal the agreement between God and his people at the making of the Covenant.

The Mount of Olives: 22:39–46 ●●●

After the meal, Jesus and the disciples go to the Mount of Olives. Jesus asks the disciples to keep watch while he goes to pray. His words are full of intense emotion:

→ Jesus prays by kneeling on the ground – a sign of great spiritual anguish.
→ He addresses God with the formal use of the word 'Father'.

- He asks that 'the cup' of suffering might be taken from him.
- Jesus says he will carry out God's will.
- An angel comes to strengthen him.
- Jesus returns to the disciples and finds them sleeping.

The arrest: 22:47–62 ●●●

The arrest of Jesus is filled with symbolic meaning:

- Judas appears with an armed crowd.
- Judas tries to greet Jesus with a kiss.
- A disciple, probably Peter, draws a sword and cuts off the ear of a servant.
- Jesus orders violence to cease.
- He rebukes the Jewish authorities for arresting him at night.

Before the Jewish authorities: 22:63–71 ●●●

Jesus is taken to the house of the High Priest for a hearing, which soon becomes a trial before the chief priests and elders. The proceedings are completely irregular and the Gospel writers make it clear that justice is not being done:

- It takes place at night.
- Jesus is not allowed to call witnesses on his own behalf.
- Proper trial procedures are not observed. Jesus tells the Council he is the Son of God.
- He is found guilty of blasphemy under the Law of Moses, which is punishable by death.

Before Pilate: 23:1–25 ●●●

- They take Jesus before Pontius Pilate, the Roman Procurator:
- They accuse Jesus of subverting the nation, opposing tax payment and claiming to be the Christ.
- Pilate asks Jesus if he is the King of the Jews.
- Pilate finds no basis for a charge against Jesus.
- Pilate sends Jesus to Herod, who also finds no basis for a charge.
- The crowd shout for Barabbas to be released instead.
- Reluctantly, Pilate condemns Jesus to death, even though he finds him innocent of any crime.

Background

The cup is a symbol of suffering, referring to the Old Testament notion of the 'cup' of the anger of God (Psalm 75).

Terminology

Remaining awake and watchful was to be an important aspect of discipleship.

Useful quotations

'Every day I was with you in the Temple Courts, and you did not lay a hand on me. But this is your hour – when darkness reigns' (22:53).

Examiner's secrets

Remember – the Jewish leaders have no authority to condemn a person to death, only the Roman political authorities could pass the death sentence or 'ius gladii'.

Checkpoint 2

What is blasphemy?

Exam question   answer: page 97

Discuss the view that it was the religious, rather than the political, authorities who were responsible for the death of Jesus.   (45 mins)

Death and resurrection in Matthew and Mark

74

This is the climax of Jesus' ministry. Crucifixion was the method of execution used by the Romans on Jewish prisoners.

The crucifixion: Matthew 27, Mark 15 ●●●

The Roman soldiers mock Jesus, and place a crown of thorns on his head. The place of execution was a hill outside Jerusalem called 'Golgotha'. The crucifixion contains many important features:

→ Jesus was forced to walk through the city, facing the abuse of the citizens en route.
→ The soldiers seize a man called Simon of Cyrene and force him to carry Jesus' Cross.
→ Jesus is nailed to the Cross and offered myrrh/wine to drink.
→ The soldiers draw lots to see who would get Jesus' clothes.
→ Above his head is a sign saying 'The King of the Jews'.
→ Jesus is mocked by the chief priests and teachers of the law.
→ Jesus is placed between two robbers.
→ Darkness covers the whole land from the sixth hour (12 noon) and lasts until the ninth hour (3 p.m.).
→ On the Cross, Jesus utters a cry which is a quotation from Psalm 22.
→ Jesus dies, taking upon himself the sins of the world.
→ Jesus dies at the ninth hour (3 p.m.).
→ The curtain in the temple is torn in two.
→ A Roman centurion declares that Jesus is the Son of God.
→ None of the disciples were present when Jesus died.
→ Some of the women followers are there.
→ Pilate agrees to let Joseph of Arimathea bury the body of Jesus in a tomb cut out of rock.
→ Pilate wraps the body of Jesus in a linen cloth.

The body could not be buried with the proper ritual at this time because the sabbath was soon to begin and Jews were not allowed to work on the Sabbath. Jesus is, therefore, buried temporarily, and after the Sabbath is over, the body will be properly prepared and buried.

Terminology

Golgotha means 'The Place of the Skull'.

Checkpoint 1

What was the religious significance of giving Jesus myrrh to drink?

Background

The giving of wine to drink is foretold in Psalm 69:21 and the dividing of his clothes is foretold in Psalm 22:18.

Background

Psalm 22:1 says: *'Eloi, Eloi, lama sabachtani?'*
This means 'My God, my God, why have you forsaken me?'

Background

The most sacred part of the temple, the 'Holy of Holies', was protected with a great curtain that acted as a barrier between God and his people. The tearing of the curtain, on the death of Jesus, meant that the barrier was now no longer needed.

Examiner's secrets

In examination answers on this topic, the most important things to include are the actions which have religious significance – make sure you know what they are.

The resurrection: Matthew 28, Mark 16

There are important variations in the accounts of the resurrection.

Mark's account

Mark's original account is very brief. It begins on the Sunday morning:

→ Three women, Mary Magdalene, Mary, the mother of James, and Salome, come to the tomb.
→ They see that the stone has been rolled away.
→ A man wearing a white robe tells them that Jesus has risen.
→ He tells them to go and inform the disciples that Jesus will meet them in Galilee.
→ The women run away.
→ No disciples are present.

The ending of the Gospel is strange because the risen Jesus is not seen at all and the reaction of the disciples is not known.

Matthew's account

Matthew's account differs from Mark's in that:

→ Only two women go to the tomb, Mary Magdalene and another Mary.
→ There is an earthquake and the guards are petrified.
→ An angel opens the tomb.
→ The angel tells the women that Jesus has risen and will meet the disciples in Galilee.
→ The women then meet Jesus personally.
→ The women worship Jesus.
→ The chief priests bribe the guards to spread the story that the disciples have stolen the body of Jesus.

In Galilee, Jesus gives the disciples the great commission: 'Therefore go and make disciples of all nations' (v. 19).

Background

Mark's Gospel originally ended with the words 'They said nothing to anyone because they were afraid' (16:8).

Scholars' views

Some scholars believe that the early Church may have added on several verses at the end of Mark to complete the story, including the resurrection appearances and Jesus giving the disciples the great commission to '*Go into the world and preach the good news to all creation*' (v. 15).

Checkpoint 2

Why have the women come to the tomb?

Exam question   answer: page 97

What are the main differences between Matthew and Mark's accounts of the crucifixion?   (30 mins)

Death and resurrection in Luke

This is the climax of the ministry of Jesus. The Romans used crucifixion as the method of execution for condemned Jews.

The crucifixion: 23:26–56

The place of execution was a hill outside Jerusalem called 'Golgotha'. There are many important religious features:

→ Jesus, like all condemned prisoners, was forced to walk to Golgotha, facing the abuse of the citizens.

→ The soldiers seize a man called Simon of Cyrene and force him to carry Jesus' Cross.

→ A large crowd follows and Jesus quotes the prophet Hosea to them.

→ He is placed between two robbers, traditionally called Zoathan and Chammatha.

→ In fulfilment of the prophecy written in Psalm 69:21, the soldiers draw lots to win Jesus' clothes.

→ The soldiers and the people mock him.

→ Jesus forgives those who are crucifying him: 'Father, forgive them, for they do not know what they are doing' (23:34).

→ Jesus is nailed to the Cross and offered wine vinegar to drink as a painkiller.

→ Above him is a notice which reads 'This is the King of the Jews'.

→ Darkness covers the whole land from the sixth hour (12 noon) until the ninth hour (3 p.m.).

→ On the Cross, Jesus utters the cry 'Father, into your hands I commit my spirit' (23:46).

→ Jesus dies at the ninth hour (3 p.m.).

→ The curtain in the temple is torn in two.

→ A Roman centurion praises God.

→ None of the disciples were present when Jesus died.

→ Some of the women followers were there.

→ Pilate agrees to let Joseph of Arimathea bury the body of Jesus in a tomb cut out of rock.

→ The body could not be buried with the proper ritual at this time because the sabbath was soon to begin and Jews were not allowed to do work (i.e. burying a body) on the sabbath because of the commandment in Exodus 20:8: 'Remember the Sabbath day by keeping it holy'.

The body was buried temporarily until a proper burial could be carried out after the sabbath.

Terminology

This darkness may be symbolic of the darkness that fell on Egypt in the Old Testament during the time of Moses as a sign of God's displeasure (Exodus 10:22).

Checkpoint 1

What does Jesus say which gives salvation to one of the criminals?

Terminology

The most sacred part of the temple, the 'Holy of Holies', was protected with a great curtain, which acted as a barrier between God and his people. The tearing of the curtain, on the death of Jesus, meant that the barrier was now no longer needed.

Background

Jesus' last words are a quotation from Psalm 31:5 and, interestingly, were commonly used by Jewish mothers as a prayer taught to children before they went to sleep at night.

Examiner's secrets

In exam answers to this section, remember that the religious symbolism is the most important thing. Make sure you understand all the symbolic actions and their meaning.

The resurrection: 24:1–53

●●●

Luke's account has interesting features:

→ Three women go to the tomb – Mary Magdalene, Mary, the mother of James, and Joanna.
→ The stone has been rolled away.
→ They encounter two men at the tomb, dressed in gleaming clothes, who tell them that Jesus has risen.
→ The women go to the disciples to tell them.
→ The disciples do not believe the women.
→ Peter rushes to the tomb to see for himself.

Luke then includes an account of Jesus meeting two men on the road to Emmaus. This account is only found in Luke's Gospel:

→ On the road to Emmaus, the risen Jesus meets two believers, one of whom is called Cleopas.
→ They do not recognise Jesus.
→ Jesus talks to them at some length about the Christ.
→ After he breaks bread, the men see who he is and he leaves them. The men return to Jerusalem and tell the disciples.
→ Jesus appears to the disciples and proves his bodily presence.
→ Jesus explains how his mission has fulfilled the Scriptures.
→ Later, at Bethany, Jesus blesses the disciples and then ascends into heaven.

Background

Luke's account of the resurrection concentrates on how Jesus has fulfilled the prophesies of the Old Testament – see v. 45–47.

Useful quotations

'Why are you looking for the living among the dead? He is not here; he has risen!' (24:5–6).
'Did not the Christ have to suffer these things and then enter his glory?' (24:26).
'This is what is written; the Christ will suffer and rise from the dead on the third day and repentance and forgiveness of sins will be preached in his name to all nations' (24:47).

Checkpoint 2

Why did the women go to the tomb?

Exam question   answer: page 98

Examine the key features of Luke's account of the crucifixion.   (30 mins)

The authorship of the Fourth Gospel

There are many arguments concerning the possible authors and they may be summarised as follows.

John the Apostle

Arguments in favour

→ St Irenaeus (140–210 CE), the Bishop of Lyons, wrote that the author was 'John, the disciple of the Lord'.
→ The Gospel writer claims to be a disciple (21:24).
→ Irenaeus said his information came from a Polycarp, the Bishop of Smyra, who claimed to have heard it from John himself.
→ Polycrates, the Bishop of Ephesus, said in a letter in 190 CE that 'John, who reclined on the breast of the Lord, was a witness and teacher'.
→ The Muratorian Fragment, dating from 170 CE, gives a list of books regarded as Holy Scriptures. It states that John approved the writing of the Gospel.
→ The language of the Gospel suggests that it was written by a Jew.
→ The details suggest that it was written by an eyewitness (e.g. 18:15; 19:13; 21:11).
→ Some of the details could only have been known to a disciple who was present, e.g. the Last Supper and the resurrection narratives.
→ Irenaeus said that John lived until the reign of the Emperor Trajan (98–117 CE).

Arguments against

→ John the Apostle would have been very old by the time of the reign of Trajan, probably over 90.
→ Would his memory be reliable?
→ There is a tradition that John was killed, along with his brother James, about four years after the death of Jesus (Acts 12:2).
→ Irenaeus does not actually say John wrote the Gospel, only that it was written with his authority.
→ Some of the events are in a different order to those in the other Gospels (e.g. cleansing of the temple).
→ Some of the facts are wrong, e.g. the Sea of Galilee was not called the Sea of Tiberius at the time of Jesus (6:1).

→ If John was a fisherman, was he educated enough to write the Gospel?

→ Would he have had access to the High Priest's house (18:15)?

Other possible authors ●●●

John the Elder

John the Elder lived in Ephesus from 70 CE until 146 CE.

→ The early historian Eusebius quoted from Papias, the Bishop of Hierapolis, who suggested that John the Elder was the likely author since he lived through the reign of Trajan.

→ Two New Testament epistles called 2 John and 3 John begin with the phrase 'the Elder'.

John Mark

John Mark lived in Jerusalem at the time of Christ and he was several years younger than Jesus.

→ He came from a priestly family and had a good knowledge of the temple and may have had access to the High Priest.

→ He was wealthy man and accompanied St Paul on his first missionary journey and was known to the disciples (Acts 12:12–15).

→ However, he would still have been very old at the time of Trajan.

The beloved disciple

There are references in the Gospel to 'the disciple whom Jesus loved' (13:23; 20:2) and this disciple is referred to in 21:21–24 as the one who wrote the Gospel.

→ Some scholars have suggested that this term refers to John himself, because he is not mentioned by name in the Gospel.

→ Others have suggested that it might be Lazarus, whom Jesus raised from the dead and who was referred to as the one Jesus loves.

However, all the evidence is unreliable and it is impossible to know for certain who the author of the Fourth Gospel was.

Examiner's secrets

Don't forget, the claim in the Gospel that the author is John appears in Chapter 21, which some scholars believe is not part of the original text.

Background

John the Elder is referred to by some writers as 'the Presbyter'.

Background

John Mark may have been the mysterious young man who fled naked from the scene of Jesus' arrest in Mark 14:51–52.

Checkpoint 2

What is an epistle?

Exam question   answer: page 98

Examine the evidence for and against the view that the author of the Fourth Gospel was John the Apostle.   (45 mins)

Date, origin and influences

The date of the Gospel can only be based on circumstantial evidence.

Arguments in favour of a first-century dating are:

→ In 212 CE, Clement of Alexandria declared that the fourth Gospel was the last to be written.
→ The 'Rylands Fragment', dating from about 150 CE seems to have parts of Chapter 18 of the Gospel enscribed upon it.
→ The 'Egerton Papyrus' contains passages similar to the Fourth Gospel.
→ The Gospel contains precise details, indicating an eyewitness.
→ It contains ideas similar to first-century Essene writings.
→ The author of the Gospel seems to make references to the excommunication of believers from Judaism in 85–90 CE (9:22, 12:42 and 16:2).

The arguments in favour of second-century authorship are:

→ The Fourth Gospel was used by Ptolemaeus and other second-century Gnostics.
→ The Gospel was used by the writers of the 'Gospel of Peter' and the Valentinian 'Gospel of Truth' around 150 CE.
→ There is no reference in historical records to the Fourth Gospel before 150 CE.

The place of origin of the Fourth Gospel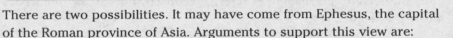

There are two possibilities. It may have come from Ephesus, the capital of the Roman province of Asia. Arguments to support this view are:

→ Ephesus was the main centre used by St Paul for his mission and had a thriving Christian community.
→ Irenaeus said John the Apostle lived in Ephesus.
→ The language of the Gospel contains phrases common to the area.

The alternative is the city of Antioch:

→ The Syrian writer Ephraim Syrus (306–370 CE) said Antioch was 'the home of the gospel'.
→ It was the third city of the Roman Empire.
→ Antioch was the place where the followers of Christ were first called 'Christians' (Acts 11:26).

The Fourth Gospel gives indications that it was influenced by both Greek and Jewish ideas.

Background

Most scholars believe that the Gospel was published some time between 85 and 150 CE.

Examiner's secrets

The importance of knowing the date is that it allows us to consider how accurate the Gospel is. The earlier the date, the more likely the writer knew Jesus or was an eyewitness.

Checkpoint 1

What is excommunication?

Background

Although the place of origin of the Gospel is less important than the date, it is, nevertheless, an important factor in deciding on the authenticity and reliability of the Gospel text. Many scholars believe it originated from Ephesus.

Greek influences on the Gospel ●●●

At the time of Christ, most educated people could speak Greek, allowing the Christian message to reach educated people throughout the known world. There were many strands of Greek thought in the Gospel:

→ **Platonism** – this world of time and space would pass away and that behind it was an eternal and changeless world, called 'the world above'.
→ Philo said that the aim of the religious person was to bring their life into relationship with reality and achieve immortality. This is done by bridging the gulf between divine ideas and the physical world.
→ The Gospel writer portrays the logos as the image of God.
→ The logos will enable humanity to find the ultimate truth and develop a relationship with God.
→ **Stoicism** – people must follow their conscience, which is inspired by reason.
→ Reason is God (logos) and, in some sense, the universe.
→ The divine logos is found in the minds of people, but the individual must choose to do something about it.
→ The Gospel writer says that the relationship between God and humanity is achieved when humanity lives according to the logos.
→ **Gnosticism** – only those who have the divine light will reach the spiritual world.
→ This light comes with knowledge ('gnosis').
→ The Fourth Gospel uses Gnostic notions of light, evil, the physical and the spiritual worlds.

Jewish influences on the Gospel

→ The author makes reference to the Old Testament.
→ Much of the action revolves around the temple and during Jewish festivals.
→ The Gospel contains Essene notions of light and dark, good and evil (12:31 and 12:36).

Terminology

The influence of Greek culture is known as 'Hellenism'.

Checkpoint 2

What is stoicism?

Take note

Gnostics believed that there were two worlds – the world of the spirit, where God is, and which is pure and holy, and the world of physical matter, where humanity dwells and which is evil and corrupt. Humanity's only escape is in death, when the soul leaves the physical world behind.

Examiner's secrets

Remember, there are no right and wrong answers here – you need to weigh up the arguments on all sides.

Exam question   answer: page 98

Examine the evidence concerning the date of the Gospel.   (30 mins)

The purpose of the Fourth Gospel

Background

The author uses Old Testament prophecies to show how the work of the promised Messiah will be fulfilled in Jesus.

Background

The prophecy concerning the triumphal entry is Zechariah 9:9: *'Do not be afraid, O daughter of Zion; see, your king is coming, seated on a donkey's colt.'*

Background

Jesus' claim to be the Son of God led directly to the charge of blasphemy levelled against him by the Jews: *'We have a law, and according to that law he must die, because he claimed to be the Son of God'* (19:7).

Background

R.V.G. Tasker notes: *'His whole incarnate life is, in fact, meaningless apart from "the hour" to which it is inevitably moving, and that hour is none other than the hour of His passion'.* (*John* (1960)).

Examiner's secrets

This is a popular question and usually requires the candidate to consider not only the author's stated purpose, but also other possible purposes.

Checkpoint 1

What does the word Messiah mean?

The author of the Fourth Gospel states his purpose in 20:31: 'But these are written that you may believe that Jesus is the Christ, the Son of God, and that by believing you may have life in his name'.

The textual narrative supports this in the following ways.

'Jesus is the Christ . . .'

The Gospel highlights the fact that Jesus is the Christ, the Messiah who will bring salvation. This is seen in the following incidents:

→ Jesus clears the temple (2:13–17) – a promised Messianic action, reflected in Psalm 69:9: *'Zeal for your house will consume me'*.
→ The healing at the pool, which took place on the sabbath (5:1–16).
→ The disciples will recognise him as Messiah (1:41, 49).
→ Jesus tells the Samaritan woman he is the Messiah (4:25–26).
→ There are Messianic overtones when he feeds the people (6:1–15).
→ He makes a triumphal entry into Jerusalem riding a donkey in fulfilment of prophecy (12:12–19).
→ The Jewish authorities refuse to accept him as the Messiah (5:18, 7:47, 10:33, 19:7).
→ The disciples' acknowledgement of Jesus as Messiah (1:41, 1:49, 6:68–69, 7:41).

'The Son of God . . .'

There are several references to Christ as the Son of God:

→ John the Baptist testifies that *'I have seen and have borne witness that this is the Son of God'* (1:34).
→ Jesus refers to his intimate relationship with God.
→ He knows the Father's will.
→ Jesus and the Father are one (3:35, 5:19–20, 8:4, 14:10).

'. . . that by believing you may have life in his name'

Eternal life comes from believing in the teaching of Christ:

→ He lays down his life for the sheep (10:11).
→ He is *'the Lamb of God, who takes away the sin of the world'* (1:29).
→ He is lifted up and draws all to him (12:32).
→ Those who accept him receive eternal life (3:16).
→ He sacrifices himself in order that humanity may have life (10:10, 12:24).

Some scholars believe the author may have other purposes too.

A spiritual Gospel   ●●●

Some scholars believe the author wrote a spiritual Gospel. The purpose of this was not to write an accurate biography of Jesus' life but to express vital truths about Jesus in order to lead his readers into the belief that Jesus was the Son of God. The author does this in the following ways:

→ He alters the historical sequence of events in Jesus' life to highlight important theological points.
→ For example, the cleansing of the temple occurs at the start of Jesus' ministry (2:12–25), whereas in the synoptic Gospels it occurs near the end.
→ The author highlights the importance of worship in spirit and truth (4:24).
→ Jesus is the place where humanity meets with God (1:51, 2:21).
→ He alters the timing of Jesus' death with events brought forward by 24 hours.
→ Jesus' death on the Cross is the fulfilment of Scripture.
→ The author emphasises Jesus' divinity.
→ He uses witnesses to support this, for example, John the Baptist (1:29) and the Samaritan woman (4:25–26).
→ The author emphasises the relationship between Jesus and the Father.
→ He shows how Jesus is in control of all the events leading up to the Cross.

Other possible purposes?   ●●●

→ To counteract the doctrines of Docetism and Gnosticism.
→ To bring the message of Christ to Jews in Gentile nations (Barrett).
→ To convert Jews to Christianity (Robinson).
→ To preach salvation to all humanity (Smalley).

Background

'Last of all, John, perceiving that the external facts had been made plain in the Gospels, being urged by his friends and inspired by the Spirit, composed a spiritual Gospel' (Clement of Alexandria). B.F. Westcott, comparing the Fourth Gospel with Luke's Gospel, suggested that: '*The real difference is that the earliest Gospel contained the fundamental facts and words which experience afterwards interpreted, while the latest Gospel reveals the facts in the light of their interpretation.*' (*The Gospel According to St John* (2001)).

Checkpoint 2

What is religiously significant about Jesus dying on the Day of Preparation?

Useful quotations

'*Now my heart is troubled, and what shall I say? "Father, save me from this hour?" No, it was for this very reason I came to this hour. Father, glorify your name!*' (12:27–28).

Exam question   answer: page 98

To what extent is it fair to say that the Fourth Gospel is a spiritual Gospel?

(30 mins)

The Prologue

The introduction to the Fourth Gospel is called the Prologue (1:1–18). Everything the reader needs to understand the Gospel narrative, plot and events is provided by the Prologue.

What is the Prologue?

Scholars have differing views concerning the Prologue:

→ **Robinson** claims that it is a later addition to the Gospel and was put in to bring things to a conclusion.
→ **Burney** says it is an Aramaic hymn.
→ **Stanton** suggests it is the 'lens' through which to view the rest of the Gospel.
→ **Morna Hooker** describes it as a 'key' which unlocks the Gospel.

The Word (*Logos*)

In the Prologue, the writer says that Jesus Christ is God himself, who came into the world as a human being. The story of Jesus is the story of the *Logos* or Word. The Logos worked alongside God in creation and came into the world as Christ. There is much religious significance:

→ The author brings from Judaism the idea of God's creative breath (*ruah*) – his speech, wisdom and purpose from which creation comes.
→ The Jews identified the Word of God with the Torah, the Word was God's wisdom, embodied in the law and the Word gave meaning to life.
→ The author incorporates the Hellenistic notions of the ideal world and the ideal human.
→ The Word is a living, distinct being within the Trinity.
→ It is the source of light and life.
→ The Word was with God 'in the beginning' (v. 1).
→ The Word is the eternal purpose of God – it is that which gives meaning to life. The author is trying to show to the readers the fact that, in Jesus, the whole purpose of God and creation has meaning.

Useful quotations

'. . . the preface to the Fourth Gospel, with its movement from the Word to the Son of God, is both an introduction and a conclusion to the whole work. The relation between creation and salvation, prophets and apostles, history and that beyond history, time and eternity, law and grace, death and life, faith and unbelief – these are the themes of the Fourth Gospel' (E. Hoskyns and F. Davey, The Fourth Gospel (1947)).

Background

The term logos links together concepts from the Old Testament, the Jewish Rabbinic tradition, Hellenistic and Stoic thought and early Christian theology.

Useful quotations

'Through him all things were made; without him nothing was made that has been made. In him was life . . .' (John 1:3–4).
'. . . that life was the light of men. The light shines in the darkness, but the darkness has not understood it' (John 1:4–5).
'He came as a witness to testify to the light, so that through him all men might believe' (1:7).

Checkpoint 1

What is the Torah?

John the Baptist

The one sent from God to announce the coming of the light into the world.

→ He bridges the gap between the Old Testament and the New.
→ He shows humanity how to recognise Jesus as the Word.
→ He is a witness offering testimony to the light and the testimony of a witness was crucial in establishing truth. John shows that the 'light' of the Scriptures is fulfilled in Christ, the incarnate Word of God.

The Word Incarnate

The message of the Prologue is that humanity must recognise Christ as the Word Incarnate. However, this is not easy:

→ The people live in darkness and do not recognise him.
→ Some did receive him. To these are given the right to become 'children of God' (1:12).
→ It is not a physical birth, but a spiritual one, achieved through faith in Jesus Christ.
→ God became fully human through the Word.

Law, grace and truth

→ Jesus is the incarnate word of God, which has existed from the beginning – this is the notion of pre-existence.
→ The Word becoming flesh is a gift from God to all who believe.
→ Humanity will not be saved by obeying the law, but through the grace and truth of God.
→ God has become human so that humanity can truly know him.

Terminology

The testimony of a witness is crucial in establishing the truth of a claim. The Word of God is known through testimony – from God himself, or from his divinely inspired messengers.

Useful quotations

'He came into the world, and though the world was made through him, the world did not recognise him. He came to his own, but his own did not receive him' (John 1:10–12).

Background

To become children is a gift of God. This is to be the difference between the Jews – God's chosen people by birth – and Christians, chosen through God's grace.

Checkpoint 2

What does incarnate mean?

Examiner's secrets

The Prologue is a popular area, but the questions require a really detailed knowledge of the text and background as well as the views of scholars. Only attempt the question if you really know the material!

Exam question answer: page 98

What are the differing views of scholars concerning the Prologue? (45 mins)

The Holy Spirit and women in the Fourth Gospel

Useful quotations

The Holy Spirit is present from the beginning of Jesus' ministry, setting him aside as the one anointed for God's purpose, fulfilling John's testimony that *'the man on whom you see the Spirit come down and remain is he who will baptise with the Holy Spirit'* (1:33).

Background

The opening verses of the Gospel – *In the beginning was the Word* – echo Genesis 1:1–2, where we read that *'In the beginning . . . the spirit of God moved over the face of the waters'*.

Action point

Read the account of Saul's empowering with the Holy Spirit in 1 Samuel 11.

Useful quotations

'The concept of the paraclete is a stroke of genius . . . It gave the Christians a distinctive way of thinking about the presence of God, answered the nagging question of the delay of the Parousia, and solved the problem of the growing temporal separation from the historical revelation' (Robert Kysar, *John, the Maverick Gospel* (1993)).

Checkpoint 1

To whom does Jesus say they must be born again of water and spirit?

Terminology

There are four primary ways of translating paraclete:
An advocate – *one called to the side of another to assist.*
A defence counsel – *one who intercedes for another.*
A comforter – *one who comforts and consoles.*
A proclaimer – *one who exhorts and encourages.*

Unlike in the synoptic Gospels, the Holy Spirit is described as both *pneuma* and *paraclete*, two Greek terms which express different, but related, functions of the Spirit.

The term *pneuma* is used to speak of the Spirit prior to the Passion to describe the role of the Spirit in the life and ministry of Jesus. In the Old Testament God's Spirit empowers Israel's judges and kings, equipping them in times of crisis. However, they possessed the Spirit temporarily, whereas it 'remains' on Jesus (1:32). Thus, the coming of the Spirit on Jesus points to the fulfilment of the Old Testament prophecies (Isaiah 42:6–67) and Jesus, sent by God, who will baptise with the Holy Spirit. For the Fourth Evangelist, the *pneuma* Spirit is the way in which man's longing for God will be satisfied, quenching his thirst for God (Psalm 42:1). The Fourth Evangelist makes explicit the link between water and spirit in 7:37–39, explaining that 'rivers of living water' flowing from the heart of the believer is the Spirit which will be poured out on them after Jesus's death.

In the Farewell Discourses a new dimension to the teaching on the Holy Spirit is revealed through the use of paraclete. The concept adds to the Gospel's understanding of eschatology. So valuable was the presence of the Spirit in the midst of the Johannine community, that they were able to claim that future blessings had already become a present reality.

The paraclete will be 'another' like Jesus (14:16) and fulfil the roles and functions which Jesus performed when on earth – hence, the paraclete is *'the presence of Jesus when he is absent'* (Raymond Brown). It will dwell in the disciples and yet the world will not be able to accept it (14:17), but for the believer it will intercede, guide and teach – leading them into a deeper knowledge of Jesus' own words. The paraclete is integral to eschatology: *'And when he comes he will convince the world concerning sin and righteousness and judgement'* (16:8). This brings into focus the other central function of the paraclete: it is the Johannine church's solution to the problem of the delay of the Parousia. Rather than look to the future, he urges them to look to the present and see that Jesus is already among them and that the Parousia has occurred already. In this way all believers have as direct an access to Jesus as the first and the paraclete keeps alive the revelation of God in Christ so it is available to all.

Women

Distinctively, the Fourth Gospel gives women disciples a position comparable with that of the Twelve, and he chooses five female characters to present this important development.

Jesus' mother is never named, and appears only twice, at the beginning and end of Jesus' ministry, witnessing its commencement and fulfilment. At Cana, she bears witness to his authority through her confident appeal to Jesus that '*they have no wine*' (2:3) and, despite his apparently discouraging reply, she orders the servants to '*Do as he tells you*' (2:4). At the foot of the Cross she must have seen the spear thrust, the final sign, and she is part of the foundational witness on which the Johannine community is based.

The Samaritan woman is arguably a prototype of the ideal woman disciple, appearing briefly, and with none of the obvious advantages that Nicodemus had. Her response to Jesus is initially clumsy, but subtly she is revealed as a true disciple by her desire to know more of Jesus and her witness to her fellow Samaritans.

The woman caught in adultery serves as a foil for a conflict scene with the Pharisees. It is not clear whether the woman becomes a disciple but she emerges as a sympathetic figure.

Martha and Mary. The closest parallel in the Fourth Gospel to Peter's synoptic confession is Martha's threefold identification of Jesus at 11:27, as '*Christ, the Son of God, the one who is coming into the world*'. Mary comes into her own at the anointing at Bethany (12:1–8). Although she does not speak, her act of extravagant devotion to Jesus receives the highest praise, and she has perceived what none of the male disciples have grasped – that he must die. She serves as a foil to the deceitful Judas and Jesus interprets her action as prophetic (12:7).

Finally, it is to ***Mary Magdalene*** that Peter loses the pre-eminence as the first to testify to having seen the risen Jesus. She is then free to take to the male disciples the word of the Gospel – that Jesus Christ has been raised from death.

Useful quotations

'Thus, if other Christian communities thought of Peter as the one who made a supreme confession of Jesus as the Son of God and the one to whom the risen Jesus first appeared, the Johannine community associated such memories with heroines like Martha and Mary Magdalene' (Raymond Brown, *The Community of the Belared Disciple* (1979)).

Action point

Make a list of the male disciples in the Fourth Gospel and note how they compare in their actions and words to the women.

Checkpoint 2

Why was the Samaritan woman a despised figure?

Background

Deuteronomy 22:23 prescribes the death penalty for adultery.

Exam question   answer: page 98

Outline and evaluate the role of (i) the Holy Spirit and (ii) women in the Fourth Gospel.   (45 mins)

The early ministry of Jesus

In the first part of the Fourth Gospel, the author highlights Jesus' teaching concerning himself and the nature of salvation. These teachings are sometimes accompanied by signs or 'I am' sayings.

The wedding at Cana: the first sign 2:1–11

The story of the wedding at Cana shows how Jesus has come to replace the old Jewish rituals with the new way – with life through him. It contains much symbolism:

→ It takes place 'on the third day', with echoes of the resurrection.
→ Jesus is invited to the wedding – the Messiah comes to his people.
→ Jesus turns water into wine.
→ The six stone jars contained the water that was needed in the Jewish purification rites.
→ Jesus changes the inadequate water into excellent wine and the feast is complete.

The meaning of the first sign is clear – the water of Judaism is inadequate for salvation – the wine/blood of Christ is the path to eternal life.

Cleansing the temple: 2:12–25

The temple market was where faithful Jews could buy animals for sacrifice, in the belief that this could lead to the forgiveness of their sins ('atonement'). Jesus is angry because God's message in the Old Testament was that he did not want animal sacrifices, but worship from the heart (Psalm 51:16). Jesus' message is that salvation will not come through the sacrifices, but from faith in the salvation Jesus brings.

Jesus and Nicodemus: 3:1–21

The conversation between Jesus and Nicodemus shows the struggle between traditional Judaism and the teaching of Jesus.

→ He comes to Jesus at night, symbolising the 'darkness' he lives in.
→ He accepts Jesus as a teacher who has come from God.
→ Nicodemus' knowledge of the law and the Scriptures is not enough for salvation.
→ Nicodemus can see God's power but he cannot truly experience a personal relationship with God.
→ To do this he must be born again.
→ Jesus is saying that the Jewish rituals will not lead to salvation – rebirth in the Spirit is necessary.

Background

In the Old Testament, God was depicted as the bridegroom and Israel was the unfaithful bride (Isaiah 54:5; Hosea 2:19). At this wedding, Jesus is the bridegroom returning back to Israel.

Background

In the Old Testament, it had been foretold that the Lord would one day come and cleanse his temple (Malachi 3:1; Isaiah 56:7).

Take note

Nicodemus represents the best of Judaism. He is a Pharisee and, probably, a member of the Sanhedrin. He is a Jew who would like to follow Jesus but cannot because he is hampered by his religious situation.

Checkpoint 1

What is atonement?

Useful quotations

'For God so loved the world that he gave his one and only Son, that whoever believes in him shall not perish but have eternal life' (3:16).

Jesus and the Samaritan woman: 4:1–45 ●●●

In this meeting, Jesus highlights the faith of a Samaritan woman and also reveals his identity to her – something he had not done with his male disciples. He also shows her that the religious traditions of the Samaritans, like those of Judaism, were insufficient for salvation. The main religious points are:

→ The action takes place at Jacob's Well, the place where the patriarch Jacob changed his name to 'Israel'.
→ Jesus asked her for a drink. She was surprised, for a Jew would not speak to a Samaritan woman.
→ He told her that he had 'living water' (v. 10).
→ He told the woman to call her husband, but she has no husband. 'Husband' refers to God.
→ The woman called him a 'prophet' (v. 19).
→ Jesus told her that he is the Messiah (v. 26).
→ She acts as a disciple should, going to her people and telling them the 'good news'.
→ The townsfolk received Jesus and accepted him.

Jesus and the official's son: the second sign: 4:46–54 ●●●

The official was probably a Roman administrator. He asked Jesus to heal his sick son. Jesus does so with the words 'You may go. Your son will live' (v. 50). The official had such great faith in Jesus that he was able to accept his word without question and went home to his healed son. The meaning of the sign is that true belief means obedience and trust in the word and power of Christ.

The healing at the pool: the third sign: 5:1–30 ●●●

Jesus met a crippled man on the sabbath. Jesus asked him if he wanted to be healed. This caused problems with the Jewish authorities who said it was against the Law of Moses. Moreover, when the Jewish authorities questioned Jesus, he told them of his unique relationship with God and that, as God's Son, he did what God required him to do. He told them that God will bring judgement and that humanity has been given a chance of eternal life, by following Jesus.

> I tell you the truth, whoever hears my word and believes him who sent me has eternal life and will not be condemned. He has crossed over from death to life. (v. 24)

Terminology

The Samaritans were Jews who had intermixed with foreigners and were despised by those who believed themselves to be the true Jews for having abandoned their Jewish faith and traditions.

Useful quotations

'Whoever drinks the water I give him will never thirst. Indeed, the water I give him will become in him a spring of water welling up to eternal life' (4:14).
'All that John says about the Gospel of Jesus Christ is ultimately concerned with salvation' (Stephen Smalley, *John: Evangelist and Interpreter* (1978)).
'The farther Jesus moves from Jerusalem . . . the more he receives the sort of response that he seeks' (John Marsh, *St John* (1968)).

Take note

The crippled man had been there for 38 years, the same length of time that the Israelites had wandered in the desert under Moses (Deut. 2:14).

Checkpoint 2

Who were the Samaritans?

Examiner's secrets

When writing your answer, remember that the important thing is not to retell the story, but to explain its meaning and significance.

Exam question answer: page 99

Examine and comment on the meaning and symbolism of two of the 'signs'.

(45 mins)

Jesus' later ministry

The later part of Jesus' ministry is characterised by the 'I am' sayings and signs.

The feeding of the five thousand: the fourth sign: 6:1–15

With only five small loaves and two fish, Jesus miraculously fed a crowd of 5,000 (v. 11). The disciples gathered up 12 baskets full of fragments. Sadly, the people did not understand the message of the sign. They thought Jesus was a great prophet and wanted to forcibly crown him as king.

Jesus walks on water: 6:16–24

Later, the disciples were on a boat in rough weather on the lake and Jesus miraculously walked on the water to them. Jesus is proving to the disciples that he possesses God's authority and power.

'I am the bread of life': the first 'I am' saying

Jesus proclaims his divinity by describing himself in a series of 'I am' sayings ('ego eimi'). Jesus tells the people that:

→ Under Moses in the desert God gave the people 'bread from heaven' (v. 32).
→ Jesus is the bread to satisfy their spiritual hunger.
→ This will be understood after his resurrection.
→ 'Whoever eats my flesh and drinks my blood has eternal life and I will raise him up at the last day' (v. 54).

The woman caught in adultery: 8:1–11

A woman guilty of fornication, an offence punishable by death under the Law of Moses (Deut. 22:23), was brought to judgement before Jesus by the Jews. Jesus saves her with the words 'If any one of you is without sin, let him be the first to throw a stone at her' (v. 7).

The woman is saved, but Jesus does not excuse her sin. Instead he suggests the law is not wrong, but it should not be imposed in such a strict and unfeeling way.

'I am the light of the world': the second 'I am' saying: 8:12–30

This saying has much symbolic significance:

→ Humanity lives in darkness and sin.
→ Jesus has come with God's light to show humanity the truth.
→ Those who follow Jesus will never walk in darkness again.

The Pharisees could not grasp the spiritual significance. Jesus told them the light he will bring would show everyone the truth of their situation. Jesus told them that just being 'Sons of Abraham' would not be enough. To be freed from the darkness of sin they must believe in him.

Healing the blind man: the fifth sign (Chapter 9) ●●●

The blind man probably begged at the gate of the temple. Jesus restored the man's sight by spitting into some clay and anointing the man's eyes with it. Note the following:

→ God used clay in Genesis 2 to create Adam.
→ Jesus was making the blind man into a new person.
→ The man washed his eyes and received his sight.
→ He had been cleansed in 'living water', and the 'light of the world' had entered into him.
→ The Pharisees said that Jesus could not be from God because this healing happened on the sabbath.
→ The man was 'thrown out' of the synagogue.
→ Jesus told the man who he was.
→ He worshipped Jesus – he had received both physical 'sight' and spiritual 'sight'.
→ Jesus told the Pharisees they were spiritually blind.

'I am the gate for the sheep': the third 'I am' saying: 10:1–10 ●●●

In these sayings Jesus declared that he and not the chief priests, was the real leader of God's people.

→ A shepherd protects the sheep and guards the entrance to the sheepfold.
→ Jesus is the real shepherd, the chief priests are false shepherds, who enter by stealth and use threats.
→ Jesus is the 'gate' through which the sheep (people) will pass in order to find safety and life.

'I am the good shepherd': the fourth 'I am' saying: 10:11–42 ●●●

→ A good shepherd sacrifices his own life for his sheep.
→ He said, 'I lay down my life for the sheep' (v. 15).
→ Jesus spoke of 'other sheep that are not of this sheep pen' (v. 16) in reference to the Gentiles, who will also become part of his flock.
→ He said, 'I and the Father are one' (v. 30).
→ The Jews tried to stone him. He was forced to leave.

Terminology

Popular belief at that time was that blindness was a punishment from God because of the sins of the person or his parents. Jesus said that this was not true.

Terminology

To be 'thrown out' of the synagogue meant 'excommunicated' and was the most severe of punishments. It meant that no other Jew could associate with him and that God would 'reject' him forever.

Checkpoint 2

Why was the figure of the shepherd of religious significance?

Exam question   answer: page 99

What is the meaning of the sayings 'I am the good shepherd' and 'I am the gate for the sheep'?   (30 mins)

The road to the Cross

The last days of Jesus' ministry are concerned with miracles and signs of what is to come.

The raising of Lazarus: the sixth sign (Chapter 11) 'I am the resurrection and the life': the fifth 'I am' saying: 11:25

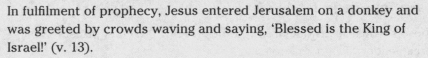

Lazarus had been dead and buried for four days before Jesus arrived. Note the most important features:

→ Martha believed that Jesus could raise Lazarus.

→ Jesus said: 'I am the resurrection and the life. He who believes in me will live, even though he dies, and whoever lives and believes in me will never die' (v. 25).

→ Lazarus is raised from the dead – he heard the voice of Christ and lived.

→ The Sanhedrin condemned Jesus as a danger to Judaism.

→ The High Priest Caiaphas said, 'It is better for you that one man die for the people than that the whole nation perish' (v. 50).

The triumphal entry (Chapter 12)

In fulfilment of prophecy, Jesus entered Jerusalem on a donkey and was greeted by crowds waving and saying, 'Blessed is the King of Israel!' (v. 13).

→ This angered the Jewish leaders.

→ Inside the city, Jesus spoke to Jews and Gentiles, indicating that his message was for all people.

→ He told them of the judgement to come, when only those who follow him will be saved.

The Last Supper (Chapter 13)

The final part of Jesus' ministry begins with a supper.

→ First, Jesus washes the disciples' feet, showing that he had come as a humble servant.

→ Jesus gave bread to Judas who then went to betray him.

→ Jesus told the disciples that he was soon to leave them.

→ Peter offered to lay down his life for Christ.

→ Jesus foretells that Peter will deny him three times.

→ Jesus told his disciples to trust in God. He highlighted his unique role with the Father.

Background

Marsh said the raising of Lazarus is the crux of the Gospel. It symbolised the end of the old Israel and the birth of the new. Lazarus died as a member of the old Israel and was raised through belief in Christ. The action points to the resurrection of Jesus and the bringing of his people out from death to eternal life.

Useful quotations

R.V.G. Tasker notes:
'It was His claim to bestow upon believers the gift of eternal life by raising them from spiritual death which led to His crucifixion.' (*John* (1960)).

Checkpoint 1

Who was the prophet who foretold the triumphal entry into Jerusalem on a donkey?

Background

The believer must accept Christ's offer of help and service, otherwise there can be no true relationship of salvation. In the same way, Christ's followers must serve others humbly.

Useful quotations

'A new commandment I give you: Love one another. As I have loved you, so you must love one another. By this all men will know that you are my disciples' (13:34–35).

Examiner's secrets

It is crucial if you want to do well in this section to make sure you know all the relevant Old Testament references.

'I am the way and the truth and the life': the sixth 'I am' saying: 14:1–14 ●●●

Still at the supper, Jesus shows his unique relationship with God. He told the disciples that he and the Father are one. The only way to reach the Father is through the Son, Jesus Christ.

The Holy Spirit: 14:15–31 ●●●

Jesus told them he was not going to leave them alone:

→ To help them to carry on his work, the Father would send the Holy Spirit.
→ 'But the Counsellor, the Holy Spirit, whom the Father will send in my name, will teach you all things and will remind you of everything I have said to you' (v. 25–26).
→ The Spirit lives within the disciples (v. 17).
→ Jesus told the disciples that anything they ask for in his name would be given to them.
→ He told the disciples to obey his words and trust in God (v. 23) and not to be afraid (v. 27).

'I am the true vine': the seventh 'I am' saying: 15:1–17 ●●●

Jesus says he is the true vine that will produce fruit – all people will know God. He said:

→ Believers in Jesus would be the 'branches'.
→ They receive life from the vine and they will bear fruit.
→ They will need pruning and cutting back.
→ A branch cannot bear fruit on its own – and neither can believers. They must stay in the love of Jesus.

Terminology

The Holy Spirit is a 'counsellor' ('paraclete'). The Holy Spirit is equal to Christ himself and will enable the disciples to understand the truth.

Useful quotations

'And I will do whatever you ask in my name, so that the Son may bring glory to the Father. You may ask for anything in my name, and I will do it' (14:13–14).

Terminology

In the Old Testament, the figure of the 'vine' was sometimes used to symbolise the nation of Israel (Psalm 80:8) and the prophet Jeremiah said that Israel had become a 'corrupt, wild vine' (2:21).

Useful quotations

'No branch can bear fruit by itself; it must remain in the vine. Neither can you bear fruit unless you remain in me' (9:4).

Checkpoint 2

What did Jesus mean by saying he was one with the Father?

Exam question answer: page 99

What is the meaning of the sayings 'I am the true vine' and 'I am the way, the truth and the life'? (30 mins)

The death of Jesus

The last hours of Jesus' life are enacted out in fulfilment of prophecy and Scripture.

The demands of discipleship

At the Last Supper he prepared his disciples by telling them:

→ To be obedient to his words and teachings.
→ To love each other.
→ That they had been especially chosen.
→ Life would not be easy.
→ The world would hate them.
→ They would suffer persecution.
→ The Holy Spirit will be with them.
→ The Holy Spirit will help them to preach about Jesus and the love, righteousness and judgement of God.
→ The disciples would not need to despair.

The 'High Priestly Prayer' Chapter 17

The 'High Priestly Prayer' was very special. In it, Jesus asks for God's blessing on himself, as sacrifice, and the disciples.

→ Jesus is the priest praying for consecration.
→ Jesus is the sacrifice to be consecrated.
→ He prays that his death would be a time of glory.
→ He asks God to bless the disciples and keep them, and the church to come, strong in faith.
→ Jesus prays for future believers.

The Passion: the seventh sign (Chapter 18)

After the Supper, Jesus and the disciples spend the evening in a garden outside Jerusalem. Note the symbolism here:

→ Creation began in the Garden of Eden and the scene of the final conflict is in a garden too.
→ Judas came at night (symbolic of darkness and evil).
→ As Jesus says 'I am . . .' the soldiers fell to the ground, just as the enemies of God did in the past.
→ Peter denied three times that he knew Jesus.
→ Jesus told Annas, who questioned Jesus, that he had taught openly, for everyone to hear (v. 20).
→ When Pilate asked what the charges against Jesus were, the Jews were very vague, saying he was a 'criminal'.
→ Pilate's first reaction was to free Jesus. He could not understand what was wrong with Jesus.
→ He offered to set Jesus free by using the custom of releasing one prisoner at Passover.
→ The Jews asked Pilate to release Barabbas instead.

The crucifixion (Chapter 19)

The crucifixion is filled with symbolism. Note the Old Testament references:

➜ Pilate ordered Jesus to be flogged and humiliated, but the Jews were not satisfied.
➜ They told Pilate that Jesus had to die because he claimed to be the Son of God (v. 7).
➜ They told Pilate that if he freed Jesus – the King of the Jews – then Caesar would be angered.
➜ Pilate handed Jesus over to be crucified.
➜ Jesus carried his own Cross.
➜ He was crucified between two criminals (Isaiah 53:12).
➜ His clothes were divided among the soldiers (Psalm 22:18).
➜ He was offered vinegar to drink (Psalm 69:2).
➜ His garment is seamless, like the High Priest's (Exodus 28).
➜ As with the Passover sacrificial lamb, Jesus' bones were not broken (Exodus 12:6).
➜ Blood and water flow from a spear wound on his side (Zechariah 12:10).
➜ On the Cross, he quotes from Psalm 22 – foretelling the death of the Messiah.

The resurrection (Chapter 20)

The resurrection is the final and greatest sign:

➜ Mary finds the empty tomb and tells the disciples.
➜ This fulfilled the requirement of the law that two adult male witnesses were needed to 'prove' the truth.
➜ Mary saw two angels.
➜ She saw the risen Christ and greeted him with the word 'Rabboni' (v. 16).
➜ Jesus told her to tell the disciples that he had risen.
➜ Jesus gave the gift of the Holy Spirit to the disciples.
➜ He gave them the authority to act in his name to forgive sins.

Background

The trial ends strangely – when Pilate asked the chief priests, *'Shall I crucify your king?'* (v. 15), their reply was *'We have no king but Caesar'* – the ultimate blasphemy!

Useful quotations

'The contrast between Jesus as light and his enemies – who are also the enemies of God – as darkness, is sustained throughout the Gospel, particularly in the debates between Jesus and "the Jews"' (Stephen Smalley, *John: Evangelist and Interpreter* (1978)).

Terminology

Mary's use of the term 'Rabboni' is unusual, for it meant more than just teacher – it was used at that time exclusively to address God himself.

Background

The author concludes the chapter by summing up the message and purpose of the Gospel:
'But these are written that you may believe that Jesus is the Christ, the Son of God, and that by believing you may have life in his name' (v. 31).

Checkpoint 2

What is the religious significance of Mary seeing angels?

Exam question   answer: page 99

Examine the meaning and significance of three acts of religious symbolism in the crucifixion.   (45 mins)

Answers
New Testament

The background to the life of Christ

Checkpoints

1 The Jewish sabbath lasts from 6 p.m. on Friday night until 6 p.m. on Saturday night.
2 It comes from the Greek 'Christos' and means 'anointed one'.

Exam question

You will need to explain what the Law of Moses was and why it was important. This will require reference to the Old Testament and, in particular, Exodus 20. It also involves the Covenant and notions of holiness and righteousness. It was the key to the Jews' relationship with God. For the temple, there needs to be reference to what the temple meant for the people – the dwelling place of God. You must include detailed discussion and the views of scholars.

The birth and infancy narratives

Checkpoints

1 Bethlehem was the city of David and the prophet Micah had foretold that the redeemer would be born there.
2 Gentiles meant all those peoples that were not Jews.

Exam question

It is important here that you don't fall into the trap of retelling the Christmas story! The question requires discussion of the religious features such as the birth being in fulfilment of prophecy, humble surroundings, shepherds and so on. The views of scholars and the background to the birth narratives are important here.

Parables in Matthew and Mark

Checkpoints

1 Parable means 'alongside story' – that is, a story based on real life that has a religious or moral message.
2 The Messianic Banquet was a feast that the Jews believed they would eat with the Messiah at the dawning of the new age of the kingdom of God.

Exam question

Don't spend too much time retelling the parable! The important aspect of this question is to discuss the parable's message about judgement. To answer this, first define judgement and then look at the aspects of the parable. Stick closely to the textual narrative and include the views of scholars.

Parables in Luke's Gospel

Checkpoints

1 Jesus taught in parables to bring his teaching into a real-life context. He also left his audience to work out the meaning for themselves – he made them think!
2 Sin is that which separates God and humanity.

Exam question

Do not spend time retelling the parable in detail! Instead, look at the meaning – it is concerned with sin, forgiveness, love and salvation and should be discussed in these contexts. You will need to define and use these technical terms and look at the parable not just from the lost son's perspective, but also the father's and the eldest son's – and ask yourself who do these characters represent? Don't forget the views of scholars.

Miracles in Matthew and Mark

Checkpoints

1 Faith is to be certain of what we hope for and to be sure of the things we cannot prove. It means trust in God.
2 Jesus makes the woman admit to what she has done so that she herself knows that it was her faith that enabled Jesus to cure her.

Exam question

Be careful here – this miracle has symbolic meanings that you must discuss – such as the Old Testament notions of God stilling storms and bringing his people safely home. Remember to say what this tells us about the person of Jesus – that he is the Son of God.

Examiner's secrets

Examiners dread marking some exam scripts on the synoptic Gospels because the standard is so low and based around overly simplistic Sunday School material, which is often taken by the candidate from the wrong Gospel. There is no excuse for this after one or two years of study.

Miracles in Luke's Gospel

Checkpoints

1 It was difficult to accept because Jesus healed the man by forgiving his sins – something only God could do.
2 Ritual uncleanliness meant that a person was unacceptable to God because they had either not performed the correct rituals or were in an unclean state, for example, they had recently touched a dead body.

Exam question

Begin by defining what a miracle is – and remember Jesus used miracles in a number of important ways in his ministry – to display love, the power of God and to teach a message. Give a couple of brief examples. Don't forget to mention scholars and quote from the textual narrative.

The Sermon on the Mount

Checkpoints

1 The kingdom of God is the time when God will reign over all things and evil and suffering will be no more.
2 Righteousness means good conduct and a proper relationship of love and obedience with God.

Exam question

You will need to be selective in your material. Don't try to write about every incident involving the disciples. What is needed is a look at what discipleship meant – obedience, faith, trust in God and being prepared for prosecution, rejection and ill-treatment. Stick closely to the textual narrative and, in particular, the words of Jesus concerning discipleship. Remember to quote and to mention the views of scholars.

Religious themes in Luke's Gospel

Checkpoints

1 The word Gospel means 'good news'.
2 To repent means to seek forgiveness for sins and to seek to live in accordance with the teachings of Christ.

Exam question

To do this question you must first explain what prayer and salvation are and then examine Jesus' teaching on them. Do not simply retell the narrative, but look into the detail of what Jesus says and what he means by it. The key to a good answer lies in in-depth discussion of the meaning behind the words. Scholars will be particularly useful.

Social themes in Luke's Gospel

Checkpoints

1 Tax collectors were despised because, often, they were Jews who worked for the Romans. Also, sometimes they charged the people too much and exploited them.
2 A disciple is a pupil, who learns from a teacher; an apostle is one who has learned and now teaches.

Exam question

This is a popular question. It requires you to highlight Jesus' teachings, but you must avoid the trap of simply retelling the narrative. Look for good examples and highlight the words of Jesus and the meaning behind them. Address such issues as: is it wrong to be wealthy? Why is it difficult for the wealthy to enter the kingdom? You will also be expected to quote – Jesus gives many famous examples.

The Passion in Matthew and Mark

Checkpoints

1 The message was that animal sacrifices were not needed for salvation.
2 The Sanhedrin was the Supreme Jewish Council, led by the High Priest.

Exam question

Make sure you keep the religious authorities distinct from the political one – the Romans. The question requires you to weigh up the evidence, so you will need a detailed knowledge of not only the trial of Jesus, but also the issues between Jesus and the authorities that led to his arrest. Try to consider the motives of the authorities – what were they trying to do and why? Old Testament references will help, as will the views of scholars.

The Passion in Luke

Checkpoints

1 If they arrested Jesus during the festival it might have provoked trouble with the people.
2 Blasphemy is words or actions that deliberately display contempt for God.

Exam question

Keep a distinction between the religious authorities and the political ones. You will need to examine the motives behind the actions of both and consider the incidents that led up to Jesus' arrest and trial. Ask why things happened as they did. You will need to stick closely to the textual narrative and may find scholars and Old Testament references useful.

Death and resurrection in Matthew and Mark

Checkpoints

1 Myrrh was one of the gifts given by the Wise men to the infant Jesus.
2 The women had come to the tomb to prepare the body of Jesus for a proper burial.

Exam question

Do not retell the two accounts here. Instead look to highlight the differences and try to show the significance – what message is each Gospel writer trying to give to the readers? Highlight the important ones – the women, the angels, the details of the crucifixion. Use Old Testament references, quote from the textual narrative and use the views of scholars.

Death and resurrection in Luke

Checkpoints

1 Jesus tells him that on this day, he will be with him in paradise.
2 The women go to the tomb to anoint the body of Jesus and prepare it for burial.

Exam question

Do not retell the story, but instead highlight the key features – select about three, for example the women, the angels, the resurrection appearances. Say what they are and why they are significant – refer to the symbolism, Old Testament prophecy and so on. Quote carefully from the text and use the views of scholars.

The authorship of the Fourth Gospel

Checkpoints

1 He was John, son of Zebedee, one of the 12 disciples of Jesus.
2 An epistle is a letter.

Exam question

This is a very popular question. Make sure you consider the evidence for and against. Be selective – you won't be able to discuss all the evidence in detail. You will need to make extensive reference to the views of scholars as well as the textual narrative and the historical and cultural evidence. You may, briefly, consider the other possible candidates.

Examiner's secrets

Candidates often have so much to write about this question that they take too long and run out of time to write a proper, full second answer. Practice your timing on this very carefully.

Date, origin and influences

Checkpoints

1 Excommunication means being thrown out of a religious faith or grouping.
2 Stoicism is a philosophical notion based on the belief that the world depends for its existence on reason (logos).

Exam question

This is a popular area for candidates. Consider the pros and cons of both first- and second-century authorship, including the age of the author, eyewitness accounts, the views of the early Church writers and later scholars. Weigh up the evidence and highlight the most convincing arguments on both sides.

The purpose of the Fourth Gospel

Checkpoints

1 Messiah means 'anointed one'.
2 The day of Preparation was when the Passover lamb was killed – just as Jesus, the Lamb of God, dies as a sacrifice for humanity's sins.

Exam question

This is a complex question. You will need to define what is meant by spiritual and look at the evidence, both within the textual narrative and outside, concerning the nature of the Gospel. Make extensive use of textual evidence, together with the views of ancient scholars, archaeological evidence and modern theories.

The Prologue

Checkpoints

1 The Torah is the divine teaching of God, principally contained in the first five books of the Old Testament/Jewish Bible.
2 Incarnate means 'becoming flesh' and refers to Jesus as God coming into the world in human form.

Exam question

This is a compact question, dealing with the first 18 verses of Chapter one. You need to be very familiar with these verses – almost knowing them by heart – and understand the important concepts such as logos, reason, light, grace and incarnation. It is vital in this question to include a range of scholars' views and to show an in-depth understanding of the key features.

The Holy Spirit and women in the Fourth Gospel

Checkpoints

1 Nicodemus.
2 Because Samaritans and Jews were at enmity with each other since the division of the kingdom following the death of Solomon.

Exam question

Ensure that you show both good textual knowledge and an understanding of how significant both the Holy Spirit and women are in the Fourth Gospel. Distinguish clearly between uses of pneuma and paraclete and show how they demonstrate the different functions of the Holy Spirit throughout Jesus' ministry and beyond. Don't rely on stereotypical responses regarding women in the Gospel, but show that you understand their theological role in developing themes of discipleship and Christology. Don't narrate the stories, but pick out the main themes from each. Use three scholars in this essay and at least three direct textual quotations.

The early ministry of Jesus

Checkpoints

1 Atonement ('at-one-ment') is the way in which humanity is reconciled to God through the death of Jesus.
2 The Samaritans lived in the region of Samaria, north of Jerusalem. They were Jews who had intermarried with Gentiles and tolerated pagan gods. They were despised by the 'true' Jews in Judea.

Exam question

In this question, it is vital that you do not waste valuable time telling the story of the incidents surrounding the signs you have chosen. Instead get quickly to the heart of the matter – what the signs and the symbolism mean. You will need to understand the background, the Old Testament references and the views of scholars. Concentrate on the words of Jesus – and remember to quote. Choose wisely – pick the signs that have lots of obvious meaning and symbolism.

Jesus' later ministry

Checkpoints

1 The 12 baskets signify the 12 tribes of Israel.
2 In the Old Testament, the figure of the shepherd was used to represent a king or ruler.

Exam question

This is a popular question. As well as knowing the textual narrative, you will also have to understand the symbolism connected to the ideas of shepherds and sheep and, in particular, the Old Testament references. Look for the views of scholars concerning the meaning – the idea of the flock (believers) being led by the shepherd (Christ) who gives his life for the sheep. Don't forget to quote.

The road to the Cross

Checkpoints

1 The triumphal entry was foretold by Zechariah.
2 This saying highlights the fact that Jesus and God are united in a unique relationship. Jesus is God in human form.

Exam question

It is important, when answering this question, that you know and understand the meaning of the symbolism. You must use relevant Old Testament passages and imagery as well as referring back to important aspects of the Fourth Gospel itself, particularly the Prologue and the healing of the blind man. You need to quote and make reference to the views of scholars.

The death of Jesus

Checkpoints

1 They are called the Passion because they are full of intense emotion.
2 Mary sees angels at the resurrection, just as the Virgin Mary, at the Annunciation, met an angel who told her that Christ was to come into the world.

Exam question

Be careful to avoid simply retelling the story of the crucifixion. This question requires you to select three acts of religious significance – pick those which have the most symbolism, such as the breaking of the legs, the piercing of his side – and remember to link these to Old Testament prophecy. You must give important quotations, explain their meaning and highlight your answer with the views of scholars.

Revision checklist
New Testament

By the end of this chapter you should be able to:

1	Know and understand the key features of the background to the life of Christ.	Confident	Not confident. **Revise** pages 52–3
2	Understand the significance of the birth narratives.	Confident	Not confident. **Revise** pages 54–5
3	Be able to write confidently about the parables in Matthew and Mark.	Confident	Not confident. **Revise** pages 56–7
4	Be able to write confidently about the parables in Luke.	Confident	Not confident. **Revise** pages 58–9
5	Convey an understanding of the significance of the miracles in Matthew and Mark.	Confident	Not confident. **Revise** pages 60–61
6	Convey an understanding of the miracles in Luke.	Confident	Not confident. **Revise** pages 62–3
7	Know and understand the Sermon on the Mount and its meaning.	Confident	Not confident. **Revise** pages 64–5
8	Understand and evaluate religious themes in Luke.	Confident	Not confident. **Revise** pages 66–7
9	Understand and evaluate social themes in Luke.	Confident	Not confident. **Revise** pages 68–9
10	Understand the meaning and significance of the events of the Passion narrative in Matthew and Mark.	Confident	Not confident. **Revise** pages 70–71
11	Be sure of the meaning and significance of the events of the Passion narrative in Luke.	Confident	Not confident. **Revise** pages 72–3
12	Convey an understanding of the death and resurrection narratives in Matthew and Mark.	Confident	Not confident. **Revise** pages 74–5
13	Convey an understanding of the death and resurrection narratives in Luke.	Confident	Not confident. **Revise** pages 76–7
14	Know, understand and evaluate evidence for the authorship of the Fourth Gospel.	Confident	Not confident. **Revise** pages 78–9
15	Have a secure grasp on the key debates regarding the date, origin and influences on the Fourth Gospel.	Confident	Not confident. **Revise** pages 80–81
16	Have an awareness of a range of possible purposes of the Fourth Gospel.	Confident	Not confident. **Revise** pages 82–3
17	Be conversant with the nature, content and purpose of the Prologue to the Fourth Gospel.	Confident	Not confident. **Revise** pages 84–5
18	Understand the meaning and significance of the Holy Spirit and women in the Fourth Gospel.	Confident	Not confident. **Revise** pages 86–7
19	Know, understand and evaluate the key features of Jesus' early ministry in the Fourth Gospel.	Confident	Not confident. **Revise** pages 88–9
20	Know, understand and evaluate the key features of Jesus' later ministry in the Fourth Gospel.	Confident	Not confident. **Revise** pages 90–91
21	Have a clear understanding of the events on the road to the Cross in the Fourth Gospel and their significance.	Confident	Not confident. **Revise** pages 92–3
22	Be confident in dealing with issues relating to the crucifixion and resurrection in the Fourth Gospel.	Confident	Not confident. **Revise** pages 94–5

Philosophy of religion

The philosophy of religion focuses on questions of the existence and nature of God, as well as questions arising from religious belief, such as is there a life after death, how do we speak meaningfully of God, is there a problem of evil, and is it reasonable to expect God to perform miracles? These topics have been the concern of religious and non-religious thinkers for thousands of years, and you need to be aware of the contribution of a range of thinkers, ancient and modern. Your own view about these topics is interesting, of course, but must never take precedence over showing the examiner that you are able to discuss the views of scholars with confidence. Philosophy is about analysing the nature of language and the claims it makes, especially when those claims appear to be inconsistent or flawed. Philosophy of religion is particularly open to these challenges, which makes it a lively subject of debate.

Exam themes

→ Arguments for the existence of God:
  → Design
  → Cosmological
  → Ontological
  → Religious experience
  → Moral
→ Problem of evil
→ Miracles
→ The nature of religious experience
→ Life after death
→ Atheism and critiques of religious belief
→ Religious language
→ The relationship between religion and science
→ The foundations of religious belief: Plato and Aristotle
→ The foundations of religious belief: Judeo-Christian themes: God as creator; God and goodness

Topic checklist

AS ○   A2 ●

	OCR	AQA	EDEXCEL
The design argument	○	●	○
The cosmological argument	○	●	○
The ontological argument	○	●	●
The argument from religious experience	○	○●	●
The moral argument	○		
The problem of evil and suffering	○	●	○
Miracles	●	○	○
Life after death	●	●	●
Atheism and critiques of religious belief	●		●
Religious language	●		●
Religion and science	○●	○●	○
Foundations of religious belief: Plato and Aristotle	○		
Foundations of religious belief: Judeo-Christian themes	○		

The design argument

One of the classic arguments for the existence of God, the design argument has withstood the challenges of scientific interpretations of the world.

The principles of the design argument ●●●

The design argument suggests that, like human inventions, features of the universe are so perfectly adapted to fulfil their function that they display evidence of being deliberately designed by an intelligent, personal designer. Since the works of nature are far greater than the works of humanity, an infinitely greater designer, God, is suggested as the most likely explanation. The argument seeks to explain four features of the world: order, benefit, purpose and suitability for human life.

Thomas Aquinas: the Fifth Way

Aquinas observed that the beneficial order in the universe could not happen by chance and since many objects do not have the intelligence to work towards an end or purpose they must be directed by something that does have intelligence. Thus, God exists as the explanation of beneficial order.

William Paley

Paley used an analogy between a watch and the world to show how unity and purpose could not be explained by chance. Paley argued that just as the discovery of a watch on a heath could not be explained by saying it had always been there, the order in the universe also demands an explanation. Paley anticipates several criticisms against his argument, some of which had been addressed by David Hume. He does not intend to draw any conclusions about the character of the designer, or even of the design, in terms of its perfection, infinity, or rarity. Rather, he claims, even if the watch goes wrong or shows evidence of bad design or, if we have never seen a watch before we could still deduce that it had been designed, and if we cannot work out the function that individual parts contribute to the whole, it does not disprove that it has been designed.

The probability of design

Richard Swinburne supports the argument on the grounds that the probability of design is greater than chance. He identifies seven features of the world which demand an explanation: its existence; its order; consciousness; the opportunity to do good; the pattern of history; miracles; religious experience.

Useful quotations

'This proof always deserves to be mentioned with respect. It is the oldest, the clearest, and the most accordant with the common reason of mankind' (Immanuel Kant).

Terminology

The design argument is also known as the teleological argument, from the Greek *telos*, meaning end or purpose.

Examiner's secrets

An essay on the design argument which starts with these principles rather than Paley's watch, shows a more sophisticated understanding of the argument.

Checkpoint 1

What kind of argument does Aquinas use in the Fifth Way? How is it similar to the arguments in the other four Ways?

Useful quotations

'So there is our universe. It is characterised by vast, all persuasive temporal order, the conformity of nature to formula, recorded in the scientific laws formulated by humans. These phenomena are clearly things too big for science to explain . . .' (Richard Swinburne, *Is There A God?* (1996)).

Action point

Read Paley's article, *The Watch and the Watchmaker*, so you can quote directly from his work.

Example

Examples of natural beauty, such as Niagara Falls or the Grand Canyon, illustrate the aesthetic nature of the universe – they are not essential for life, so may be evidence of a personal, loving creator.

Other forms of the argument

The argument from providence – the universe contains everything needed for human survival and benefit.
The aesthetic argument – the world is beautiful.
The anthropic principle – the purpose of the universe appears to be to support human life.

Criticisms of the design argument ●●●

→ The features of the universe could be the result of one huge coincidence, a cosmic happening which produced a result which merely *appears* to be designed. Richard Dawkins suggests that although the universe may be difficult to explain as the result of one chance, it could easily be the result of many smaller chances.

→ The premises of the argument are flawed: not everyone *will* perceive design in the universe; why is God the only explanation for design, if it is there?

→ Evolution and natural selection could provide just as likely an explanation for the character and appearance of the universe as divine design. As species adapt to their environment they will inevitably appear to be designed to suit it, otherwise they would not survive.

→ The aesthetic argument is unconvincing since beauty is subjective, and what one person perceives as beautiful, another does not. Further, since we have no other world to compare, how do we know this world *is* beautiful?

Paley's argument fails on several counts:

→ *The analogy is unsound*: natural things are different to human designs; the world is more like a vegetable than a machine.

→ *God is made more human*: if the analogy is sound, then God must be similar to humans and so it could not be concluded that he is infinite or perfect.

→ *The problem of evil*: John Stuart Mill argued that the most we can claim is that the designer of the universe might be loving, but the existence of evil and suffering suggests that he could be or must be seriously limited in power.

The argument from probability is not convincing. Probability usually refers to the chance that something random might happen or that something is likely because of past events. However, when talking about the probability that God exists, neither of these is meant. What then does the claim 'It is probable that God made the universe' mean?

Useful quotations

'God being omnipotent is able to produce a world orderly in these respects. And he has a good reason to choose to do so: a world containing human persons is a good thing . . . God being perfectly good, is generous. He wants to share' (Richard Swinburne, *Is There A God?* (1996)).

Useful quotations

'In crossing a heath, suppose I pitched my foot against a stone, and were asked how the stone came to be there, I might possibly answer . . . it had lain there forever . . . But suppose I found a watch . . . I should hardly think of the answer which I had before given' (William Paley in John Hick (ed.), *The Existence of God* (1964)).

Terminology

To be a **proof** (i.e. to convince everyone) the argument must be valid and have **true premises**. In terms of **logic** the argument is not **valid** as the existence of God is not a necessary conclusion.

Terminology

An argument which compares God to humans is guilty of **anthropomorphising** God.

Checkpoint 2

Consider what it means to say that the universe is 'religiously ambiguous' and how that might affect the design argument.

Useful quotations

Richard Dawkins said of natural selection: *'It has no vision, no foresight, no sight at all. If it can be said to play the role of the watchmaker in nature, it is the blind watchmaker.'* (*The Blind Watchmaker* (1986))

Exam questions   answers: page 136

(a) Outline the key features of the design argument for the existence of God.

(b) Evaluate the view that the weaknesses of the argument outweigh its strengths.   (45 mins)

The cosmological argument

Useful quotations

'The question is: is there an unanswered question about the existence of the world? Can we be puzzled by the existence of the world instead of nothing? I can be and am; and this is to be puzzled about God' (Herbert McCabe in Brian Davies (ed.), *The Philosophy of Religion* (2000)).

Action point

Find out about the famous radio debate between Bertrand Russell and F.C. Copleston in 1947. They discussed the cosmological argument and other arguments for the existence of God. Learn some quotations from it.

Terminology

Contingent beings are capable of existing or not existing – they may or may not be. A necessary being cannot not be – it cannot go in and out of existence.

Terminology

Aquinas called motion 'the reduction of something from potentiality to actuality'.

Checkpoint 1

Supporters of the argument often appeal to Ockham's Razor. What is Ockham's Razor and how may it apply to the cosmological argument?

Useful detail

The Islamic form of the argument, known as the Kalam Argument and which goes back to al-Kindi (*c* 870) and al-Ghazali (1058–1111), and which proposes a cosmological argument is as follows:

P1: Whatever comes into being must have a cause.
P2: The universe came into being.
C: The universe must have a cause.

The cosmological argument is an *a posteriori* one. It assumes that the universe has not always been in existence but is ultimately explained by a necessary external agent.

The principles of the argument

The cosmological argument is based on the claim that everything that exists in the universe exists because it was caused by something else, and that something was itself caused by something else. However, it is necessary for something to have started this all off – something which did not, itself, need to be caused. The argument is based on three main questions:

→ Why is there something rather than nothing?
→ Why does the universe possess the form it does, and not some other form?
→ How can the series of events that culminate in the universe be explained?

Aquinas and the Five Ways

The first three Ways are cosmological arguments:

→ *The First Way – motion*: Things in the world are in motion (a state of change), but since nothing moves itself, there must be a first mover who began the chain of motion.

> *In the world some things are in motion. Now whatever is moved is moved by another. But this cannot go on to infinity . . . Therefore it is necessary to arrive at a first mover, moved by no other; and this everyone understands to be God.*

→ *The Second Way – cause*: Nothing causes itself, so if the universe was to exist at all there needs to be a first cause which began the chain of cause and effect.

> *In the world of sensible things we find there is an order of efficient causes. There is no case known in which a thing is found to be the efficient cause of itself; for so it would be prior to itself, which is impossible . . . Therefore it is necessary to admit to a first efficient cause, to which everyone gives the name of God.*

→ *The Third Way – necessity and contingency*: The universe is contingent, and so could not be the cause of its own existence. Only a necessary being has the power to bring it into existence.

> *We find in nature things that are possible to be and not to be, since they are found to be generated, and to be corrupted, and consequently, it is possible for them to be and not to be . . . Therefore if everything cannot be then at one time there was nothing in existence.*

Other forms of the argument

Leibniz explained the cosmological argument in terms of the *principle of sufficient reason*. He said that even if the universe had always been in existence, it would still need a sufficient reason for its existence. By going backwards in time forever we will never arrive at such a complete explanation since there is nothing within the universe to show *why* it exists.

Richard Swinburne argued that since there ought more reasonably to be nothing rather than something the fact that there is something suggests a creator:

> It is extraordinary that there should exist anything at all. Surely the most natural state of affairs is simply nothing: no universe, no God, nothing . . . If we can explain the many bits of the universe by one simple being which keeps them in existence, we should do so – even if inevitably we cannot explain the existence of that simple being.
> (*Is There A God?* (1996))

Criticisms of the cosmological argument ●●●

David Hume proposed the classic criticisms of the cosmological argument in *Dialogues Concerning Natural Religion*:

→ Why assume we need to find a cause?
→ Why look for an explanation for the whole universe?
→ Is the concept of a necessary being meaningful?
→ If it is, why should it be God and not the universe itself?
→ The argument begins with a familiar concept but reaches conclusions about things that are outside our experience.
→ It is not reasonable to look for a cause for the whole chain if we can satisfactorily explain each item in the chain.
→ Even if specific instances of things in the universe require an explanation, it does not follow that this must be the case for the universe as a whole – we cannot work from the specific to the general.
→ **Russell** claimed that some things are *just there* and require no explanation and the universe is a *brute fact*.

Does the argument work?

Although it is perfectly reasonable to propose as a hypothesis that there is a God who created the universe, the argument will only work if it reduces the number of unanswered questions. Ultimately, the argument cannot explain God, only offer God as a possible explanation, and if we are not satisfied with the idea of God as a being who himself requires no explanation, the argument will fail.

Useful quotations

'If one does not wish to embark on the path which leads to the affirmation of a transcendent being . . . one has to deny the reality of the problem, assert that things "just are"; and that the existential problem is a pseudo-problem. And if one refuses even to sit down at the chessboard and make a move, one cannot, of course, be checkmated' (F.C. Copleston in John Hick, *The Existence of God* (1964)).

Useful quotations

Bertrand Russell challenged the attempt to move from the particular to the general: *'Every man who exists has a mother, and it seems to me your argument is that therefore the human race must have a mother, but obviously the human race hasn't a mother – that's a different logical sphere.'* (in John Hick, *The Existence of God* (1964))

Checkpoint 2

Why may the cosmological argument be said to have 'perennial value'?

Exam question   answer: page 136

Explain and evaluate the cosmological argument for the existence of God.

(30 mins)

The ontological argument

An *a priori* argument, the ontological proof arose from Anselm's quest for an argument which would prove everything about God, his nature and existence.

The principles of the argument

The ontological argument is **deductive**, hence its conclusion necessarily follows from its premises. The argument is also **analytic** – the truth (or falsity) of an analytic statement is completely determined by the meanings of the words and symbols used to express it – and **a priori** – known to be true independently of experience (though some experience may be necessary to understand what the statement means). The argument is based on the principle that the word 'God' is an analytic term, which conveys everything there is about God, including his necessary existence, which derives from his supreme perfection.

Anselm's form of the argument

Anselm devised two forms of the argument:

(i) First form

P1 God is that than which nothing greater can be conceived.
P2 That than which nothing greater can be conceived must contain all perfections, including the perfection of existence.
P3 If God exists only as a contingent being then a greater being could be imagined that has necessary existence.
C   Thus God must exist.

Hence, it is a contradiction to be able to conceive of something than which nothing greater can be thought and yet to deny that that something exists.

(ii) Second form

P1 God is the greatest possible being.
P2 It is greater to be a necessary being then a contingent being.
P3 If God exists only as a contingent being then a greater being could be imagined has necessary existence.
P4 This being would then be greater than God.
P5 God is therefore a necessary being.
C   God must necessarily exist.

Anselm and the fool

Anselm maintained that it was impossible for the atheist to meaningfully deny the existence of God, since to even use the word 'God' had to convey understanding of what it means. Since 'God' *means* a supremely perfect being that cannot not exist, the atheist must understand this at least intellectually. Once they had grasped the full significance of the term, they would no longer be able to deny God's existence.

Weaknesses of Anselm's argument

➜ Anselm assumes that 'God' functions as an analytic term, and that his definition of God is beyond question.

➜ Anselm treats existence as an analytic term. However, statements about existence are synthetic, since existence is a contingent concept and yet he assumes that it is meaningful to make an exception for God, and declare him necessarily existent by definition.

➜ Why is existence a 'great making property'? Why is something great simply by virtue of it existing? Aren't there some existing things which would be greater if they didn't exist?

➜ Existence does not describe anything, it merely indicates the actuality of an object. Bertrand Russell argued that to say 'Cows are brown' and 'Cows are brown and exist' is to say the same thing. Their existence is assumed in the first statement, hence existence adds nothing to our understanding of them.

Gaunilo

Anselm's contemporary, Gaunilo, demonstrated that Anselm's argument attempted to define things into existence, and would lead to absurd conclusions if applied to anything other than God:

P1 I can conceive of an island that than which no greater island can be thought.
P2 Such an island must possess all perfections.
P3 Existence is a perfection.
C   Therefore the island exists.

Anselm argued that the principle was intended to apply only to God, since only he has the quality of necessary existence.

Descartes

Descartes argued that necessary existence belonged to God as three angles belong to a triangle – it cannot be separated from God's nature and definition. Furthermore, if God is a perfect being, he must exist to put the idea of his existence into the minds of imperfect humans, who could not otherwise conceive of him.

Malcolm

Norman Malcolm argued that the very nature of God meant that if he did not exist necessarily, he could not exist at all. Since it is contradictory to say that God does not exist, then he must exist necessarily.

Plantinga

Alvin Plantinga furthered the argument, by claiming that since God is maximally great and perfect, he must exist in any and all conceivable worlds.

Checkpoint 2

What does it mean to say that existence is not a predicate? This was a key criticism raised by Kant.

Terminology

The argument is sometimes supported because it is effective as an **anti-realist** argument – this means that it is meaningful to those who already hold beliefs about God and its claims are consistent with other claims they hold about God. It is compatible, therefore, with a **coherence theory of truth**.

Terminology

The ontological argument maintains that God exists necessarily *de dicto* – this means by definition, literally, of words.

Exam question   answer: page 136

'The Ontological Argument can never succeed as a proof for the existence of God.' Discuss and evaluate this claim. (45 mins)

The argument from religious experience

Terminology

Rudolph Otto coined the term 'numinous' to describe the 'holy other' nature of religious experience.

Terminology

Williams James used the term 'noetic' to describe the way in which religious experiences reveal something to the experient.

Checkpoint 1

Identify some problems raised by corporate experiences.

Useful quotations

'God establishes himself in the interior of this soul in such a way, that when I return to myself, it is wholly impossible for me to doubt that I have been in God and God in me' (Teresa of Avila).

Action point

Study some key religious experiences from the Bible: Moses' encounter at the Burning Bush (Ex. 3:2ff); Isaiah's vision in the temple (Is. 6:1ff); Paul's conversion (Acts 9:1ff); the Transfiguration (Mark 9:2ff) are all useful.

Useful quotations

'When a fellow Monk', said Luther, 'one day repeated the words of the Creed: "I believe in the forgiveness of sins", I saw the Scripture in an entirely new light; and straightaway I felt as if I were born anew'.

Action point

Use the Internet to find out about a famous religious experience, for example, the visions of Bernadette at Lourdes in 1858.

Religious experiences – in which God, rather than physical objects, is experienced – are beyond ordinary empirical explanation and are most likely to take place within a context of religious expectancy and hope. Is it reasonable to treat them as evidence for the existence of God?

Types of religious experience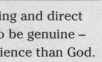

Religious experience may serve to be the most convincing and direct proof of the existence of God, if they could be proven to be genuine – that is, that there is no better explanation for the experience than God. There are several types of religious experience, which are not mutually exclusive:

Mystical – an overwhelming awareness of the presence of God, leading to wonder and awe. In *introvertive mysticism* the mystic looks inwards and understands his own oneness with the divine. In *objective mysticism* the mystic contemplates outward circumstances.

Conversion – an experience which leads to a changed perspective on life and the world.

Corporate – an experience shared by more than one person, often in the context of a religious meeting.

Charismatic – an experience involving gifts of the Holy Spirit, such as speaking in tongues or words of knowledge.

St Teresa of Avila was a famous Spanish mystic who identified three tests of religious experience: it should conform to the teaching of the Church; it should lead to increased humility; it meets with the approval of a person in spiritual authority.

William James published *The Varieties of Religious Experience* (1902) in which he identified four characteristics: ineffability (cannot be expressed); noetic (gives insight); transiency (it lasts a short time); passivity (the experient feels helpless).

Paul Tillich described two stages in a mystical experience: an event or encounter, followed by a special understanding of that event which reveals its religious significance.

Richard Swinburne identified five types of religious experience: seeing God in a place or object everyone can see; seeing God in a public place, but in an unusual way; a private experience which can be described in everyday language; a private experience beyond expression; a private belief about a person's relationship with God.

Can religious experience prove the existence of God? ●●●

Richard Swinburne argues that a loving God has reason to make himself known. Swinburne draws the conclusion that since it has been the case that many millions of people have had an experience of what *seems to them* to be of God, then it is a basic principle of rationality that we should believe them. This is what Swinburne calls the **principle of credulity** – unless we have overwhelming evidence to the contrary, we should believe that things are as they seem to be. In addition, Swinburne argues for the **principle of testimony** – we should work on the assumption that people tell the truth. '*In the absence of special considerations the experiences of others are (probably) as they report them.*'

Swinburne suggests three reasons why we might *not* believe a person's account: the circumstances surrounding the experience render their account unreliable; we have good evidence that things are not as they are reported; there is evidence that the experience was not caused by God.

Brian Davies argues that we cannot use the fact that not everyone shares a religious experience as grounds to dismiss them. He compares it to a team of explorers discovering an unknown animal in the jungle. A second team goes in search of it, but does not find it. However, this does not prove that the first team did not see it.

Religious experiences may prove the existence of God for those who have good reasons to interpret them as proof of his existence – this makes them highly subjective. If the experient allows nothing to count against his claim to have experienced God he could be said to have a **blik**, but this does not make his experience meaningless. However, it is not surprising that religious believers have religious experiences, since they are more likely to know how to identify them.

Arguments against religious experience as proof of God

→ If God does not exist, there can be no experience of him.
→ How do we know if we are actually experiencing God?
→ There are no tests for verifying that an experience has been one of God.
→ The testimony of religious believers may be biased.
→ Religious experiences may reveal psychological needs.
→ If there is a God, why doesn't everyone experience him?

Useful quotations

'In the absence of special considerations the experiences of others are (probably) as they report them' (Richard Swinburne, *Is There A God?* (1996)).

Useful quotations

'An omnipotent and perfectly good creator will seek to interact with his creatures and in particular, with human persons capable of knowing him' (Richard Swinburne, *Is There A God?* (1996)).

Checkpoint 2

Suggest circumstances which would fit into Swinburne's three reasons to doubt the testimony of religious experience.

Terminology

The term **blik** was coined by R.M. Hare, who used it to describe the unfalsifiable nature of a religious believer's claims.

Useful quotations

'I suggest that the overwhelming testimony of so many millions of people to occasional experiences of God must, in the absence of counter evidence, be taken as tipping the balance of evidence decisively in favour of the existence of God' (Richard Swinburne, *Is There A God?* (1996)).

Exam question   answer: page 137

'Religious experiences are only fantasy and prove nothing'. Discuss.   (45 mins)

The moral argument

The relationship between religion and morality is, for many people, taken for granted. However, the link between the two is a complex one: are religion and morality linked and does morality therefore prove the existence of God or are they totally separate?

Are morality and religion linked?

Are things good because God commands them or does God command that which is good? (Plato's Euthyphro Dilemma)

The link between religion and morality depends on whether morality comes from God or humans. J.H. Newman argued that moral laws had their origin in a personal lawgiver who imposes moral demands upon us; our experience of morality leads us to conclude the existence of a lawgiver, otherwise our moral experience makes no sense. God gives commands and what he commands is good because God is the perfect form of the good, and all lesser standards of goodness (such as human goodness) are judged by reference to him.

How do humans discover God's moral law? Believers will look in the Scriptures to establish God's will – e.g. the Ten Commandments (Exodus 20:1–17), God's law given to his people many centuries ago, but still relevant and applicable today. These commandments are very general, e.g. 'Do not murder', but can be applied to a range of modern dilemmas such as abortion and euthanasia. In the New Testament the teachings of Jesus, such as the Sermon on the Mount (Matthew 7), offer more flexible guidelines, based on love.

Does morality prove the existence of God?

In *The Critique of Practical Reason*, Kant argued that the existence of a morality and moral law depended on the existence of God. He maintained that everyone could understand moral law, which was the highest form of good, and that humanity had a *duty* to seek the perfect state of affairs, which he called the **summum bonum**. This duty is a **categorical imperative**. But, Kant acknowledged, the perfect state could not be achieved in this life, and so it needs God to bring it to fulfilment in an afterlife, so there could be no morality without God and religion.

Kant's argument is an a priori one since it is not humanity's experience of the world which points to the existence of God but, by reason, morality demands his existence. Moral behaviour would not be invalid if God did not exist, but Kant maintained that if the goal of morality was to be achieved, then it would need God to bring it about.

Aquinas

Aquinas claimed that the realities of which the human mind is aware are merely pale copies of a greater, unseen reality, which is eternal. The goodness, virtue or truth found in human beings is a reflection of the supreme or perfect goodness of God. God, being perfect in goodness, is also perfect in his very being, or existence. His moral perfection and authority are evidence for his existence, and all lesser forms or reflections of goodness were striving towards the ultimate good that is their cause.

The weaknesses of the argument ●●●

Morality can only prove the existence of God if we can prove he is the only source of moral authority. But if God's commands determine what is moral then whatever God commands is morally right, regardless of what it is. So, to say that something is morally right because God has commanded it is not enough. Similarly, there are weaknesses in Kant's argument. His suggestion that humanity *ought* to do good, implies that they *can* do good, yet he claims that we are not able to do so, and assumes that God is the only agent capable of doing so.

Are religion and morality totally separate?

Even if there are **objective moral laws**, which require the existence of a moral lawgiver, they can be explained without God. Owen argued that it may not even be necessary to consider a *personal* source of morality. Furthermore, if all religions have a moral code which comes from God, why is there disagreement over matters of morality?

It may come down to considerations of probability: is it more or less likely that God is the source of morality? If moral commands are merely expressions of approval or disapproval, or if they are relative to our culture, then they cannot prove the existence of God.

Useful quotations

'Among beings there are some more and some less good, true, noble and the like . . . there must also be something which is to all beings the cause of their being, goodness, and every other perfection, and this we call God' (Aquinas in John Hick (ed.), *The Existence of God* (1964)).

Useful quotations

'I do think that all goodness reflects God in some way and proceeds from him, so that in a sense the man who loves what is truly good, loves God even if he doesn't advert to God' (F.C. Copleston in John Hick (ed.), *The Existence of God* (1964)).

Action point

Look at the story of Abraham and Isaac in Genesis 22. This is often cited as an example of God commanding something morally unacceptable. What do you think?

Checkpoint 2

Explain the error of reasoning committed by Kant.

Action point

Find out about the differences between two Christian denominations on an important moral issue.

Useful quotations

Bertrand Russell argued: *'I love the things that I think are good, and I hate the things that I think are bad. I don't say that these things are good because they participate in the Divine goodness.'* (In John Hick (ed.), *The Existence of God* (1964)).

Exam questions   answers: page 137

(a) Examine the view that morality proves the existence of God.

(b) Evaluate the claim that there are more convincing reasons to suggest that morality does not derive from God.   (45 mins)

The problem of evil and suffering (1)

'Either God cannot abolish evil or he will not: if he cannot then he is not all-powerful, if he will not, then he is not all good' (St Augustine).

What is the problem?

There are two types of evil – **natural evil**, which is the malfunctioning of the natural world, and **moral evil**, which is the result of morally wrong human actions. The problem of evil challenges the notion of an all-loving, all-powerful God. The dilemma is: If God is **omnipotent** (all-powerful) then he can do anything. This means he could create a world that is free from evil and suffering and he could stop all evil and suffering. If God is **omniscient** and knows everything in the universe then he must know how to stop evil and suffering. If God is **omnibenevolent** (all-loving) then he would wish to end all evil and suffering. No all-loving God would wish his creation to suffer for no reason. Yet evil and suffering do exist, so either God is not omnipotent or omnibenevolent *or* he does not exist.

(a) God's omnipotence

(c) Evil exists   (b) God's goodness

J.L. Mackie observed that these three propositions constitute an ***inconsistent triad***: the conjunction of any two entails the negation of the third.

Is there a solution?

It may be that if God's goodness is different from human goodness, he allows evil to exist as part of his greater plan of love. This view has led to the development of theodicies to justify the existence of a loving God in the face of evil.

The Augustinian theodicy

Augustine argued that the Bible shows that God is wholly good and created a world perfectly good and free from defect, evil and suffering. Evil is really the going wrong of something that is good, which came from angels, and humans who turned their backs on God. Consequently, perfection was ruined by human sin and natural evil came about through the loss of order in nature, and moral evil from the knowledge of good and evil which humanity had discovered through their disobedience. God is right not to intervene since the punishment is justice for human **sin**. Technically, everyone would get their full and rightful punishment in hell, but in love God sent his son Jesus to die so that those who accepted him could be saved.

Example

Examples of natural evil may be disease, earthquake or famine. Examples of moral evil may be rape, murder or assault.

Useful quotations

'But the name of God means that He is infinite goodness. If, therefore, God existed, there would be no evil discoverable; but there is evil in the world. Therefore God does not exist' (Aquinas in John Hick (ed.), *The Existence of God* (1964)).

Useful quotations

'From these it follows that a good omnipotent thing eliminates evil completely, and the propositions that a good omnipotent thing exists, and that evil exists are incompatible' (J.L. Mackie, *Evil and Omnipotence* (1955)).

Checkpoint 1

Why can the problem of evil lead to qualification of God's nature?

Terminology

Theodicy comes from the Greek words *theos* and *dike*, meaning righteous God. A theodicy attempts to justify God's failure to remove evil and suffering from his creation.

Useful quotations

'God saw all that he had made, and it was very good' (Genesis 1:31).

Terminology

Augustine called evil the **privation** of good.

Criticisms of the Augustinian theodicy

→ It is a logical contradiction to say that a perfectly created world had gone wrong.

→ Augustine's view that the world was made perfect and damaged by humans is contrary to the theory of evolution.

→ Suffering is essential to survival – things must die in order that others might eat and live – so God must bear the responsibility for this.

→ The existence of hell as a place of eternal punishment seems a contradiction for an all-loving God.

The Irenaean theodicy (later developed by John Hick)

Irenaeus also suggested that evil was due to human free will, but claimed that God did not make a perfect world in which evil has a valuable part to play. God created humans imperfectly so they could develop into perfection. Goodness had to be developed by humans themselves, through willing cooperation with God so that evil and suffering will be overcome and humanity will develop into God's perfect likeness and willingly come into a love relationship with him. To achieve this, God had to create human beings at an **epistemic distance** from him – a distance of knowledge – otherwise humans would be overwhelmed by God and have no choice but to obey. The world has to be imperfect if humans are to make genuine choices and develop the positive qualities of love, honour and courage. Hick suggests that the world is a place of soul making, that is, a world where humans have to strive to meet challenges in order to gain perfection.

Criticisms of the Irenaean theodicy

→ The Irenaean theodicy allows room for the concept of evolution and avoids some of the problems associated with Augustine. However, it still has many criticisms.

→ The theodicy gives no ultimate reason to be good, since he offers the hope of the afterlife in which everyone will be brought to perfection.

→ Does the world really need such severity of suffering, such as experienced by the Holocaust, to produce good, especially when there is no guarantee that good will prevail?

However, Irenaeus held that there would be an afterlife that ultimately solves the problem because:

→ God's purpose would never be fulfilled without an afterlife.

→ Only a supremely good future in heaven can justify the magnitude of suffering.

→ Many apparently evil people cannot be held responsible for their actions, and they cannot be punished for eternity.

Checkpoint 2

Where in the Bible would you find the passages that are crucial for an understanding of Augustine's theodicy?

Terminology

The Irenaean theodicy exposes the **counterfactual hypothesis**: the view that God could continually make everything good. If he constantly interfered in such a way then humans simply could not develop.

Useful quotations

D.Z. Phillips argued that love could never be expressed by allowing suffering to happen: *'What are we to say of the child dying from cancer? If this has been done to anyone that is bad enough, but to be done for a purpose planned from eternity – that is the deepest evil. If God is this kind of agent, He cannot justify His actions and His evil nature is revealed.'* (*The Concept of Prayer* (1976)).

Action point

Identify some key ways in which the different world religions tackle the problem of evil.

Exam questions   answers: page 137

(a) Explain what is meant by the problem of suffering?

(b) Outline two theodicies and evaluate the view that neither succeed in offering a solution to the problem.   (45 mins)

The problem of evil and suffering (2)

'But the name of God means that He is infinite goodness. If, therefore, God existed, there would be no evil discoverable; but there is evil in the world. Therefore God does not exist' (Aquinas).

Examiner's secrets

Not as many candidates write about process theodicy as about the other solutions to the problem. It is worthwhile having it at your fingertips.

Useful quotations

David Griffin observed: *'God is responsible for evil in the sense of having urged the creation forward to those states in which discordant feelings could be felt with greater intensity'.* (*God, Power and Evil: A Process Theodicy* (1976)).

Checkpoint 1

Why have some thinkers argued that process theodicy is a heresy?

Action point

Compare the process theodicy with the Augustinian model. Make a note of the crucial differences in approach to the nature of God.

Further solutions to the problem of evil

Process theodicy

Process theodicy stems from the views of **A.N. Whitehead** and **David Griffin**. It is a radical theodicy in so far that it suggests that God, who is not omnipotent, did not create the universe, an uncreated process of which God is himself a part. God is also bound by natural laws, and suffers when evil occurs. God began the evolutionary process that led to the development of humans but, since God does not have total control, humans are free to ignore him. God cannot stop evil since he lacks the power to change the natural process, yet he bears some responsibility for it. God's actions are justified on the grounds that the universe has produced sufficient good to outweigh evil.

Process theology argues that the reality of God is still developing, and that God is 'bipolar', having two poles, one mental and one physical. The physical pole is the material world itself, which acts almost as God's 'body'. God is partly distinct and partly immersed in the world; hence any suffering in creation is also undergone by God. Creation itself is a cooperation between God and all other beings which God cannot force, but can only influence.

Does God have to be omnipotent?

The claim that God is omnipotent is equivalent to the claim that God possesses the logical limits of power. If this is this case, Whitehead argued that no being could be omnipotent. However, **Hartshorne** and Griffin argued that while God possesses the *greatest possible power*, that power is not sufficient to bring about a world containing no instances of evil. This is because:

→ A being of maximal power has no possible superior and possesses all the power there is to possess.
→ Griffin claims that in any conceivable world there must be beings which have power to determine to some degree their own activities and the activity of others.
→ However, if there were a being that possessed all the power that there is to possess, any other beings would possess no power at all.
→ Thus, if some beings can determine their own actions, the notion of a being which possesses all the power is not coherently conceivable.

Criticisms of process theodicy

Process theodicy denies the monopolistic view of God's omnipotence which is fundamental to the traditional classical theistic view of God. Is a limited God actually a being worthy of worship? Although it *may be* that an omnipotent being might prevent all genuine evil in the world, an omnipotent being cannot be the *sufficient cause* of that state of affairs, and hence cannot guarantee it; whether or not it occurs will be partly due to the activities of others. It removes the problem of why God does not put an end to evil and suffering – he simply lacks the power to do so. However, the theodicy may appeal because the fact that God suffers too means that he can identify with the suffering of humanity and believers are encouraged to fight alongside God against evil.

The free will defence

All the traditional theodicies, as well as process theodicy, depend on the notion that humans have free will. The free will defence can run independently of any of the specific theodicies, however. If this world is the logically necessary environment for humans to develop and it does so by providing freedom in the form of real choices, the production of both good and evil is inevitable. Without such choices we would not be free and not be human. God cannot intervene because to do so would compromise human freedom and take away the need for humans to be responsible and thus humans would not be able to develop.

However, as **J.L. Mackie** observed, God had to have been able to make a different world:

> *God was not, then, faced with a choice between making innocent automata and making beings who, in acting freely, would sometimes go wrong: there was open to him the obviously better possibility of making beings who would act freely but always choose right.* (*Evil and Omnipotence* (1955))

On the other hand, **Richard Swinburne** argued:

> *A generous God will seek to give us great responsibility for ourselves, each other, and the world, and thus a share in his own creative activity of determining what sort of world it is to be . . . The problem is that God cannot give us these goods in full measure without allowing much evil on the way.* (*Is There A God?* (1996))

Terminology

Process theologians refer to God as *'the fellow sufferer who understands'*.

Useful quotations

'The less he allows men to bring about large scale horrors, the less freedom and responsibility he gives them' (Richard Swinburne, *Is There A God?* (1996)).

Checkpoint 2

Why does monism claim to solve the problem of evil?

Exam question   answer: page 137

'The problem of evil can never be solved'. Discuss.   (30 mins)

Miracles

A philosophical examination of miracles must include consideration of the definition of the term, and reasons for and against the belief that it is possible for miracles to occur.

Scholars generally agree that a miracle must contain three features:

1 A breaking of the laws of nature.
2 The event has a purpose and significance.
3 The event may be interpreted religiously.

Although it is possible to use the term miracle in other ways – to describe a scene of great natural beauty, or to speak of some particularly fortuitous event, or of a change for the better in someone's personality – a miracle is most commonly defined as an event which includes these essential three criteria.

Definitions of miracles

David Hume defined a miracle as '*a transgression of a law of nature by the volition of the deity . . .*' **Thomas Aquinas** identified three kinds of miracles, all of which he defined as '*Those things . . . which are done by divine power apart from the order generally followed in things.*'

1 Events done by God, which nature could never do, e.g. stopping the sun (Joshua 10:13).
2 Events done by God, which nature could do, but not in that order, e.g. exorcisms (Mark 1:31).
3 Events done by God, which nature can do, but God does without the use of natural laws, e.g. healing by forgiving sins (Mark 2:5).

Aquinas's definitions infer an ***interventionist*** God, who only acts on random occasions. **Mel Thompson** argues that '*The idea of a miraculous event introduces a sense of arbitrariness and unpredictability into an understanding of the world*'. **Richard Swinburne** claims that the laws of nature are reasonably predictable and that if an apparently 'impossible' event happens then it is fair to call it a miracle. Some events which are no more than coincidences may be described as miracles by those who find a religious significance in them.

The problem of definition

These definitions are very subjective and it is not clear whether the concept of miracle must include a violation of a natural law and whether such laws are fixed. An anti-realist view of miracles, which suggests that any event with religious significance to the experient may be defined as a miracle, is very open ended.

Problems with accounts of miracles ●●○

Serious criticisms against miracles can be raised on moral and theological grounds. **Peter Vardy** observes:

> A God who intervened at Lourdes to cure an old man of cancer, but does not act to save starving millions in Ethiopia – such a God needs, at least, to face some hard moral questioning. (*The Puzzle of the Gospels* (1995))

David Hume argued that it would always be impossible to prove that a miracle has happened:

→ 'There is not to be found in all history, any miracle attested by a sufficient number of men, of such unquestioned good sense, education and learning, as to secure as against all delusion.'

→ 'It forms a strong presumption against all supernatural and miraculous relations that they are observed chiefly to abound amongst ignorant and barbarous nations.'

→ 'In matters of religion, whatever is different is contrary . . . every miracle, therefore, pretended to have been wrought in any of these religions . . . destroys the credit of those miracles.'

Problems with Hume's view

→ Hume does not say what would constitute a sufficient number, or what 'unquestioned good sense, education and learning' actually means. Do only religious people see miracles and are they always unreliable?

→ Earlier in his work, *An Enquiry Concerning Human Understanding*, Hume had argued that any regular event could happen differently. In his chapter on miracles, he contradicts this by claiming that miracles, as breaks in the regular order of things, cannot occur.

→ Hume argues that the probability of a person lying is greater than the probability of a miracle occurring, but unless the probability is zero it does not automatically discount all testimonies to miracles. How high we rank the probability of a miracle occurring depends on our pre-existing beliefs.

Other arguments in support of miracles

Richard Swinburne claims that it is reasonable to consider that sometimes the best explanation for an event is that it is a miracle. The principle of *Ockham's Razor* could be applied here – that the simplest explanation for an unusual event is the most philosophically viable explanation. Swinburne proposes a ***principle of credulity***: 'We ought to believe things as they seem, unless we have good evidence that we are mistaken.' (*Is There A God?* (1996)).

Useful quotations

'It seems strange that no miraculous intervention prevented Auschwitz or Hiroshima whilst the purposes apparently forwarded for some of the miracles acclaimed in the Christian tradition seem trivial by comparison' (Maurice Wiles, *God's Action in the World* (1986)).

Checkpoint 1

When was Hume writing? What intellectual movements influenced his ideas?

Action point

Check Chapter 10 of Hume's *Enquiry Concerning Human Understanding* for more of his criticisms of accounts of miracles.

Terminology

A **sceptic** questions the reality of human experience when it does not concur with what regularly occurs.
An **empiricist** trusts in what can be encountered by use of the senses rather than that which is beyond the physical world. Hume is a well-known sceptic and empiricist.

Checkpoint 2

Briefly explain the claim that miracles breach the epistemic distance between God and humanity.

Useful quotations

'If there is a God, one might well expect him to make his presence known to man, not merely through the overall pattern of the universe in which he placed them, but by dealing more intimately and personally with them' (Richard Swinburne, *Is There A God?* (1996)).

Exam questions   answers: page 138

(a) Explain what is meant by the term 'miracle'.

(b) Consider the view that the arguments raised against miracles are stronger than those in their support. (45 mins)

Life after death

Earthly, physical life must eventually end, but is there life after death? This great mystery is not just a religious issue, since many people who are not religious believers find the prospect of a post mortem existence highly desirable.

Why believe in an afterlife?

→ We find it hard to accept that this short life is all that there is; in an afterlife human potential could be fulfilled.

→ The moral law needs to be balanced, good rewarded and evil punished.

→ The Bible promises an afterlife as a gift from God and foreshadowed in the resurrection of Jesus.

→ Our personal identity is so strong that it must be able to survive the death process.

Evidence of an afterlife?

→ Mediums claim that it is possible to communicate with a post mortem spirit world. This is easily open to fraud, however.

→ Near death experiences are relatively frequent among people who have been brought back from a state of being clinically dead. There are, however, many neurological or chemical explanations, and so they cannot decisively prove an afterlife.

Forms of the afterlife

Immortality of the soul (or disembodied soul)

Plato suggested that the body belonged to the physical world and would thus decay, but the soul belonged to a higher realm where eternal truths, such as justice, love and goodness will endure forever. Once freed by death from the physical world, it would return to the realm of the Forms, where it will spend eternity contemplating the truth. **Descartes** maintained that non-physical existence was more certain than physical, thus any post mortem existence would have to be in a non-physical form: '*Our soul is of a nature entirely independent of the body, and consequently . . . it is not bound to die with it. And since we cannot see any other causes which destroy the soul, we are naturally led to conclude that it is immortal.*' **Kant** further maintained that '*The summum bonum is only possible on the presupposition of the immortality of the soul.*'

The philosophical problems of dualism revolve around whether or not a disembodied soul is really us. Many Christian theologians disagree and suggest that personal identity is strongly linked to the physical body. **Aquinas** believed that the soul (the *anima*) gave the body life while for the soul to become individual it needs the body: '*The natural condition of the human soul is to be united to the body.*'

Gilbert Ryle in *The Concept of the Mind* criticised dualism for committing a category error by proposing a *ghost* (soul/mind) *in a machine* (the body), and claimed instead that all mental events are really physical events interpreted in a mental way.

The resurrection of the body

Bodily resurrection is nothing to do with resuscitating corpses; it is the re-creation by God of the human individual as a spiritual body. Paul explains that the resurrected body is spiritual and eternal: '*For the trumpet will sound, the dead will be raised imperishable, and we shall be changed. For the perishable must clothe itself with the imperishable, and the mortal with immortality*' (1 Corinthians 15:52). Those who support the resurrection of the body largely do so on the basis that it is meaningless to speak of body and soul as separate entities, as this is not consistent with our experience. **John Hick** supported the view that God can create a replica resurrection body, consistent in all ways with the body that has died '*in a different world altogether, a resurrection world inhabited only by resurrected persons.*' (*Faith and Knowledge* (1966)).

The heart of the problem lies in the matter of what constitutes personal identity and, so, what makes a person? The body is the means by which we can know the identity of a person – even if the body fails and goes into a coma, we still regard that individual as a person. On the other hand, is a person to be limited in their identity to the body? While a great sportsperson may be identified by their body, a playwright is identified by their mind.

Philosophical problems of the afterlife

→ Is it meaningful to speak of life after death, since life and death are mutually exclusive? Can personal pronouns be used to identify people in the afterlife, or do they belong exclusively to life in this world? Perhaps talk of life after death is meaningful only to those who are part of the appropriate language game, but is incorrectly used outside it.

→ Lack of verification; evidence of the decay of the body; it is merely a comfort for those afraid of death; it is used as a device to keep people satisfied with their lot in this life.

→ Perhaps the idea of life after death is necessary to cope with the prospect of death and, hence, is merely a psychological device.

Exam question   answer: page 138

Outline (i) immortality of the soul and (ii) bodily resurrection and evaluate which presents a stronger case for life after death.   (30 mins)

Atheism and critiques of religious belief

There are many reasons why people may hold an atheistic position. Some may hold alternative spiritual views that do not allow room for the God of classical theism. Others may feel that the religious belief is irrational and can be explained in terms of other phenomena or social structures.

While an atheist claims that there are good reasons to argue that God does not exist, or that belief in God is irrational, the agnostic may well claim to be open to the possibility of knowledge leading to belief rather than non-belief, but may not be able to say what it would take for them to make that move.

Arguing for the non-existence of God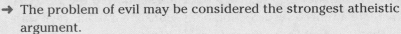

→ The problem of evil may be considered the strongest atheistic argument.

→ Science and rationalism have made a significant contribution to atheistic belief since the Enlightenment. It is possible to explain the world religiously and non-religiously, and therefore the existence of God cannot be decisively proved by referring to the evidence provided by the natural world.

→ Modernism rejects the literal use of terms such as heaven, hell or demons, claiming that they are merely representations of outdated mythological concepts.

→ Advances in biblical criticism and analysis, which discouraged a literal interpretation of the text and revealed the writers' use of sources and the way in which they had been influenced by their cultural environment, could give grounds to argue that the Bible cannot therefore contribute in any way to proving the existence of God.

→ The argument that religious explanations are immature and even intellectually degrading: *'Faith is the great cop-out, the excuse to avoid the need to think and to evaluate evidence'* (Richard Dawkins).

Critiques of religious belief: key features

→ 'God' is the name given to something else – e.g. society.

→ Religious beliefs and practices are functionally or projectively explained.

→ The existence of religion serves to maintain a social structure of benefit to some, but not others.

→ The existence of religious belief prevents the individual from realising the full potential of their humanity.

→ Religious beliefs serve to deceive the individual or the group as to what is truly real.

Terminology

Atheism literally means 'no God'. Weak atheism amounts to scepticism regarding the existence of God, possibly based on the problem of evil or other grounds for doubt. Strong atheism is an explicitly held belief that God does not exist.

Example

Richard Dawkins is a well-known example of a strong atheist, or an anti-theist, who holds an objection to religious belief per se.

Action point

Find some useful quotations from modern atheists such as Peter Atkins or Richard Dawkins.

Terminology

Some may argue that agnosticism is a form of atheism

Useful quotations

'In matters of the intellect, follow your reason as far as it will take you, without regard to any other consideration. In matters of the intellect, do not pretend that conclusions are certain which are not demonstrated or demonstrable' (T.H. Huxley, *Agnosticism*, 1889).

Checkpoint 1

Is this an atheistic view? *'It is impossible to use electric light and the wireless, and to avail ourselves of modern medical and surgical discoveries, and at the same time to believe in the New Testament world of demons and spirits'* (Rudolph Bultmann in S. Fergusen and D. Wright (eds), *The New Dictionary of Theology* (1988)).

Sociological approaches

Functionalist theory of religion argues that religion plays a function in society: to unite and preserve the community. **Durkheim** likened a religious community to a primitive clan which worshipped a totem, symbolising God and the unity of the clan. The clan and God are one and the same, hence there is no separate entity called God, but rather, a unified social system which believes that it owes its being to God. This belief is expressed in shared rituals, values and identity, and discourages change.

Karl Marx argued that God was an invention of the human mind in order to satisfy emotional needs, declaring that '*The first requisite for the happiness of the people is the abolition of religion.*' The ruling classes used religion, a human creation, to dominate and oppress their subjects, offering them an illusion of escape. He observed that religion was an alienating force, prescribing to God powers that man in fact possessed. Marx maintained that when a revolution overthrew the ruling class, and religion was abolished, the oppressed masses could be liberated. Ironically, religion had originated in revolutionary movements but, once detached from its roots, it had been used by the ruling classes to dominate and oppress. Inequality was legitimised in the name of religion, discouraging the subject classes from recognising their real situation and seeking to rise above it. Although religion offered a release from distress, it was a false release, and thus, claimed Marx, was '*the opium of the people*'.

Psychological approaches

Freud argued that religion is a projective system, a 'universal neurosis' which should be disregarded as illusory. Like Durkheim, Freud also saw the origins of religious belief as lying in the primitive horde. The tension between the dominant male and the subordinate males led to the overthrow of the father (a manifestation of the Oedipus Complex), but the subsequent guilt of the sons leads them to elevate his memory and to worship him. The super-ego takes the place of the father as the source of authority, which is derived from the family, education and the Church. Freud maintained that man was still dependent upon religion to '*make his helplessness tolerable*'.

Useful quotations

Durkheim defined religion as: '*A unified system of beliefs and practices relative to sacred things . . . beliefs and practices which unite into one single moral community called a church, all who adhere to them.*' (*The Elementary Forms of Religious Life* (1954)).

Useful quotations

Karl Marx believed that religion '*eased pain even as it created fantasies*'. He was convinced that '*religion is so fully determined by economics that it is pointless to consider any of its doctrines or beliefs on their own merits.*' (in Brian Davies, *Introduction to the Philosophy of Religion* (1982)).

Action point

Find out more about Marx's political solution to the oppression of the working classes.

Checkpoint 2

Identify three weaknesses of the sociological critiques of religion.

Examiner's secrets

Many candidates do not make a clear distinction between arguments for the non-existence of God and critiques of religious belief. They are two very different things and you should be able to explain why.

Checkpoint 3

Identify two strengths of the psychological critique of religion.

Exam questions   answers: page 138

(a) Outline two critiques of religious belief.

(b) Evaluate the view that they are more characteristic of agnosticism than atheism.   (45 mins)

Religious language (1)

Religious language is language which deals with God and other theological matters. It includes terms which we ascribe only to God in their primary context and words which are about religious beliefs. However, even when we speak of religious issues we almost always also have to use everyday language and this raises problems of a particular kind.

The problem of religious language

Cognitive language makes factual assertions that can be proved true or false, or are treated as if they can be proved true or false: e.g. God exists; God loves us; God will execute a final judgement. These are not: '*Crypto-commands, expressions of wishes, disguised exclamations, concealed ethics, or anything else but assertions*' (Antony Flew, *Theology and Falsification*).

Non-cognitive language makes claims or observations that are to be interpreted in some other way, as symbols, metaphors, ethical commands, or other non-literal modes of expression. It is language which serves some other function than expressing factually, objectively true claims since they cannot be verified or falsified and are not intended to be treated as if they can.

Some thinkers argue that religious language is not meaningful because it does not deal with factually verifiable assertions. Others argue that it is meaningful because it can be verified, at least to the believer's satisfaction, if not the non-believer, but also because not all religious language is intended to function cognitively.

Non-cognitive, anti-realist language

Symbol

Symbols identify – point to the concept they are conveying – and participate – share in some way in the meaning of that concept. Symbols may be pictorial, abstract, verbal, or active (a symbolic action). So, for example, the Cross (a central symbol in the Christian tradition) immediately identifies for believers the death of Jesus, but it does more than simply point to it in a factual way. It participates in it by bringing to the believer's consciousness what Jesus' death signifies.

Symbols express what the believer feels about what that symbol conveys. Signs are to do with facts; symbols transcend facts and should therefore not be interpreted literally. This leads only to misunderstanding. Symbols are therefore subtle modes of communication which do not belong exclusively to religious language, but are of particular value to discourse which deals with issues that are beyond the factual and objective.

Checkpoint 1

Identify the problems raised by the following claims:
(i) God loves us as a father loves his children.
(ii) God appeared to me in a dream.
(iii) God created the world.
(iv) There will be a last judgement.

Terminology

Cognitive language can also be called realist language.
Non-cognitive language can also be called anti-realist language.

Examiner's secrets

Many candidates fail to use these technical terms in their essays on religious language. This is a shame as they show a real understanding of the principles.

Useful quotations

'*A pattern or object which points to an invisible metaphysical reality and participates in it*' (Erika Dinkler-von Schubert, *A Handbook of Christian Theology* (1960)).

Checkpoint 2

Suggest six things which the symbol of the Cross may represent to the Christian.

Problems of symbolic language

→ Symbols are useful ways to communicate truths which go beyond the factual world; their interpretation can pose difficulties since they can become the focus of worship in themselves, or they can become trivialised and their original meaning lost.

→ Symbols can become outdated. Paul Tillich wrote: '*It is necessary to rediscover the questions to which the Christian symbols are the answers in a way which is understandable to our time.*' (In S. Fergusen and D. Wright, *The New Dictionary of Theology* (1988)).

Myths

Myths embody and express claims that cannot be expressed in any other way, frequently making use of symbol, metaphor and imagery in a narrative context to convey concepts which go beyond basic true–false descriptors to express that which is other worldly. Mythological language was used by the biblical writers to explain puzzling features of the world and to speak of the events they anticipated would take place at the end of time.

Rudolph Bultmann identified a key problem with mythological language in religious discourse in that the mythological form tended to obscure the religious teaching in the narratives. He argued that it was necessary to access the *kerygma*, or the abiding truth of the authoritative word, which kindled faith and came close to revelation, and to do this religious language must be **demythologised**.

However, it may not be so easy to dismiss mythological language; since it is so deeply engrained in theological discourse, it may be impossible to dispense with it. Furthermore, if religious language is anti-realist – that is, not concerned with making true or false statements about objective reality – then it need not be a burden to communication. Myths are clearly an important part of a religious language game and it is important to understand how they should be interpreted rather than being concerned with trying to establish what really happened in a literal way.

Action point

Identify a range of biblical myths and work out what their meanings may be.

Useful quotations

'It is impossible to use electric light and the wireless and to avail ourselves of modern medical and surgical discoveries and at the same time, to believe in the New Testament world of demons and spirits' (Rudolph Bultmann in S. Fergusen and D. Wright, *The New Dictionary of Theology* (1988)).

Watch out!

Questions on religious language could be linked with other topics in the Philosophy of Religion. Consider how problems of language are connected with life after death, critiques of religious belief or religious experience.

Exam question   answer: page 138

Explain and evaluate the contribution of myth and symbol to religious language.   (45 mins)

Religious language (2)

Religious language is language which deals with God and other theological matters. It includes terms which we ascribe only to God in their primary context and words which are about religious beliefs. However, even when we speak of religious issues we almost always also have to use everyday language and this raises problems of a particular kind.

Cognitive, realist language ●●●

Much religious language has to make use of terms with which we are familiar in everyday talk, and the challenge is to demonstrate how these are meant differently when applied to God, and yet retain enough of their common meaning so we can understand how they are being applied. Language can be used **univocally**, when we employ a term in exactly the same way in two different contexts, or **equivocally**, when we employ it to speak of two entirely different things in entirely different ways. When we use language of God and man, which is intended? Both are problematic.

The *via negativa*

One solution to this problem is the *via negativa*. This approach works by taking the least appropriate attributes of God and negating them. Hence, rather than saying that God is love, for example, one would say that he is *not-love*, because he is ultimately so much more than what this term can convey that it would be better to say that he is not that term at all. However, used on its own the *via negativa* cannot distinguish theism from atheism, since to say that God can only be spoken of in negatives effectively denies God altogether. Nevertheless, negation does emphasise the unknowability of God and Aquinas observed that an affirmative statement has to have a subject, and God, who is above all things, and existentially different from them, cannot be a subject.

Aquinas wrote in the *Summa Theologica*:

> But no name belongs to God in the same sense that it belongs to creatures; for instance, wisdom in creatures is a quality, but not in God. Now a different genus changes an essence, since the genus is part of the definition; and the same applies to other things. Therefore whatever is said of God and of creatures is predicated equivocally. (In John Hick (ed.), *The Existence of God* (1964)).

Analogy

> *Analogies are proportional similarities which also acknowledge dissimilar features.* (D. Burrell, *A Dictionary of Christian Theology*)

Useful quotations

'Wisdom, thought, design, knowledge – these we justly ascribe to him because those words are honourable among men, and we have no other language by which we can express our adoration of him' (David Hume, *Dialogues Concerning Natural Religion* (1998)).

Checkpoint 1

What are the problems of both univocal and equivocal language in reference to religious language?

Useful quotations

'I try to show the restless iconoclastic character of belief in God, which continually strives after intelligible content, and yet must by its own inner dialect always negate any proposed specific content' (Don Cupitt in S. Fergusen and D. Wright, *The New Dictionary of Theology* (1988)).

Terminology

An analogy identifies the similarities **and** the differences between two analogates – the items or beings being compared.

Action point

Look at William Paley's analogy of the watch and the watchmaker to see how an analogy can be used as the basis for a proof of the existence of God.

Aquinas showed that all good and worthy things in man belong first to God and so are analogously related to him:

Among beings there are some more and some less good, true, noble and the like. But more and less are predicated of different things according as they resemble in their different ways something which is the maximum . . . so that there is something which is truest, something best, something noblest . . . Therefore there must also be something which is to all beings the cause of their being, goodness, and every other perfection, and this we call God. (In John Hick (ed.), *The Existence of God* (1964)).

For example, because God is the cause of good things in man we can use the description good of both God and man, but as the cause of man's goodness, God's goodness is greater. The effects resemble their cause, and thus, their goodness is related but different.

Analogies work in several ways:

→ Analogy of proportion: all good qualities belong proportionately to God and to man, thus we know that proportionately they must exist pre-eminently in God.

→ Analogy of attribution: God is the cause of all good things in man and other beings and thus attributes to them what belongs to him first in a greater and higher sense.

→ Upwards analogies work from the secondary to the primary analogate.

→ Downwards analogies work from the primary to the secondary analogate.

→ The principle of remotion and excellence: if we remove all creaturely concepts from a word and project what is left on to God then we learn that God is without limit.

→ Models and qualifiers (**Ian Ramsey**). We take a human attribute (the model) and ascribe it to God, qualifying it to make clear that it is infinitely enhanced when applied to God, and leading us to an understanding of the infinite nature of God. Note that this is a positive rather than a negative act of qualification, as criticised by **Antony Flew**.

Action point

Identify three problems of analogical religious language.

Example

Upwards analogy: man's wisdom is less than God's but it can be understood by working up from man to God and understanding that God is the cause of man's lesser wisdom.

Example

Downwards analogy: God possesses supreme wisdom, from which we can work downwards to the lesser wisdom of man.

Examiner's secrets

Not many candidates use quotations from Aquinas in their discussion of analogy. It will enhance your answer to do so.

Checkpoint 2

Explain the difference between positive and negative qualification of God's nature.

Exam question   answer: page 139

Identify and discuss the value of analogy to religious language.   (30 mins)

Religious language (3)

Religious language is language which deals with God and other theological matters. It includes terms which we ascribe only to God in their primary context and words which are about religious beliefs. However, even when we speak of religious issues we almost always also have to use everyday language and this raises problems of a particular kind.

Action point

Find out about the members of the Vienna Circle who were leaders in logical positivist thinking in the 1920s–30s.

Examiner's secrets

A candidate who can refer specifically to the work of A.J. Ayer and use some quotations from his book will gain valuable extra marks.

Checkpoint 1

What is the status of the following statements?

(i) God answers prayers.
(ii) Harry Potter plays rugby.
(iii) Abortion is a sin.

Meaningful and meaningless statements

Language may be true *and* meaningful. It is possible to confuse these terms. When discussing whether a sentence is meaningful we are only interested in whether it makes sense, not whether it actually is the case. 'Today is Wednesday' is meaningful and true if it *is* Wednesday, but it would still make sense even if it were Thursday. However, we need to distinguish between 'meaning' – what a statement *says* – and 'meaningful' – whether a statement makes sense.

Meaningful statements may be either analytic or synthetic. An analytic statement is one which is true by definition (i.e. a circle is round) or tautologous (i.e. all dogs are dogs), or a mathematical statement (2 + 2 = 4). An analytical statement cannot be false and contains the means of its own verification. Such a statement is a logical proposition and they are necessarily true or false; for example, 'A bachelor is an unmarried man' is necessarily true, while 'A spinster is a married woman' is necessarily false. A synthetic statement is verified or falsified by subjecting it to testing. If it can be verified or falsified by use of the senses then it is a meaningful statement. Arguably, if it cannot then it is not meaningful. An analytic statement contains the subject contained in the predicate. No new information is therefore contained in an analytic statement and so whether it is true or false is determined by the meaning of the words.

A synthetic statement can add new information and whether it is true or false is determined by empirical evidence. Hence, although 'John is a bachelor' is analytically true (if he is male and unmarried), 'John is happy' needs to be confirmed by further evidence, and it has nothing to do with whether he is a bachelor.

The verification principle stated that only assertions that were in principle verifiable by observation or experience could convey factual information. Assertions that there could be no imaginable way of verifying must either be analytic or meaningless. The logical positivists were concerned to find a distinction between sense and nonsense and the key was that of meaningfulness. An empirical proposition which could be known through observation and is contingently true or false would be meaningful. Empirical propositions include all facts about the world since, conceivably, any fact about the world could have been otherwise – there is no logically necessary reason why they should be as they are – hence, they are synthetic rather than analytic. In this way, the logical positivists applied the principles of science and mathematics to all language statements. However, if a statement could theoretically be verified then it passed the criteria of meaningfulness as laid down by the logical positivists: 'There are mountains on the dark side of the moon' was not verifiable in 1936 when A.J. Ayer wrote *Language, Truth and Logic*, but it was theoretically possible to construct a means of verifying it, hence the weak verification principle allowed for it to be considered meaningful.

Implications for religious language

→ Statements about God are neither analytically true, nor open to verification by observation, and are therefore rendered meaningless.

→ Claims to have experienced God are subjective, not universal, and there no reliable grounds for testing them, hence they cannot be the basis for empirical propositions about God.

→ The question 'Does a transcendent God exist?' is rejected since, although it seems to be cognitive (asking a question about an objective reality), our experience of the world does not admit of transcendent things.

Wider implications

→ All statements which express unverifiable opinions or emotions are rendered invalid, as are ethical statements.

→ Universal statements such as 'All ravens are black' cannot conclusively be verified since in theory it is possible that one day someone will encounter a white raven.

Action point

Consider why a statement may be meaningful *despite* lack of verification.

Checkpoint 2

Identify the problems of these religious language claims:

(i)   Muhammad is God's final messenger.
(ii) God is my rock.
(iii) Jesus said, 'I am the light of the world'.

Useful quotations

'People began to realise that this glittering new scalpel was, in one operation after another, killing the patient' (Bryan McGee, *Confessions of a Philosopher* (1997)).

Exam question   answer: page 139

'Lack of verification renders religious language meaningless.' Discuss.

(30 mins)

Religious language (4)

Religious language is language which deals with God and other theological matters. It includes terms which we ascribe only to God in their primary context and words which are about religious beliefs. However, even when we speak of religious issues we almost always also have to use everyday language and this raises problems of a particular kind.

The view that religious language is meaningless is based on three suppositions about language:

→ **Empiricism**: the view that sensory experience is the primary source of knowledge. Religious language claims are essentially non-empirical as they cannot be tested using the five physical senses.
→ **Science**: a discipline that appears to be based on objective truth. Science could assert facts and know things, while religious language is based on faith.
→ **The work of Ludwig Wittgenstein**: at a time when philosophy seemed to be stagnating, Wittgenstein published *Tractatus Logico-Philosophicus* in which he presented the picture-theory of language, arguing that language derives from our picture of the world, hence it is all based on sense experience.

Language games

Initially, Ludwig Wittgenstein maintained language had to correspond to a picture to be meaningful. However, later he proposed that language is anti-realist, expressing a form of life, without making statements which are true or false. Language can be correctly or incorrectly used within the rules of the game, but its primary purpose is not to make factual statements. Thus, it is non-cognitive. All forms of life have their own language and, hence, stand alone from each other. The player of one language game cannot criticise the player of another, or enter into the game without first learning the rules and conventions of the language. Wittgenstein illustrated the principle thus:

> *Suppose someone is ill and he says: 'This is a punishment', and I say: 'If I'm ill, I don't think of punishment at all.' If you say, 'Don't you believe the opposite?' – you can call it believing the opposite, but it is entirely different from what we would normally call believing the opposite. I think differently, in a different way. I say different things to myself. I have a different picture.* (In Basil Mitchell (ed.), *The Philosophy of Religion* (1971)).

Action point

Make a list of statements which are based on empirical knowledge of the world and which can be pictured.

Action point

Ask your teacher to show you the film *Wittgenstein*. It is directed by Derek Jarman, and can be ordered from Amazon.

Examiner's secrets

Strong candidates are able to understand the problems of religious language within the wider context of linguistic philosophy.

Checkpoint 1

Suggest three other religious language claims which are meaningful only as part of a religious language game.

The two understandings of illness described in this conversation reflect different forms of life, neither necessarily right nor wrong. They use language in different ways and need to be understood in that context. If we misunderstand the way religious language claims are made then we will respond in the wrong way.

The falsification principle ●●●

Antony Flew used Wisdom's parable of the gardener to illustrate how believers were guilty of not allowing evidence that failed to prove the existence or love of God to actually count against their theological statements. If a believer is reduced to saying 'God's love for us is incomprehensible' because he cannot explain why God is apparently allowing a child to die of an inoperable illness, then Flew maintains he is simply allowing his definition of God to '*die the death of a thousand qualifications.*' Similarly, to say 'God exists' must include the possibility that he might not exist or that he might not exist in the way that the believer maintains.

R.M. Hare proposed that a believer's statements were **bliks**: ways of regarding the world which are in principle neither verifiable nor falsifiable. However, because it makes a significant difference to his life, the believer's claims are not meaningless. They matter.

Basil Mitchell offered the parable of the partisan and the stranger to demonstrate that believers do recognise challenges to faith without allowing them to be conclusively falsified. Mitchell observed that there are three ways in which the believer treats their claims:

→ Provisional hypotheses to be discarded if experience tells against them.
→ Vacuous formulae . . . to which experience makes no difference and which makes no difference to life.
→ Significant articles of faith.

Since believers' claims about God fall into the third category, Mitchell claims that they will neither abandon them nor qualify them.

Richard Swinburne also argues that statements which cannot be falsified are still meaningful to those who use them:

> *. . . there are plenty of examples of statements which some people judge to be factual which are not apparently confirmable or disconfirmable through observation. For example: Some of the toys which to all appearances stay in the toy cupboard while people are asleep and no one is watching actually get up and dance in the middle of the night and then go back to the cupboard, leaving no traces of their activity.* (Cited in *Philosophy of Religion*, ed. B. Davies)

Action point

Identify a range of strengths and weaknesses of language game theory.

Useful quotations

'In order to say something which may possibly be true, we must say something which may possibly be false' (John Hick, *Faith and Knowledge* (1996)).

Useful quotations

'Now it often seems to people who are not religious as if there was no conceivable event . . . the occurrence of which would be admitted by sophisticated religious people to be a sufficient reason for conceding . . . "God does not really love us then"' (Antony Flew in John Hick (ed.), *The Existence of God* (1964)).

Action point

Access via the Internet or in book form the university debate between Flew, Hare and Mitchell on the falsification of theological statements.

Checkpoint 2

Give two more examples of statements about God which may 'die the death of a thousand qualifications'.

Exam question   answer: page 139

'Religious language can only be understood in the context of religious belief'.
Discuss.   (45 mins)

Religion and science

The two disciplines of religion and science are often held to be in direct opposition to each other, one dealing with faith and the other with fact. However, it is possible to argue that they are complementary as much as contradictory.

What is the conflict?

The apparent conflict between science and religion exists because it is possible to have a consistent religious interpretation of the universe and a consistent atheistic interpretation of the universe. Nothing in the universe points decisively towards the existence of God but nothing points decisively away from it either. Both atheist and theist take a step of faith that their interpretation is the best, most likely, or simplest one, but neither can claim that their interpretation of the origin of the universe is more decisive.

Both interpretations of the world are concerned with finding an explanation for the existence and features of the universe. This is based on the presumption that the universe is not self-explanatory. For strong atheists such as Richard Dawkins, religious interpretations can never provide an explanation – they are non-explanations which prevent us from finding real explanations. However, while some religious believers discount the findings of science, more will accept that there is good reason to identify the connections between the two.

What is a religious explanation?

→ The facts of creation cannot be fully explained without reference to God.
→ God intervened to bring something out of nothing (creation *ex nihilo*).
→ Creation is the result of God's supernatural intervention.
→ Creation reflects God's nature, and his purpose for the universe and human agents.
→ No single, agreed religious explanation.

Why does science challenge this position?

→ Religious views often depend on narrative interpretations that have questionable origins.
→ Religious believers have been slow to accept that while narrative or doctrinal views of creation have some truth value, it is not necessarily factual value.

What constitutes a scientific explanation?

→ No personal direction.
→ No metaphysical purpose or meaning.
→ No intelligent design.
→ No supernatural intervention.
→ Independent physical, chemical and biological processes.

Why does religion challenge this position?

→ It allows too much to chance.
→ It does not explain all the features of the universe.
→ The law of probability is not in its favour.
→ The universe is reduced to an unintelligible, brute fact.

Ways to reconcile these positions

John Polkinghorne, a physicist and an Anglican minister, claims that the natural world exhibits a carefully balanced order which cannot be simply explained or dismissed. Natural theology enables us to understand that order. He supports the anthropic principle which observes that the slightest variation in the conditions which led to the Big Bang would have made it impossible for human life to develop. This points to a God who created the world rather than a random, impersonal event, and suggests that religious and scientific explanations are complementary, not conflicting.

Less convincing is *concordism*, which attempts to find evidence that the Bible supports scientifically observable facts about the universe. Even the opening verses of Genesis – '*In the beginning when God created the heavens and the earth*' – could be used by a concordist to argue that the Bible teaches that there must have been a singular event by which the universe began.

Teilhard de Chardin attempted to synthesise evolutionary biology and theology, arguing that the universe was driven by an evolutionary process which became increasingly complex and works towards what he called an Omega Point, when the meaning of the whole process will be revealed. This point was reached in the life of Christ. Thus, it is the end of the process of evolution, not the start, which is important for understanding the relationship between God and the world. Although this view is interesting, it is a matter of speculation and could be thought to be too mystical to be a reasonable explanation of the potential compatibility of science and religion.

Action point

Practise writing a short précis of at least two scientific explanations of the universe, for example the Big Bang and evolution by natural selection.

Useful quotations

'*Even if the whole universe consisted of organic soup, the chance of producing the basic enzymes of life by random processes without intelligent direction would be approximately one in 10 with 40,000 zeroes after it . . . Darwinian evolution is most unlikely to get even one polypeptide right, let alone the thousands on which living cells depend for survival*' (Dave Hunt, *In Defence of the Faith* (1996)).

Example

Psalm 102:25–26 claims: '*Long ago you laid the foundation of the earth, and the heavens are the work of your hands. They will perish, but you will endure; they will all wear out like a garment. You change them like clothing and they pass away*'. Concordism might claim that this verse supports the law of entropy.

Checkpoint 2

Explain what is meant by the claim 'God is an unnecessary hypothesis in the quest for an explanation of the universe.'

Exam questions answers: page 139

(a) Outline the main features of a religious and a scientific interpretation of the origin of the universe.

(b) Evaluate the claim that they are utterly irreconcilable. (45 mins)

Foundations of religious belief: Plato and Aristotle

The foundations of monotheistic religious beliefs lie deep in the pre-Christian philosophical traditions of Plato and Aristotle. Their thinking sheds important light on many key aspects of later theology.

Examiner's secrets

You must avoid treating questions on Plato and Aristotle as an opportunity to relate their life story. Narrative is not important, but an understanding of their thinking is.

Terminology

The Socratic Method is a means of discourse which draws out from opponents the error of their reasoning.

Action point

Read the Allegory of the Cave in Plato's book *The Republic*.

Terminology

In an allegory the apparent meaning of the characters and events is used to symbolise a deeper moral or spiritual meaning.

Useful quotations

H.D.F. Kitto observed that *'It was Greek philosophy, notably, Plato's conception of the absolute, eternal deity, which prepared the world for the reception of a universal religion'*. (*The Greens* (1951)).

Checkpoint 1

How might Aquinas's Fourth Way provide a useful basis for beliefs about the God and morality?

Plato

Plato, a follower of Socrates, left Athens after his teacher's execution, not returning until 387 BCE, believing that the only hope for the world would be when '*kings were philosophers or philosophers were kings.*' Plato's works consist of a series of dialogues between Socrates and others presented in a highly characteristic style, known as the Socratic Method. The works of Plato are a useful foundation for an understanding of the nature of reality and knowledge, and the distinction between body and soul.

Plato uses his famous ***Allegory of the Cave*** to draw attention to the difference between the world of appearances and the real world. Only what is permanent can be the source of true knowledge, not the objects of the physical world which are always changing. The unchanging realities are those that Plato believed could only be apprehended by the mind, since those we experience through the senses are only imperfect copies. However, the unthinking man simply accepts what he hears, and never questions whether it is valuable, good or true, rather than overcoming the difficulties of achieving the goal of perfect reality.

Plato's ***Theory of the Forms*** develops ideas about goodness and reality. The prisoners in the cave would always be condemned to accepting a pale copy of the truth as reality, and so would never be able to apprehend the true, absolute Form of the Good. Aquinas's Fourth Way was clearly influenced by Plato, pointing to the need for a highest source of goodness, truth and nobility, which Aquinas identified as God. These unchanging concepts could never be encountered in the physical world, but Plato believed we have an instinctive, if imperfect, appreciation of them. This, he believed, indicated that man has an immortal, pre-existent soul, which has encountered these forms before becoming imprisoned in the physical body. Upon the death of the physical body the soul will re-enter the eternal realm from which it came.

Aristotle

●●●

Aristotle was an empiricist philosopher who was devoted to deepening his understanding of experience. Aristotle looked for scientific explanations and asked important questions about the nature of scientific explanation. Although none of the works he prepared for publication survived, for hundreds of years his work constituted the largest systematic body of knowledge.

Aristotle rejected Plato's Theory of the Forms, believing that reality lay within the empirical world. Aristotle sought to answer the question 'What does it mean for something to exist?' Aristotle identified four causes of a thing, which constituted a complete explanation of what caused something to exist:

→ **The material cause** of something answered the question *What does it consist of?*
→ **The efficient cause** answered the question *How did it happen?*
→ **The formal cause** answered the question *What are its characteristics?*
→ **The final cause** answered the question *Why is it here?* or *What is its purpose or telos?*

Once all four causes had been established, the complete explanation for the existence of an item had been found. The most important was the final cause, which was ***teleological***.

Aristotle was also interested in tracing all movements back to a first mover. Aristotle observed that a chain of movers had to begin with an Unmoved or Prime Mover, something which was not itself moved, but which could cause other things to move. He concluded that there had to be a necessary first mover, which he called God, a final cause in itself, and which causes things to be not simply through physical or mechanical momentum, but through an act of love. All things are drawn towards God, the necessary being which is eternally good and on whom all other things depend.

Aristotle saw the relationship between soul and body as a psycho-physical unity of soul and body. The human soul was essentially the body and its organisation, but Aristotle did identify another quality that it possessed – reason, the means by which men could develop intellectually and morally.

Useful quotations

Bryan Magee observes that Aristotle was *'working always from inside experience, never trying to impose abstract explanations on it from the outside.'* (*Confessions of a Philosopher* (1997)).

Action point

Find out how Aristotle's thinking laid the foundation for virtue ethics.

Checkpoint 2

Where else in the philosophy of religion is the notion of a first mover and a telos important?

Exam question   answer: page 139

Outline Plato's Theory of the Forms and examine and evaluate the effectiveness of this theory.   (30 mins)

Foundations of religious belief: Judeo-Christian themes

The biblical writers portray God very differently to the ancient Greeks, and although he is a transcendent and sovereign creator, his creation of humanity and the universe is for a purpose and sets the scene for the relationship between God and humanity and which has its culmination in an eschatological future.

Examiner's secrets

Resist the temptation to write out a long narrative of the creation accounts in Genesis. It will earn you few marks.

Terminology

A myth is a symbolic, approximate expression of truth.

Links

Also refer to pages 130–1 on religion and science.

Checkpoint 1

Explain the claim that creation accounts address difficult questions about the world.

Action point

Look up these verses in Genesis: 1:26; 1:27; 2:7; 2:9; 2:15; 2:19.

Useful quotations

The Psalmist testifies to God's continued sustaining of the created order: *'Who by thy strength has established the mountains . . . who stills the roaring of the seas?'* (Psalm 65:6–7).

Checkpoint 2

Identify two problems of interpreting the biblical creation narratives.

God as creator

The narratives of Genesis 1–2 share remarkable similarities to the creation myths in the Babylonian traditions, especially the epic *Euma elish*. There are also allusions to Baal's defeat of the sea monster Leviathan in the Canaanite texts from Ugarit, which may have influenced the Genesis account.

There are two distinct accounts of creation in Genesis 1 and 2. The first account, from the priestly tradition is characterised by repeated phrases, and creation takes place over six days. Traditionally, creation is thought to have been *ex nihilo*. The second account is narrative in style, and possibly older. It is linked directly with the events of the fall in Genesis 3 and it begins to address why, if God had created a perfect universe (1:31), there are imperfect things and situations in the world. There are common features in both accounts:

→ Humanity is the goal of God's creative work.
→ Humanity is distinguished from the rest of creation, being in the image of God and given life by the direct and personal action of God's spirit.
→ Humans are given authority over the animals and the opportunity to participate in God's creative work.
→ Everything necessary for humanity's survival is in the garden in which God places him.

The theme of creation runs throughout the Old Testament, and is expressed vividly in the Psalms and the wisdom literature. When Job questions God's plans and purposes, God rhetorically replies: *'Where were you when I laid the foundations of the earth?'* (Job 38:4). Above all, Isaiah expresses the utter sovereignty of God who cannot be challenged by man or by the false gods which man, in his ignorance, carves and worships. *'I am the Lord, and there is no other. I form light and create darkness, I make weal and create woe, I am the Lord, who does all these things'* (Isaiah 45:6–7).

God's goodness

The goodness of God is expressed through the standards God sets for humans and how he responds to their attempts to live up to those standards. Does God create moral standards that he issues as commands, or does he command that which he already knows as good? This dilemma is difficult to solve, since religious believers tend to use God's commands as a guide to decide what is good, but are aware that sometimes this causes problems. The classic example of someone who was called by God to do something which society would condemn as wrong is Abraham's call to sacrifice Isaac. Peter Vardy observes that because Abraham trusted his relationship with God he was able to hold to two contradictory facts: God's promise to him that he would have many descendents through Isaac, *and* that he would sacrifice Isaac as God commanded him to do so. For the Israelites, God's goodness was experienced through his Covenant relationship with them, first revealed in the giving of the Law, including the Decalogue. Acceptance of them indicated the willingness of the people of Israel to enter into a Covenant relationship with God, but the highest standards of behaviour were expected of Israel. For the New Testament writers, the ultimate demonstration of God's goodness is, of course, in the sending of Jesus whereby he provides the means of redemption.

God at work in the world

The biblical writers believed that God is *immanent*, and can be known through human experience and the world. This runs counter to the equally important view that God is *transcendent*. This means that God is beyond the limits of any human experience. The Judeo-Christian picture is something of a paradox:

> The God of the Bible stands above the world as its sovereign Lord, its Creator and its Saviour; but he appears in the world to set men tasks to do, speaking to men in demand, in promise, in healing and fulfilment.
> (John A. Hutchinson, S. Fergusen and D. Wright, *The New Dictionary of Theology* (1988))

Throughout the Bible, God's action in the world is illustrated by accounts of miraculous events in which God suspends the laws of nature to accomplish his purpose. The biblical writers had no concept of natural law that determined how the universe operates and so when God intervenes in the course of events, it is never portrayed as a violation of natural laws. Whatever the interpretation of biblical events when God directly intervenes, the narratives characteristically attribute all events – natural and supernatural – to divine providence.

Exam questions

answers: page 140

(a) Outline the ways in which God may be known in the world.

(b) Evaluate the problems which arise from the claim that God's transcendence means he cannot be known. (30 mins)

Useful quotations

'I am the Lord, and there is no other. I form light and create darkness, I make weal and create woe, I am the Lord, who does all these things' (Isaiah 45:6–7).

Terminology

This dilemma is called the **Euthyphro Dilemma**.

Links

Look also at pages 110–11 on God and morality.

Action point

Read Genesis 22 for the story of Abraham and Isaac.

Terminology

A covenant is an agreement ratified between two parties.

Useful quotations

'You only have I known of all the families of the earth; therefore I will punish you for all your iniquities' (Amos 3:2).
'I will not execute my fierce wrath against them, I will not return to destroy Ephraim: for I am God and not man; the Holy one in your midst' (Hosea 9:11).
'For God so loved the world that he gave his only Son, so that all who believe in him should not perish but have eternal life' (John 3:16).

Links

Look also at pages 116–17 on miracles.

Terminology

Natural law – that which happens regularly within nature.

Answers
Philosophy of religion

The design argument

Checkpoints

1 Aquinas uses an *a posteriori* argument. Like the other ways, it argues from a general principal to a specific conclusion, using inductive reasoning based on observation of the world. The conclusion to every argument is that God must exist to fulfil the purpose outlined in the premises – first mover, first cause, necessary being, and so on.

2 The world is religiously ambiguous because it can be interpreted religiously or non-religiously. The evidence of the world does not point conclusively in one direction or the other. It affects the design argument in so far as the apparent evidence of design could be interpreted as leading to a divine designer or, just as easily, as being the result of natural selection.

Exam questions

Outlining the key features of the argument should convey some understanding of the general principals of the argument as well as being able to accurately recount the contributions of the main thinkers – Aquinas, Paley, Swinburne, and others you may have covered. Avoid starting with the traditional outline of the argument, however, but rather start with showing that you understand the notion of features of the world needing an explanation. Also show that you are aware of the specific forms of the argument too – aesthetic and anthropic principles, for example.

In part (b) you have to show an understanding of both strengths and weaknesses in order to answer the question. Remember that you have to reach a conclusion – *Do* the weaknesses outweigh the strengths or not? You will have to use the word 'because' a lot here and compare the relative merits of reasons to support the argument and reasons to reject it.

> **Examiner's secrets**
>
> A lot of people will do this question very poorly. Practise it until you are confident that you have shown a more sophisticated understanding of the topic.

The cosmological argument

Checkpoints

1 The principle of Ockham's Razor is the philosophical methodology that the simplest explanation is the most likely, or the most reasonable – '*What can be done with fewer assumptions is done in vain with more*'. The cosmological argument works on the principle that God is the simplest explanation for the existence of the universe. It could be explained in other ways, but God, as an omnipotent, necessary being demands no further explanation himself and thus is a more economical explanation for the world.

2 'Perennial value' means that it continues to have value throughout the ages. The cosmological argument could be said to have perennial value because we are always interested in the question of origins, however far our knowledge has extended over the years.

Exam question

The words 'explain and evaluate' are your instructions here. 'Explain' means show your knowledge in a way that demonstrates your understanding of the argument. So, avoid just writing out scholars' approaches to the argument without some reference to the principles which underlie the argument – issues of explanation again are important here, and whether an explanation is needed at all. Show that you understand how the premises of the various forms of the argument lead to an inductive conclusion. When evaluating the argument, you must show whether it is ultimately more or less convincing as a philosophical argument, or whether it is satisfactory only to religious believers. Does it simply confirm what they already believe or does it provide a convincing reason to believe in God?

The ontological argument

Checkpoints

1 In this quotation, Brian Davies draws attention to the fact that the word 'God' may appear to have a universal interpretation, but it does not. People understand the notion of God in different ways, hence there is some danger in using a definition of God as the basis of an analytic argument.

2 A predicate is a defining word, which describes a characteristic which may be possessed or lacked. Kant argued that 'exist' was not a defining or describing word so it could not add anything to our understanding of an object or being. Hence, to say that God exists does not describe an attribute of God.

Exam question

This question demands that you refer to its wording in your answer. Many candidates will rush into a blow-by-blow write-all-they-know answer, and won't address the question of whether the argument succeeds or not, except in their final paragraph. To avoid this, you could address the issue in your *first* paragraph, setting out what would be necessary for the argument to be successful. Only then work through the argument, all the time pointing out whether it has the necessary foundations to succeed in proving the existence of God, and if not, why not. Keep your evaluation flowing through the essay.

The argument from religious experience

Checkpoints

1 Corporate experiences may be the result of mass induced hysteria, encouraged by bringing people together in an

atmosphere of anticipation where they *expect* to have a religious experience. In such an environment, people may be reluctant to say they haven't had an experience, and may fabricate the features of an experience in order to be united with the group.

2 If the experient was under the influence of drugs, alcohol or illness; if they were demonstrably not where they claimed to be; if there are good reasons to believe that the experience didn't happen as they claim; if they have a history of fabricating experiences.

Exam question

Your answer must refer precisely to the wording of the question here otherwise you will gain few AO2 marks. Don't just recite descriptions of religious experiences, but tailor your information to the task – do religious experiences *prove* anything? You could consider whether the claims of experients are reliable and, if so, what do they prove – that they believe that they have had an experience of God, or that God exists and has demonstrated his existence through the experience? The two are quite different positions.

The moral argument

Checkpoints

1 Human law is rooted in religious law; non-religious people often still adopt religious moral codes, suggesting a universal moral law rooted in all humans; the existence of the conscience as a God-given means of moral guidance.

2 To say that something is an obligation and yet the agent under obligation cannot fulfil it is a contradiction. It is only logical for us to be obliged to fulfil an action we are capable of fulfilling. Kant also commits the naturalistic fallacy: to say that it *is* good to do our duty does not mean that we *ought* to do it. He moves from a statement of fact to a statement of value without further justification.

Exam questions

You can refer to several scholars' arguments in the first part of the question, outlining several ways in which the existence of morality may point to the existence of God. Keep it an academic argument, and remember that if morality derives from religion it doesn't necessarily prove the existence of God, since the development of religion has been in human hands. In (b) you need to evaluate the arguments raised in (a) and consider whether they are more or less convincing than the view suggested. Remember to evaluate all the way through the answer – use plenty of evaluative terms: because, however, nevertheless . . .

The problem of evil and suffering (1)

Checkpoints

1 If religious believers try to excuse God's lack of action in dealing with the problem of evil by arguing that although he loves humans his love cannot be understood, or that by loving them it means he has to allow them to suffer,

his nature is qualified. The problem here is that God is no longer the God initially described and is something less than religious believers originally described him.

2 Genesis, Chapters 2–3. These describe the events of creation and the fall of humans from a perfect relationship with God, the world and each other.

Exam questions

Make sure that you have plenty to say when explaining the problem of evil. Include details such as the inconsistent triad and the problem of qualification. Be clear about the different kinds of problems raised by different kinds of evil and suffering and show you understand the philosophical problems raised – the problem of conflicting claims, for example. In (b) don't get so carried away with outlining the theodicies that you don't answer the question otherwise you won't get your evaluation marks. You must draw clear conclusions as to whether *neither* theodicy outlined solves the problem or not.

The problem of evil and suffering (2)

Checkpoints

1 Because it denies the omnipotence of God, a vital attribute of the God of classical theism.

2 Monism argues that there is only one nature and hence all things are good. Evil and suffering are thus an illusion and cannot therefore have any real power.

Exam question

This question needs careful structuring since you need to explain what the problem of evil is before demonstrating by use of theodicies whether the claim made in the title is correct or not. Highlight two or three areas of the problem which are fundamental and which present the greatest challenges and consider whether the theodicies address them sufficiently or not. Above all don't just refer to the wording of the question in the final paragraph – keep it carefully in view throughout.

Miracles

Checkpoints

1 Hume was writing in the eighteenth century and was strongly influenced by rationalism and the development of modern science.

2 This means that miracles are the way in which God can communicate with humans although they are usually

prevented from doing so because of the gap of knowledge which separates man from God. Miracles breach the distance for a short time as God directly intervenes in human affairs.

Exam questions

(a) is straightforward, but shouldn't be underestimated. You can explain that the term miracle is often misused and that a proper philosophical understanding of the term needs to be reached. Use at least two scholars' definitions of the term and quote from them directly. In (b) you need to evaluate very carefully, showing that you understand arguments for and against the occurrence of miracles and can weigh and balance them out. Most candidates will argue against miracles, so it would be interesting to try to argue ultimately in their favour.

Life after death

Checkpoints

1 Because we are identified by our personalities more than our bodies; our emotions distinguish us more than our physical features; we place more value in the unseen aspects of who we are than the superficial bodily feature.

2 A replica is not the original and so cannot be the same person; Hick's third scenario demands that we postulate a realm utterly beyond human experience and makes an illogical leap from something conceivable to something inconceivable.

Exam question

Here you need to provide clear and well-learned outlines of the two understandings of the relationship between mind and body and how they provide the basis for an understanding of life after death. Ensure that you use scholars' views to support your explanations. In the evaluation part of the question, you need to build a case which leads to a conclusion. It doesn't matter which you think is the better foundation for talk of life after death, as long as you provide a clear argument as to why you support one rather than the other.

Atheism and critiques of religious belief

Checkpoints

1 Bultmann's view could be thought to be atheistic in so far as he implies that a supernatural view of the world is outdated and has been proved wrong by the discoveries of science. However, if he is advocating that supernatural features of religious belief need to be reinterpreted for a scientific age then, rather than being an atheistic perspective, it could be seen to be encouraging making supernatural thinking accessible and relevant.

2 Many religious believers have opposed social structures, not acceded to them; religious teaching on poverty does not necessarily encourage acceptance of it, but rather is

aimed to encourage the rich not to neglect their spiritual needs; religious believers recognise the value of the community aspect of their faith without it pointing away from the God at the centre of that community.

3 Religious believers are unlikely to deny that religious belief gives them psychological comfort; religious beliefs are often closely associated with how people have been brought up as children.

Exam questions

A straightforward AO1 part of the question demands a good knowledge and understanding of critiques of religious belief. You are strongly advised not to use the problem of evil but to stick to arguments which challenge the structure and purpose of religious belief and practice rather than propose a narrow case for the non-existence of God. In (b) your evaluative skills are being challenged further. Make sure that you have a clear understanding of both terms and can argue whether the critiques of religious belief could be used to prove the non-existence of God or whether they simply suggest that since the purpose of religion could be social or psychological religion itself cannot prove the existence of God. The evidence of religion makes it probable that God does *or* does not exist.

Religious language (1)

Checkpoints

1 (i) How can God's supernatural love be compared to human love? (ii) Does the speaker think that an objectively real God used a dream as a means of communicating with them, or that they dreamt that God existed and made himself known to them? (iii) The belief that God created the world is unverifiable, it is a faith claim, but is often held as if it were objectively true. (iv) This is only eschatologically verifiable, but has implications on the way people live their lives.

2 Salvation from sin; sacrifice and atonement; victory over death; the defeat of Satan; God's love for the world; Christian hope of eternal life.

Exam question

Outline the problem and nature of religious language first to give yourself a foundation to work from and quickly introduce the special nature and function of non-cognitive language in religious discourse. Few candidates can write at length and well on myth and symbol, so pack your answer with scholarship and concise examples – avoid storytelling. Conclude with whether myth and symbol make religious language easier or harder to interpret.

Religious language (2)

Checkpoints

1 Univocal language does not sufficiently highlight the distinctiveness of God, while equivocal language provides

little point of comparison between God and man to make him accessible.

2 To positively qualify God we enhance his attributes: God's love is infinitely greater than man's love. To negatively qualify God we justify or adapt his attributes to compensate for apparent difficulties. For example, to avoid the problem of evil by claiming that God's love is beyond human understanding rather than tackling the question of why a loving God does not intervene to heal human suffering.

Exam question

This very targeted question demands that you have a good deal of material on analogy at your fingertips, including scholarly quotations and contributions from a range of scholars. Again you need to highlight the problems posed by religious language before considering whether analogy addresses them effectively or whether it simply makes religious language more obscure.

Religious language (3)

Checkpoints

1 (i) Meaningless, because it cannot be verified according to any of the criteria laid down by the logical positivists. (ii) Meaningful – if Harry Potter exists we can verify whether or not he plays rugby; however, Harry Potter's fictional status makes it meaningful only within the language game of Harry Potter novels. In such a case it is meaningful, but not true, because Harry Potter plays Quidditch, not Rugby. (iii) This is an opinion and therefore meaningless. The concept of sin could be said to be meaningless because it is based on the belief that God makes judgements of human behaviour, which is unverifiable.

2 (i) This is a belief held only by Muslims and so either contradicts or cancels out the claims of Christianity and Judaism. On what authority is the claim based? (ii) This is metaphorical or symbolic language which could be said to be meaningless. What does it mean for God to be a rock if he is not a literal rock? (iii) This is another symbolic claim which needs to be interpreted within its context. If Jesus is the light of the world, why cannot that light be seen?

Exam question

This targets the verification principle specifically, but you can refer to the nature of religious language which makes it unverifiable and so make use of material on myth and symbol as well. Demonstrate a good knowledge and understanding of the logical postivists' position and why it falls prey to its own demands. A workable conclusion would be that much religious language is unverifiable (and unfalsifiable) but it has a significance, none the less, which means it cannot be dismissed as meaningless.

Religious language (4)

Checkpoints

1 'You are washed in the blood of the lamb'; 'This is the body of Christ'; 'The sabbath is a holy day'.
2 To say that God is all powerful and yet say that because of human freedom he cannot stop atrocities committed by humans. To say that God is all knowing and yet he cannot be the cause of all human actions.

Exam question

This is a question which leads you specifically to a discussion of language games, but which needs you to demonstrate a good knowledge of different types of religious language and why they may or may not be meaningless only within the context of religion. You should allude to the claim that religious language is meaningless and consider whether language game theory and its 'use not meaning' approach solves the problem.

Religion and science

Checkpoints

1 A brute fact needs no explanation and the question 'why does it exist?' or 'why is it so?' is redundant.
2 An unnecessary hypothesis complicates the search for answers and goes against the principle of Ockham's Razor. For the atheist, God is an unnecessary hypothesis since it does not lead to any answers about the origin of the universe.

Exam questions

It is so important that you do not fall into the storytelling trap here. Features, not a blow-by-blow account, of a religious interpretation of the origin of the universe are required. Show that you are aware of the general principles of both religious and scientific interpretations and gain marks by emphasising the reasons why they approach the question of origins differently. In (b) you can gain considerable credit for use of scholarship to show why the two interpretations need not be incompatible but, in fact, are complementary.

Foundations of religious belief: Plato and Aristotle

Checkpoints

1 In the Fourth Way, Aquinas argues that all that is good, true, noble and the like owe their origin to an initial source of goodness, truth and nobility, and this must be God.
2 In the cosmological and design arguments.

Exam question

Your AO1 marks can be easily earned by a good explanation of the content and principles of the Theory of the Forms, but you will only ensure a high grade by solid evaluation. You must consider fully whether it presents a view of the world – spiritual and physical – which seems philosophically and religiously reasonable.

Foundations of religious belief: Judeo-Christian themes

Checkpoints

1 Questions about how the world came to take the form it did, how humans relate to the rest of creation, and how and why evil and suffering came into the world are all addressed in some way in the creation narratives.

2 Should they be taken literally or symbolically; there are two different accounts which suggest a different order to creation.

Exam questions

(a) gives you the chance to cover a range of possibilities, including the moral law, miracles and religious experience and the nature of the world. In (b) you must show straight away that you understand the term 'transcendence' and can build up a clear argument for or against the claim that a transcendent God cannot act in the world.

Revision checklist
Philosophy of religion

By the end of this chapter you should be able to:

1	Have a strong foundational knowledge of the contribution of Plato and Aristotle to the philosophy of religion.	Confident	Not confident. **Revise** pages 102–3
2	Be aware of the key traditions within the Judeo-Christian understanding of God.	Confident	Not confident. **Revise** pages 104–5
3	Know, understand and evaluate the key features of the Cosmological Argument.	Confident	Not confident. **Revise** pages 106–7
4	Have a clear knowledge and understanding of the Design Argument and be able to evaluate its strengths and weaknesses.	Confident	Not confident. **Revise** pages 108–9
5	Demonstrate an understanding of the Ontological Proof for the existence of God.	Confident	Not confident. **Revise** pages 110–11
6	Understand and discuss how religious experience might serve as a proof for the existence of God.	Confident	Not confident. **Revise** pages 112–15
7	Display an understanding of the key features of the moral argument for the existence of God.	Confident	Not confident. **Revise** pages 116–17
8	Be aware of the challenges raised by the problem of evil and be able to discuss possible solutions.	Confident	Not confident. **Revise** pages 118–19
9	Discuss the meaning of the term 'miracle' and evaluate arguments for and against their occurrence.	Confident	Not confident. **Revise** pages 120–21
10	Know and understand the arguments raised regarding the possible ways in which religion and science may be related.	Confident	Not confident. **Revise** pages 122–29
11	Have a clear knowledge of the key features of atheism and critiques of religious belief.	Confident	Not confident. **Revise** pages 130–31
12	Know, understand and evaluate issues relating to beliefs about life after death.	Confident	Not confident. **Revise** pages 132–3
13	Demonstrate confidence in dealing with issues of religious language.	Confident	Not confident. **Revise** pages 134–5

Religious ethics combines many topics from the study of moral philosophy and the challenge is to ensure that you make clear links with religious issues. The study of ethics attempts to clarify the meaning of what it means to be good, both by analysing claims which use evaluative terms such as good, bad, right or wrong, and attempting to understand if such claims can be made meaningfully, and by examining the nature of actions which may be thought to be good or bad. Ethical theories attempt to lay down parameters for moral action, while applied ethics examines how we make moral decisions about what we actually do. Thus, while utilitarianism, for example, may propose that what is good is what brings about the greatest happiness, or least pain, for the greatest number of people, a study of the moral problems raised by euthanasia may consider issues of the sanctity of life, or whether we have a 'right to die'.

Exam topics

Meta ethics and ethical theory
→ Utilitarianism
→ God and morality
→ Situation ethics
→ Natural law
→ Deontology
→ Biblical ethics
→ Ethical language
→ Ethical concepts: emotivism, intuitionism, objectivity, subjectivity, relativism

Applied ethics
→ Justice, law and authority
→ Medical ethics
→ Environmental ethics
→ Business ethics
→ Animal rights
→ Sexual ethics
→ The ethics of war and peace

Topic checklist

AS ○ A2 ●	OCR	AQA	EDEXCEL
God and morality	○●	●	○●
Utilitarianism	○●	○●	○
Situation ethics	○		○
Natural moral law	○●	○●	●
Kantian deontology	○●	○●	●
Authority, law and justice			●
Biblical ethics	○●	○●	
Medical ethics	○●	○●	
Environmental ethics		●	
Finance and business ethics		●	
Animal rights		●	
Sexual ethics	○●		○
War and peace	●		○
Ethical language	○●	●	●
Ethical concepts	○●	●	●

God and morality

Then tell me, what do you say the holy is? And what is the unholy? For consider, is the holy loved by the gods because it is holy? Or is it holy because the gods love it?

The problem of divine command ethics ●●●

Plato's Euthyphro Dilemma exposes the difficult relationship between God and morality. The problem is whether God defines what is morally good, or is God good because he conforms to an independent standard of goodness. If God creates morality then whatever he determines is good, even if human reasons suggest otherwise.

Many religious believers argue that conforming to the will of God is part of the meaning of their faith. **R.B. Braithwaite** claims that to be religious is to be committed to a set of moral values, which includes refraining from some actions and fulfilling others. **John Locke** maintained that since humans are created by God then they must live in tune with God's will. However, does the act of creation give God the exclusive right to decide human actions? Further, if the only reason to obey God is because he has the authority to enforce his laws, does this make it right to do so?

Furthermore, not all religious believers agree on the content of divine moral laws. Many moral issues are not addressed directly through Scripture – the primary source of revealed morality. Is it enough to say that we can infer through use of reason what God would command in such cases?

Aquinas and the Fourth Way

> Among beings there are some more and some less good, true, noble and the like. But more and less are predicated of different things according as they resemble in their different ways something which is the maximum . . . so that there is something which is truest, something best, something noblest . . . Therefore there must also be something which is to all beings the cause of their being, goodness, and every other perfection, and this we call God.

As in his other Ways, Aquinas argued that without God as a first cause, nothing else could be explained, and this applied to morality as much as to the origin of the universe. His view was supported by **F.C. Copleston** who, in discussion with **Bertrand Russell**, claimed:

> I do think that all goodness reflects God in some way and proceeds from him, so that in a sense the man who loves what is truly good, loves God even if he doesn't advert to God. (In John Hick (ed.), *The Existence of God* (1964))

However, Aquinas's Fourth Way does not suggest how good can be defined. All we know is that God is the supreme source of it and it is his every essence to be perfectly good. However, what does it mean for God to *be* perfectly good?

Terminology

Divine command ethics supports a supranaturalist view of ethics, that morality comes directly from the will of God and whatever he determines as good is good by definition.

Action point

Read Genesis 22 and consider if there is any way this episode could be morally justifiable.

Example

Religious conversions often lead to a change of lifestyle which suggests that moral behaviour reflects a person's view of their relationship with God, and will change as that relationship changes.

Examiner's secrets

Ensure that your answers on this topic include plenty of scholarly views. Don't rely on listing general reasons why a religious believer may think that morality comes from God – for example, the Ten Commandments: this is too obvious to be a primary argument at A level.

Checkpoint 1

In what way is Aquinas's view influenced by Platonic theories of good?

Action point

Make a list of moral issues on which there is a lack of agreement between Christians, or members of another faith.

An eschatological justification for morality

Kant argued that only one fact was indisputable, and that was the existence of a moral law which was meaningless unless God existed. He maintained that all men could discern a moral law evident in the universe and had a duty to seek the highest form of the good, which he coined the *summum bonum*. Nevertheless, since the moral law would never be satisfied in this life, man would never be capable of achieving the *summum bonum*, thus the existence of God was necessary if the goal of morality were to be realised.

Objective moral laws

John Henry Newman argued that there were objective moral laws which had their origin in a personal law giver: Newman is making a link between the existence of a moral law which imposes certain demands upon us and the existence of God who fixes that law and to whom we are obliged for its upkeep. **H.P. Owen** argued similarly: '*It is impossible to think of a command without a commander . . . Either we take moral claims to be self-explanatory modes of impersonal existence, or we explain them in terms of a personal God.*' (In Brian Davies, *Introduction to the Philosophy of Religion* (1982)). Christians would, in principle, claim that the conscience is given by God and that it is universal whether man believes in God or not (Romans 2:12ff). It has been affected by the fall and thus is corrupted and imperfect (Genesis 3) but can be redeemed by Jesus Christ (Romans 3:21–22).

Further problems

→ How can the existence of morality prove the existence of God any more than the existence of the world can prove it?

→ Is there any reason to believe that religious people are morally superior to non-religious people?

→ If religious people act out of fear can they perform a truly moral action?

→ Obedience to God's laws imposes on man's freedom to choose to act otherwise.

→ The conscience is not an infallible guide, and may be more easily explained by psychological or sociological factors than by the existence of God.

Checkpoint 2

What was Kant's idea of the categorical and hypothetical imperatives?

Useful quotations

'If, *as is the case, we feel responsibility, are ashamed, are frightened at transgressing the voice of conscience, this implies that there is One to whom we are responsible, before whom we are ashamed, whose claim on us we fear*' (J.H. Newman in Brian Davies, *Introduction to the Philosophy of Religion* (1982)).

Useful quotations

'*Deep within his conscience man discovers a law which he has not laid upon himself but he must obey*' (Guadium et Spes, *Catholic Truth Society* (1979)).

Links

Other spreads in this chapter make a link with this topic – look at situation ethics, deontology, biblical ethics and natural law.

Exam question   answer: page 176

Is God the best explanation for the existence of morality?   (30 mins)

Utilitarianism

Utilitarianism is an ethical theory, most often attributed to Jeremy Bentham and John Stuart Mill. It is based upon the principle of utility, which suggests that where a moral choice is to be made, the right action is the one which produces the greatest happiness or pleasure (or the least pain) for the most people.

It is a **consequentialist** and **teleological** approach, because it relies on the consequences of actions and not on the intrinsic goodness of the action itself.

Act utilitarianism and Jeremy Bentham ●●●

Bentham's theory is one of *universal ethical hedonism*: if an action brings or increases pleasure, then it is right and what is right for society is that which provides the greatest happiness for the majority of those individuals who all have an equal right to happiness. Bentham devised the *hedonic calculus* to calculate the most pleasurable action. Seven elements are taken into consideration: intensity, duration, certainty, propinquity (remoteness); fecundity; purity; extent. This is a quantitative approach which measures the *amount* of pleasure derived from an action.

Rule utilitarianism and John Stuart Mill ●●●

Mill, the son of Bentham's colleague James Mill, became disillusioned by Bentham's approach, and developed the principle further by talking about *qualitative* rather than quantitative pleasure. He argued that not all pleasures were equal and that pleasures of the mind should take precedence over physical pleasures. He believed that once individuals were 'competently acquainted' with both pleasures, they would invariably choose the higher over the lower. Once basic human requirements for survival are fulfilled, a human being's primary moral concerns should be for the higher order pleasures which fulfil human potential and give them the chance to rise from the gutter. Mill was concerned that the hedonic calculus could justify harmful lower pleasures if they were carried out by a majority on a minority and maintained that it was possible to educate people to seek higher pleasures. Bentham, on the other hand, maintained that it was a matter for each individual to decide what was good or bad and as such was egalitarian.

Instead of a hedonic calculus, Mill proposed that general **rules** should be used as guides in decision-making concerning moral actions. Certain rules that promote happiness – such as keeping promises or not stealing, for example. Rule utilitarianism suggests that a person should follow established rules and consider the practical consequences of an action before carrying it out.

Strong rule utilitarianism maintains that certain rules have universal value and should always be kept; weak rule utilitarianism argues that there will sometimes be circumstances in which it would be better to allow exceptions. Mill's approach has also been called **ideal** utilitarianism, as it includes ideals (such as compassion or justice) into his understanding of human happiness.

Negative utilitarianism argues that maximising pleasure is not as important as minimising pain; the priority is to reduce suffering in the world.

Strengths of utilitarianism

→ Utilitarian theories support the view that human well-being is always good and actions should positively reinforce it.

→ Consequences have real effects on people and should therefore be the basis for evaluating their actions, irrespective of previous precedents.

→ The principle encourages democracy. The interests of the majority are considered, and a dangerous minority is not allowed to dominate.

→ It is an approach that does not depend on religious beliefs and principles which cannot be verified or universalised.

Weaknesses of utilitarianism

→ The theory depends on accurately predicting the long-term consequences of an action.

→ Not every action done out of good will is going to result in good consequences.

→ The theory cannot be used to decide what is universally and inherently good.

→ There should be consideration of both the majority and the minority views. The rights of an individual or group can be ignored if it is not in the interests of the majority – even if their claim is fair and just.

→ The theory is too simplistic; every dilemma cannot be solved by reference to a single ethical theory.

→ It makes no allowance for personal relationships or prima facie duties.

→ Religious believers may be willing to endure pain, humiliation or self-sacrifice for a cause they believe to be true and consider happiness not to be evidence of moral value.

Action point

Find out about preference utilitarianism, most commonly associated with R.M. Hare.

Examiner's secrets

Many candidates only write about Bentham's act utilitarianism, and make a brief reference to Mill, but never include other forms. Your answer will set itself apart if you explore other developments in utilitarianism.

Exam question   answer: page 176

How far should happiness be the key to ethical decision making?   (30 mins)

Situation ethics

The 1960s were host to an enormous social, political and cultural change which led to the complete re-evaluation of the moral laws which had shaped society before the Second World War.

The development of situation ethics

The Church was not unaware of these changes and in 1963 **J.A.T. Robinson** published his controversial book *Honest to God*. It reassessed the Christian idea of the nature of God and, most challengingly, the view that ethical values were 'supranaturalist' – established by God, unchanging, and applicable to every situation, time and place. **Joseph Fletcher** had introduced the ideas of situation ethics in *The Harvard Divinity Bulletin* and in 1966 published *Situation Ethics*, responding to what he felt were the failures of **legalism** inherent in ethical systems that propose rules to govern human behaviour, while at the same time rejecting **antinomianism** – a total abandonment of rules and principles. Situation ethics essentially means that there is no ethical standard that can be uniformly or consistently applied, for each situation demands its own standard of ethics. Instead, the key to making moral decisions should be the principle of *agape* – the peculiar quality of Christian love which enables the individual to love their enemies.

Fletcher and Robinson used New Testament dialogues between Jesus and the Pharisees as an illustration of old versus new morality. Jesus, they claimed, was an advocate, albeit 2000 years previously, of new morality; the Pharisees, of the old.

Robinson argued that the ideals of situation ethics could be applied far more effectively to the then hotly debated issue of divorce law than the application of a pre-packaged moral judgement that divorce was 'always wrong'. Robinson questioned the conservative view that marriage created a supernatural bond that was impossible to break, based on the belief that behind earthly, human relationships lay quite independent, invisible structures which could not be questioned. Hence, although it may appear that marriage is about two human beings signing a legal contract, in reality 'something' happens in the metaphysical realm which binds those two people together in a relationship which is beyond the legal contract between them. The legal contract cannot be dissolved like a contract of employment, because it represents a far more binding union which has been made, witnessed and ratified in the heavenly realms. *'It is not a question of "Those whom God hath joined together let no man put asunder": no man could if he tried. For marriage is not merely indissoluble: it is indelible'.* (*Honest to God* (1963)).

Fletcher used examples from real life and from literature to illustrate his thesis: the burning house and time to save only one person – your father or a doctor with the formulae for a cure for a killer disease only in his head; the woman who kills her crying baby to save a party from massacre by Indians on the Wilderness Trail; the military nurse who deliberately treated her patients harshly so they would be determined to get fit and able to leave the hospital; the famous case of Mrs Bergmeier who deliberately asks a Russian prison camp guard to make her pregnant so she can be released to return to her family in Germany (an act which Fletcher coined 'sacrificial adultery').

Fletcher developed the notion of *agape* by describing love and justice as the same thing, '*for justice is love distributed, nothing else*'. He claimed that justice is the giving to every person what is their due, and that since the one thing due to everyone is love, then love and justice were the same.

Problems with situation ethics ●●●

Although the theory seems to be well supported with evidence, it was rejected by representatives of the Protestant and Catholic churches. **William Barclay** believed that the rejection of conservative Christian ethics marked a dangerous change: '*Thirty years ago no one ever really questioned the Christian ethic . . . No one ever doubted that divorce was disgraceful; that illegitimate babies were a disaster; that chastity was a good thing.*' (*Ethics in a Permissive Society* (1972)). He suggested that:

→ Situation ethics is based on extreme and unusual examples.
→ In practice, humans are not as free as Barclay implied – we are not just limited by moral laws but by the need for laws to ensure human survival.
→ Furthermore, past choices determine future choices in a significant and unavoidable way and affect other people: '*A man can live his own life, but when he begins deliberately to alter the lives of others, then a real problem arises, on which we cannot simply turn our backs, and in which there is a place for law as the encourager of morality*'. (*Ethics in a Permissive Society* (1972)).

Useful quotations

'If the emotional and spiritual welfare of both parents and children in a **particular** family can be served best by a divorce, wrong and cheapjack as divorce commonly is, then love requires it' (Robinson, *Honest to God* (1963)).

Checkpoint 2

What are Fletcher's four principles of situation ethics?

Useful quotations

'Whatever the pointers of the law to the demands of love, there can for the Christian be no "packaged" moral judgments – for persons are more important even than "standards"' (Fletcher, *Situation Ethics* (1966)).

Useful quotations

'It is possible, though not easy, to forgive Professor Fletcher for writing this book, for he is a generous and loveable man. It is harder to forgive the SCM Press for publishing it' (Graham Dunstan in Peter Vardy and Paul Grosch, *The Puzzle of Ethics* (1994)).

Action point

Make a list of the functions which law serves in society.

Exam question   answer: page 176

Critically assess the value of situation ethics to the resolution of ethical dilemmas.   (30 mins)

Natural moral law

Natural law was developed by Thomas Aquinas who claimed that everything in the universe has a design and a purpose that could be understood through an examination of the natural world and the Bible. Humanity was a special case, in that people were given reason and freedom to choose to follow the good, which is God's purpose for them.

Features of natural moral law

Aquinas identified four **cardinal virtues** associated with natural law: prudence, justice, fortitude and temperance. These were the fundamental qualities of a good moral life. In contrast, seven vices would lead people astray – pride, avarice, lust, envy, gluttony, anger and sloth. He added three theological virtues – faith, hope and charity – based on 1 Corinthians 13.

Natural law offers a clearly defined rule that can be applied universally – this rule may be simply put as '*an action is right or wrong in itself, without reference to the consequences*'. Natural law does not look towards the final consequences, but breaks the situation down into the various actions involved and tries to establish the moral rightness of each one.

Aquinas maintained that the purpose of natural law was to enable people to live, reproduce, learn, worship God, and order society. All things must operate in accordance with these principles to which humanity is naturally inclined. An action which takes someone closer to God is right, and an action which takes them further away is wrong. Aquinas claimed that an ideal plan for humans existed in the mind of God before creation, the fulfilment of which will lead them into the image and likeness of God.

The four laws

Aquinas identified four kinds of law: eternal law – God's will and wisdom; divine law – God's will and wisdom given in Scripture and through the Church; natural law – by which God's law is known in humans; human law – which is derived from God. Evil was a privation of good, a falling short of the ideal set by God in nature and within Scripture. Natural moral law is, therefore, a universal guide for judging the moral value of human actions. It is a very precise ethical theory – it is not based on personal preferences or on guessing the consequences of an action. It is based on a simple examination of what is from God: what is natural.

Useful quotations

'True law is right reason in agreement with nature. It is applied universally and is unchanging and everlasting . . . one eternal and unchangeable law will be valid for all nations and all times, and there will be one master and rule, that is God' (Cicero).

Terminology

Natural law is an absolute, a priori and deontological approach to ethics.

Watch out!

Be clear on the difference between natural law and laws of nature: laws of nature describe facts about the world; natural laws prescribe ways of behaving and what humans ought to do.

Background

Aquinas was influenced by Aristotle who identified living well, or flourishing, as the goal of human existence. This could be achieved by a deliberate training of the will and emotions. Aquinas incorporated the central idea that since God created the universe out of nothing (*ex nihilo*) human reason could discover God's natural law inherent in the universe.

Checkpoint 1

Identify three Papal Encyclicals based on natural law.

Examiner's secrets

Candidates rarely mention these four laws. Too much time is spent on discussing the purposes for human existence. This is important but not the only valid element in an essay on natural law.

Developments of natural law theory

Hugo Grotius used natural law as the foundation for a social contract of the state, but he rejected the theological foundation, claiming that natural law, discovered by use of reason, would exist even if God did not, and that it was entirely deductive and independent of experience. Grotius's approach became the foundation for modern just war theories. **Thomas Hobbes** believed that humans were naturally greedy, selfish and hungry for power, but agreed that it was in everyone's interests to adopt the policy of do as you would be done to. **John Locke** believed that nature had endowed human beings with certain inalienable rights that could not be violated by any governing authority.

Proportionalism

Associated particularly with **Bernard Hoose** and **Richard McCormick,** proportionalism works within the framework of natural law, but without insisting on preserving static, inflexible and absolutist interpretations if greater good is served by laying it aside. Proportionalists identify the role of ontic evils, which are not morally wrong, but which may bring about some pain and suffering, and ontic goods, such as dignity, integrity or justice, which are in themselves non-moral, but nonetheless desirable. Both should be taken into account when making a proportionate moral decision. This approach takes into account a theology of compromise – the view that since we live in a fallen world the best that human beings can strive towards is a moral compromise, not moral perfection – and allows for the principle of double effect – justifying an action for its primary effect, although its secondary effect may, in other cases, be considered immoral.

Aquinas makes several problematic assumptions

→ That all people seek to worship God.
→ That God created the universe and the moral law within it.
→ That every individual has a particular purpose to fulfil.
→ That moral law comes from God and therefore people ought to obey it – this is naturalistic fallacy, the false assumption that it is legitimate to derive an *ought* from an *is*).
→ That human nature has remained the same since creation.

However, principles which underlie natural law are challenged by evolution and by discoveries which may lead to identifying 'non-natural' states, such as homosexuality or gender dysphoria, as genetic or hormonal.

Action point

List a range of activities that violate the purposes of human existence as identified by Aquinas.

Example

Natural law provides the foundation for the UN Declaration of Human Rights 1948.

Background

Communism and capitalism were both challenged on the grounds of natural law.

Checkpoint 2

Identify a criticism of the principle of double effect.

Example

In the letter to the Romans, Paul argues that human sinfulness was the product of the fall, but that the death of Jesus could redeem humans from its curse.

Action point

Make a list of advantageous scientific advances which are unnatural according to the principles of natural law.

Exam question   answers: pages 176–7

Critically consider the view that natural law is not a practical ethical theory.

(45 mins)

Kantian deontology

Terminology

Deontology is an absolutist, a priori and objective approach to morality.

Useful quotations

'Two things fill the mind with wonder and awe: the starry heavens above and the moral law within' (Kant).
'It is impossible to conceive of anything at all in the world, or even out of it, which can be taken as good without qualification, except a good will' (Kant).

Links

Pages 144–5 on God and morality are useful here.

Checkpoint 1

Give one example of a categorical imperative and a parallel hypothetical imperative.

Useful quotations

'A rational being must always regard himself as legislator in a kingdom of ends rendered possible by freedom of the will, whether as member or as sovereign' (Kant).

Deontological theories of ethics challenge the teleological view that what is morally good can be evaluated in terms of a non-moral concept – the happiness of the majority, for example, or the goodness or badness of the consequences of an action. Deontologists claim that whether an action or a moral rule is right lies in certain features that are independent of what it brings about.

Deontological ethics is based on the belief that duty is the only invariably good motive, since it is not influenced by personal preferences and inclinations. Such duties may include duties to oneself, to others, to family, social duties and duties to God. Central to the theory too is the belief that moral actions are those which must be universalisable and equally binding on everyone. Hence, morality does not consist of exceptions or situational judgements, but is *a priori* – not based on *a posteriori* experience – because if reason were universal then moral reasoning would lead to the same results over and over again.

Kant believed that the existence of God was a necessary requirement of a just universe and for the moral law to be balanced. Kant attempted to discover the rational principle that would stand as a ***categorical imperative***, grounding all other ethical judgements. The imperative would have to be categorical rather than ***hypothetical***, since true morality should not depend on individual likes and dislikes or on abilities, opportunities or other external circumstances. Categorical imperatives express the absolute and unconditional duty to act without condition and Kant considered them to be of supreme importance to moral action.

The principle of universalisability, or the principle of the law of nature, demands that human beings '*act in such a way that their actions might become a universal law*'. Universalisable principles are those which apply not just in specific cases but to everyone. The Formula of Kingdom Ends laid down the principle that every action should be undertaken as if the individual were '*a law making member of a kingdom of ends*.' This should ensure that every individual appreciated how significant the part they had to play in establishing moral guidelines and rules. Furthermore, the Formula of the End in itself would ensure that people were valued for their intrinsic, not instrumental, worth. Finally, the Formula of Autonomy established that the *decision* to act according to a maxim is regarded as having made it a universal law.

W.D. Ross, the intuitionist philosopher, argued that our duties are part of the fundamental nature of the universe, leading to the most recent revival of duty-based ethics. Ross claimed that if we seriously consider our moral convictions we will come to understand that there are seven *prima facie* duties – duties which take precedence over all others unless a stronger duty presents itself:

Fidelity: the duty to keep promises.
Reparation: the duty to compensate others when we harm them.
Gratitude: the duty to thank those who help us.
Justice: the duty to recognise merit.
Beneficence: the duty to improve the conditions of others.
Self-improvement: the duty to improve our virtue and intelligence.
Nonmaleficence: the duty to not injure others.

It may not always be obvious which duty should take priority and in such a case Ross maintains that we must use our intuition. However, this cannot always guarantee that it will be the right action and we are still dependent on making a spontaneous decision.

Strengths and weaknesses

Strengths
Motivation is valued over consequences, which are beyond control, while a good motive is in itself worthy of value. It is a humanitarian principle in which all men are considered to be of equal value and worthy of protection so justice is always an absolute. It recognises the value of moral absolutes that do not change with time or culture and are understood to be so without the need for lengthy calculation of possible outcomes.

Weaknesses
Moral obligations appear arbitrary or inexplicable except by reference to duty. When taken to its logical extreme the principle of universalisability is absurd since not all things which are universalisable in principle would be desirable or moral if universalised. Kant argued that what is good to do is what we ought to do and that what is inherently good and intrinsically right is the way in which we ought to behave for the mutual good of all, irrespective of consequences. In this respect, critics of Kant have accused him of committing the naturalistic fallacy – of turning 'an is into an ought'.

Examiner's secrets

The addition of the thinking of W.D. Ross to a question on deontology will immediately set you apart from many other candidates.

Watch out!

Don't spend ages over these terms – there are few marks for lots of definitions. It is the understanding and evaluation of the principle which will gain you credit.

Action point

Compare deontology with emotivism and draw up a list of the key differences.

Checkpoint 2

What is a statement of fact and a statement of value?

Action point

Discuss whether Kant would claim that a person who has never been tempted to do an immoral action is a better person than one who has been tempted and yet resisted temptation.

Exam question   answer: page 177

Critically evaluate the claim that Kant is too pessimistic about human's ability to make moral choices.   (45 mins)

Authority, law and justice

Link

See pages 146–7 on utilitarianism for more on John Stuart Mill.

Authority ●●●

Authority may be defined as the power to influence, control or judge. It can be acquired in several ways: by consensus, inheritance, force, by a display of strength or charisma. Governments act with authority with the support of a legal system and the threat of punishment to those who do not obey it. When authority is legitimate and acting for the greater good of society, conformity is more likely, and laws made in accordance with religious principles may be considered by some to be more legitimate than the purely secular. Monotheistic societies have taught, in principle, that governing authorities are given by God and for this reason should be obeyed. In a theocracy, the governing powers rule in the name of God and there is no separation between divine and secular law.

Ruling authorities can influence the evolution of morality through the making of law, but in some cases laws are only accepted when they comply with independent and universal moral codes. The law should not unreasonably infringe on the freedom of those it governs, unless, according to Mill's Harm Principle, it is to protect them from harm.

Law ●●●

Law is a system of guidelines set down by the governing authority. Law cannot guarantee a just society, but it can support it: it orders society, acts as a deterrent, and offers protection to those under the law. Laws may be made democratically where those governed are allowed to contribute to the law-making process, or they may reflect the philosophies of the government. **Regulative** rules exist to aid the application of **constitutive** rules, which are instruments to human fulfilment. Law controls the exercise of freedom either negatively or positively. **Negative freedom** is understood to be the absence of constraint or restraint; **positive freedom** to be the capacity to act. Liberal ideologies emphasise the importance of protecting individual liberty from state control but law is essentially designed to influence choices rather than preferences. Laws are amended in accordance with time and experience. Laws may need to be changed or abolished to suit the society in which they are applied, and to protect its members.

Punishment

Punishment may serve one or more purposes:

Retribution/revenge – those who do wrong should bear the consequences of so doing.
Protection – to protect society from wrongdoers.
Rehabilitation – changing the offender's personality or circumstances so that they will not reoffend.

Deterrence – sufficiently severe punishment will discourage future crimes and make others think again before following the criminal's example.

Rights and duties

Wesley Hohfield identified four kinds of rights: liberty – the law does not prevent us from acting; claim – rights others have a duty to fulfil; power – the power to perform an action; immunity – we are freed from certain obligations. There are five bases on which the concept of rights are established:

Divine right – rights given by God; *Natural rights* – duties that are rooted in human nature; *Contract* – society limits the rights of individuals to ensure an ordered society; *Utilitarian* – respecting other's rights in the interest of having your own respected; *Totalitarian* – rights are exercised as long as the government permits them to be.

John Stott argues that three essential relationships based on rights and duties were established at creation: *Humanity's relationship with God* – humanity is placed in a position as to be able to love and serve God, obey his commands and understand his will. *Humanity's relationship with each other* – the right to marriage and family, peaceful assembly, and to receive respect irrespective of age, sex, race or rank. *Humanity's relationship with the earth* – the rights and responsibilities of stewardship.

Justice ●●●

Justice should oppose prejudice and discrimination and ensure that the rights of citizens are not violated. Ideally, a just society is diverse, active in its promotion of social harmony and opposed to exploitation and oppression. Justice strives for equality, which may be divided into four categories: *Fundamental equality* – all people are treated as equals by government and the legal system. *Social equality* – citizens have formal rights such as the right to vote. *Equals and unequals* – people of the same group should be treated the same, but others may need special consideration in different circumstances. *Religion and equality* – humans are made in the image of God, which remains the key principle on which human life is valued. **Charles Colson** puts forward a strong case for *restorative* or *relational justice*. He argues that when justice fails to achieve results it is because a vital element in the healing of relationships is missing.

Exam question   answer: page 177

Assess how natural law may be useful in resolving issues raised by authority and law.   (45 mins)

Biblical ethics

Biblical ethics is concerned with how the Bible lays down the foundation for moral behaviour and offers rules and commandments which control that behaviour. The key principle in the Bible is that God has authority to lay down such principles and humans are required to obey him.

Old Testament ethics

In the Old Testament, belief in the one God of Israel, living, personal and involved in the world, underlines all ethical teaching. His people are called to be responsible and obedient to his laws which releases them from commitment to other gods. Obedience brings blessing, but disobedience must be punished.

The sanctity of life

God's personal creation of humans is the basis for the principle of the sanctity of life, ratified after the flood in the provision against shedding blood, even that of animals for food. Human life is equal in status and value, and even slaves were given civil rights. Special concern is expressed for the alien, widow and orphan, and the poor are to be protected.

Israel's witness to the nations

Israel is called to an exemplary standard of moral behaviour because of their special calling. The people of Israel are to be priestly, grateful, holy, devoted to God alone, and rich in righteous and steadfast love. The prophets had a special role in calling Israel back to their Covenant responsibility to be a moral witness. The prophets are generally held to be moral reformers rather than innovators – they do not determine moral standards, but reinforce them.

Law and commandments

The law and commandments are given and accepted in response to God's salvific action in the exodus and the wilderness. God is the first priority, and society and the family are protected through commands concerning the sabbath, marriage and property. The strict Old Testament teaching on sex is part of its concern for preserving the stability of the family. The law sets a higher value on human life rather than property and punishments are controlled. The principle of *lex talionis* was intended to limit the extent to which vengeance could be extracted.

New Testament ethics

In the Gospels, Jesus appears to demand a reappraisal of the law, but he did not dismiss it entirely. Much of Jesus' teaching is presented in the context of conflict with the Pharisees over matters of the law, which may in reality have been the conflict between the early Church and Judaism. Jesus' teaching on the sabbath, tithing and divorce attempts to reinterpret the law in the light of the imminent kingdom and the new focus is love, honesty and compassion.

The Sermon on the Mount (Matthew 5–7)

The Beatitudes (5:3–11) are a form of commandments urging God-centred living and attitudes. The antitheses (5:21–47) refocus the law but make it more demanding, implying that the Pharisees did not go far enough in their application of the law, dealing only with activities and not with intent and motive. Chapter 6 places an ethical standard on the religious practices of fasting, prayer and almsgiving and the golden rule of 7:12 is a reworking of the rabbinic summary of the Torah, '*Do not do to others what you do not wish them to do to you*'. Matthew makes ethics about positive action, not just refraining from prohibited actions.

The kingdom of God

The imminence of the kingdom means that repentance is urgent and believers are required to made radical decisions. The values of the kingdom are the reverse of earthly values – in the kingdom the last will be first, the master will be the servant, and children and women are given places of importance. The disciple is called to take up their cross in obedience not to a set of laws, but to the will of God.

Pauline ethics

Paul was influenced by his Jewish background as a Pharisee, but he urged that with the coming of Christ slavish obedience to the law has ended. However, freedom from the law brings a new set of responsibilities, including concern for the consciences of others and for the health of the whole Christian community. The fruits of the Holy Spirit (Galatians 5:22) are to be the key to the believer's behaviour and which enable them to withstand temptation, self-indulgence and arrogance. Paul writes to his communities with the instruction to be '*full of goodness, complete in knowledge and competent to instruct one another*' (Romans 15:14).

Useful quotations

'*Do not think that I have come to abolish the law or the prophets. I have come not to abolish but to fulfil*' (Matthew 5:17).

Useful quotations

'*Matthew remembered Jesus and his message of the kingdom and called for a surpassing righteousness*' (*New Dictionary of Christian Ethics and Pastoral Theology* (1997)).

Action point

Read Mark 10:17–31 for an example of the radical demands of the kingdom, which transcend traditional ethical loyalties.

Useful quotations

'*All things are lawful for me, but not all things are beneficial*' (I Corinthians 6:12).

Action point

Read Ephesians 5 for Paul's understanding of the ethical relationships established by the family.

Exam question   answer: page 177

Examine and evaluate the application of biblical ethics to contemporary ethical dilemmas.   (30 mins)

Medical ethics (1)

Although abortion and euthanasia are still the front runners in terms of exam favourites, bear in mind that there are several other areas you may be required to consider including: fertility treatment; neo-natal death; organ donation; medical care; healthcare decisions; surrogacy, or genetic engineering.

Many debates within medical ethics relate to the principle of the sanctity of life. From the secular viewpoint, this means that life is of intrinsic value in itself. From the religious viewpoint, it means that life is sacred and created by God, so once God has set a life in motion, only he can end it. The principle maintains that outside certain arguable circumstances innocent human beings have the right not to be deliberately killed, nor should they seek to end their life. Life is precious to God and, while it is not necessary to preserve it at all costs, it must not be disposable for utilitarian reasons.

Abortion

Therapeutic, procured or surgical abortion is a moral issue; *spontaneous abortion*, or miscarriage, is not. Therapeutic abortion may arguably include contraceptive devices such as the IUD or the 'morning after pill' since these act as abortifacients, which prevent implantation, but is more usually carried out by surgical or medical means after the foetus has implanted in the womb. Ethical problems revolve over the issue of whether or not the unborn foetus is a human being and when life begins, influenced by the Catholic view that the foetus is a person from conception, a view which was established as late as the latter part of the seventeenth century when early microscopes first revealed that a foetus seemed to have the appearance of a tiny, but fully formed, person. Augustine, however, had stated that terminating a pregnancy before the foetus was able to feel anything was not murder, because the soul was not yet present – a time he established as before 40 days for male foetuses and before 90 days for females.

Five stages may be identified as when the foetus may be classified as a human person:

Fertilisation – the extreme conservative view. Sperm and egg unite and the full potential of the foetus is established. *Implantation* – the fertilised egg is implanted on to the wall of the womb. *Quickening* – the moment when the child moves in the womb. *Viability* – the point at which the foetus can be considered to be independent of the mother for the purposes of medical care. *Birth* – the extreme liberal view. A further question still remains of who has pre-eminent rights in the decision to have an abortion – the mother, the foetus, or even third parties, such as the father, the Church or the state.

Example

Under these principles, humans are protected from abortion, and are prohibited from voluntary euthanasia. Life should not necessarily be extended if costs are prohibitive and the outcome still fatal, but should not be prematurely ended simply to free hospital resources or to save money.

Useful quotations

'Then the Lord God formed man of dust from the ground, and breathed into his nostrils the breath of life, and man became a living being' (Genesis 2:7).
'For thou didst form my inward parts, thou didst knit me together in my mother's womb. I praise thee, for I am fearfully and wonderfully made' (Psalm 139:13f).
'Before I formed you in the womb I knew you, and before you were born I consecrated you' (Jeremiah 1:5).
'He himself gives to all men life and breath and everything' (Acts 17:35).

Checkpoint 1

What are the legal grounds for an abortion in the UK?

Checkpoint 2

Outline briefly a utilitarian and a deontological perspective on abortion.

Another significant issue in the abortion debate is that of **rights**. When a woman seeks an abortion she is asserting her right to make a choice that has implications for her, for the foetus and, indirectly, for all those who have a role to play in her life, and in that of her potential child. Pro-abortionists, or pro-choice advocates, argue that the woman has significant rights:

→ Over her body.
→ Over her life – including the next nine months, eighteen years, or fifty years.
→ Over the choices that she makes about her future.
→ Over the effect that her choices will have on others with whom she is already in a relationship.
→ Over the choices she makes about the future of a foetus which will become a dependent child.

Pro-choice advocates also appeal to compassion, citing cases in which the mother and conceivably the rest of her family are likely to suffer unbearable strain if the pregnancy were to continue. Anti-abortionists (or pro-life advocates) also appeal to justice (rights) and compassion, but on behalf of the foetus. They argue that the foetus may have rights:

→ To fulfil the potential it has to life.
→ To the life it already possesses.
→ Not to be killed.
→ To be fairly represented by an impartial third party (i.e. not the mother or father).
→ For its life – whatever its physical condition – to be considered valuable.

However, it is possible also to argue that the foetus also has the right:

→ To a life free of pain.
→ To a 'minimum quality' of life.
→ To be a wanted child.

This position would interestingly assert the case for the foetus's right *to be aborted* if it were likely that these conditions could not be met. Others might claim that even though the foetus may be a person, the rights of the mother take precedence as long as the foetus is not able to survive outside the mother's womb.

Useful quotations

*'I can think of few concepts more terrifying than saying that certain people are better off dead, and may therefore be killed **for their own good** . . . Most handicapped people are quite contented with the quality of their life'* (in John Stott, *New Issues Facing Christians Today* (1999)).

Action point

Read Judith Jarvis Thompson's article 'A Defence of Abortion' in which she argues the case of the famous violinist.

Exam question   answer: pages 177–8

'Every pregnant woman has the absolute right to choose to have an abortion.' Critically analyse this claim.   (30 mins)

Medical ethics (2)

Issues in medical ethics are constantly in the news as the boundaries continue to be drawn back and developments in gene therapy and patient care are made, and public awareness of right to life and right to die issues rise. The next generation will see patients being allowed greater choices over these and many other issues in medical ethics.

Euthanasia

Euthanasia refers to the termination of the lives of people suffering from great physical or mental handicap or a painful terminal illness. Those who support euthanasia say that it is an act of compassion and mercy, allowing a gentle and dignified death for those who are suffering. Those who argue against euthanasia say that the task of the doctor is to save life, not end it. Furthermore, if we allow the killing of the sick and elderly, such people may feel pressured to agree to die. There are five main types of euthanasia:

Active: the result of positive action on the part of a carer/doctor.
Passive: the termination of treatment that is prolonging the patient's life.
Voluntary: 'mercy killing' carried out at the express wish of the patient.
Involuntary: carried out without the express permission of the patient.
Assisted suicide: the provision of means and/or opportunity whereby a patient may terminate their life.

Support for euthanasia

Pain-free death: the assumption or expectation that death will be preceded by serious pain that can only be controlled to a limited extent by drugs gives rise to considerable support for euthanasia.
Death with dignity: many fear a prolonged death, drawn out by the application of medical technology with the express purpose of delaying death as long as possible. During this time, the patient may become increasingly dependent on others, and unable to control bodily and mental functions. An earlier death is frequently considered more desirable.
Social fears and pressures: the breakdown of traditional family structures which provides care for the elderly and ill has led to an increasing fear of the old and sick abandoned to a faceless and ill-equipped health service, or left alone to die. Medical advances too may encourage a philosophy in favour of euthanasia, as expensive, glamorous life-saving treatments are promoted way above palliative care, and yet which may ultimately prove futile. Where there is a desperate need for organs for transplantation, death may be encouraged while the body is still relatively healthy enough to harvest organs. A fear of dementia and the effects of Alzheimer's disease may encourage thoughts of euthanasia in patients and the elderly.

Useful quotations

'I will maintain the utmost respect for human life from its beginning, even under threat, and I will not use my medical knowledge contrary to the laws of humanity' (The Declaration of Geneva, September 1948 – the modern version of the Hippocratic Oath).

Useful quotations

'Euthanasia is the intentional killing by act or omission, of one whose life is deemed not worth living' (*The New Dictionary of Christian Ethics and Pastoral Theology* (1995)).

Terminology

The term euthanasia comes from the Greek words *eu-thanatos*, literally meaning easy death.

Example

The Hospice Movement exists to care for terminal patients and to educate the public and the medical profession in alternatives other than euthanasia.

Checkpoint 1

What is a living will?

Implications of euthanasia

→ Even patients in a persistent vegetative state have been known to recover. Not all illnesses diagnosed as terminal will end in death.
→ Some patients given a terminal prognosis, live significantly longer than anticipated, or recover entirely.
→ Not all terminal patients will face a painful, undignified death.

Embryo experimentation ●●●

Experimentation with embryos has enormous potential for eventually eliminating a huge range of inherited diseases and for identifying genetic traits that render an individual susceptible to particular illnesses, such as heart disease or cancer, and also for adding positive or desirable characteristics. In either case, it may be argued that human beings are meddling in matters that only belong to God. The biblical writers include prenatal life within the human community and God's knowledge and care extends to the foetus. At creation God commanded that man '*Be fruitful and multiply*' and he continues to bless man with the potential to fulfil that command. If it is thought that an embryo has life from the moment of fertilisation, then the following argument will apply:

P1 It is wrong to destroy human life.
P2 Embryos have human life.
C   It is wrong to destroy embryos.

Embryo research may be carried out in four main ways:

→ Research on human embryos that have been spontaneously aborted.
→ Research on embryos which have been produced as part of a fertility programme but which are surplus to requirements.
→ Research on embryos produced specifically for the purposes of research.
→ Research on specific embryos which will hopefully be returned to the mother after they have received gene therapy to replace defective genes.

Checkpoint 2

What are positive and negative eugenics?

Example

In Genesis 25:23, the struggle between Esau and Jacob in the womb is seen to prefigure the struggle they will have as adults.

Useful quotations

'*Surely I have been a sinner from birth, sinful from the time my mother conceived me*' (Psalm 51:4).

Action point

Watch the film *Gattaca*, which explores the consequences of a society in which genetic engineering is considered the norm.

Exam question answer: page 178

Critically assess the non-religious arguments concerning euthanasia.

(30 mins)

Environmental ethics

At the heart of the Christian attitude to the environment is the concept of stewardship. This is the view that the earth was created by God and given to human beings to care for and protect. It is also an ethical issue, since the state of the environment affects everyone living in it and decisions made concerning the environment have a widespread effect.

Pollution

Pollution is the contamination of the environment, damaging and spoiling it, so that it is no longer clean, healthy and able to provide the best possible conditions for humans and animals. Nothing on earth works independently as it is all an ecosystem in which everything depends on everything else and if one element of that cycle changes, everything in the cycle is eventually affected too. Increased technology constantly leads to the development of new products the manufacture of which often causes pollution. Most domestic waste cannot be recycled and is not biodegradable. Waste takes up space, spreads disease and releases dangerous chemicals into the environment. There are seven primary causes of pollution:

Land pollution – caused by dumping litter or household waste.
Air pollution – caused by smoke from industry and homes.
Water pollution – dumped sewage, oil or chemicals affect land, rivers, animals, birds and, ultimately, humans.
Noise pollution – loud and persistent noise from industry, loud music, traffic or aircraft causes great distress and reduces the value of property.
Acid rain – burning oil, coal and gas also releases more acid into the atmosphere so that rain becomes acidic and can burn the environment.
Radioactive pollution – produces nuclear waste, which is extremely dangerous to humans and animals.
Eutrophication – fertilisers and sewage disposal release large quantities of nitrogen into rivers and streams, encouraging plant growth and suffocating fish.

One of the major effects of pollution is the **greenhouse effect**. This is caused by burning coal and oil, releasing carbon dioxide into the air which acts like the glass of a greenhouse, allowing the sun's energy in, but not out. As a result, the temperature of the earth rises because trapped heat cannot escape and, consequently, the climate changes. Trees take in carbon dioxide, turning it into oxygen, which humans depend upon. However, because vast areas of tropical rainforest are being destroyed, there are fewer trees to deal with increasing levels of carbon dioxide.

Links

See pages 166–7 on animal rights, which also examines the concept of stewardship.

Examiner's secrets

Make sure that you maintain a strong link to religious ethics and ethical philosophy when answering questions on this topic.

Background

During the Industrial Revolution, when factories and manufacturing were developing rapidly, the advantages of these developments were more important than investigating the possible damage they could be causing and the extent of the damage could not be known or measured until many years later.

Terminology

Biodegradable goods break down naturally if buried or exposed.

Action point

List effects of global warming around the world.

Terminology

Trees not replaced causes deforestation, and so the soil in which they grew disappears and the land becomes desertified.

Background

Global organisations, such as McDonald's, are thought to be guilty of an irresponsible attitude to the environment, encouraging the destruction of forest and prairie areas to increase grazing, ultimately leading to the production of unhealthy fast food products.

Natural resources are provided by nature and can be divided into two types: renewable and non-renewable resources. **Non-renewable resources** such as coal, gas and oil cannot be replaced once they are taken from the environment. Other products which are often wasted are made from non-renewable resources: metal and plastic. **Renewable resources** are not finite, but replace themselves after they have been used. They include wind power, solar power, wave power, and water power, as well as products such as sugar cane which can be used in place of petrol.

Food resources: in many parts of the world starvation and malnutrition cause disease and death. The underlying reasons are sometimes climactic – drought and crop spoilage – and sometimes because the country cannot afford to buy food from other countries. Often deforested land is reused to grow crops, but with little success, or the land is turned over for grazing, so it loses any value it may have had to grow crops.

Religious attitudes to the environment

Creative responsibility to '*till the earth and keep it*' (Genesis 2:15) suggests that if man is to reap the benefits of the productive earth which God has given him, then he must take action himself. This is the principle of stewardship.

It is only after the fall that the task of tilling and keeping the land becomes a struggle (Genesis 3:17–18). Creation had originally been perfectly good, and would provide everything that humans needed to live well, but now it would become a challenge. However, Christians believe that they are called to reverse the effects of the fall where they can. Although perfection cannot be fully achieved until heaven, the parable of the talents suggests that each generation should leave the earth in a better condition than they found it.

Islam teaches that Muslims have been placed in a position of responsibility over the earth and its resources and have a duty to care for it according to Allah's principles.

The whole universe – humans, animals and the environment – are all in balance. One of the aspects on which humans will be judged on the Day of Judgement is how well they have carried out this responsibility. Islam also teaches that Adam was made a ruler or vice-regent over creation, to whom even the angels were subject: '*It is he who has made you custodians, inheritors of the earth*' (Surah 6:165).

Checkpoint 1

What problems are inherent in attempting to reduce the use of non-renewable resources?

Background

There is increasing concern about the prioritising of unhealthy foods in the developed world while LDCs are still struggling to provide a basic diet for much of its population. Farmers and producers in LDCs also provide basic resources to the Western manufacturers but get very little in return.

Useful quotations

'Although God put humans in charge of the resources of the universe, this power must be used with concern for the rights of neighbours and future generations' (The Catechism of the Catholic Church).

Useful quotations

'When I consider your heavens, the work of your fingers . . . what is man that you are mindful of him? You made him a little lower than the heavenly beings . . . You made him rule over the work of your hands; you put everything under his feet' (Psalm 8:3–6).

Action point

Read the parable of the talents in Luke 19 and see how it may relate to the gift of the environment.

Checkpoint 2

Why are Christians sometimes concerned about the degree to which they should show responsibility for the environment?

Terminology

Although human needs take precedence, the principle of Tawhid means that there is a unity in creation which must be respected.

Exam question   answer: page 178

Examine and evaluate the claim that religious believers should make concern for the environment a priority.   (30 mins)

Finance and business ethics

There is a close relationship between religious ethics and the role which money is intended to play in the life of the believer. Four key areas emerge: spending and consumerism; borrowing, debt and gambling; giving and tithing; the ethical use of money.

Central to all these areas is the belief that all man's resources belong to God who lends them to man out of his beneficence and love and over which man is called to exercise the responsibility of good stewardship. The expectation upon traders and consumers is that they will respect the weak, worship God, shun immoral and fraudulent dealings and recognise their ultimate dependence on God. **John Wesley** offered five reasons why Christians should not be able to afford anything other than the basic necessities: God is the true source of wealth; Christians must account to God for how they have used their money; Christians are stewards of God's money; God gives money to Christians to pass on to those who need it; the purchase of luxuries is the equivalent of throwing money away, and of taking food and clothes from those who need them.

Spending and consumerism ●●●

In economic terms, consumerism refers to the using of goods, resources or services; ethically, it tends to be used to refer to the emergence of a society which is motivated by the ownership of goods and utilisation of resources beyond those required for human survival. Consumerism contributes to generating an increasingly unequal society as those with and those without the means to consume are sharply distinguished. Those unable to gain credit to enter the marketplace are marginalised, while those who are given credit facilities face the dangers of mounting debt. '*The practical outcome of this is that many families have reached for a standard of living that is years ahead of their income and savings. They have thereby become, in some real financial and psychological ways, servants of their possessions and slaves to their creditors*' (*Dictionary of Christian Ethics and Pastoral Theology*). Secondly, consumerism increases waste as the world's resources are depleted to meet consumer need. To object to the wastage of resources is influenced by the view that money, like the world's resources, is to be used wisely, as suggested by the parable of the talents (Luke 19:11–27).

Debt and gambling ●●●

Economically speaking, debt is the obligation to pay for prior receipt of goods, services or money, but it has important ethical implications. The power of the creditor to charge escalating levels of interest is easily abused, and the charging of interest at any rate (*riba*) is forbidden by Islam. The Old Testament expressly forbids adding to the burden of a needy human being and taught that money should be loaned to the

Background

Keith Tondeur identifies four dangers of wealth for the religious believer: it separates people from each other; makes them arrogant; encourages man to forget God; and makes it harder for them to trust in him.

Checkpoint 1

Explain the following terms: beneficence; stewardship; tithing; the biblical principle of Jubilee.

Useful quotations

'*Consumerism can be a hunger within us. The more we feed it the more it grows and the more hungry we become*' (Keith Tondeur, *Your Money and Your Life* (1996)).

Action point

Find out from the Internet or a journal the average level of debt for individuals in the UK.

Action point

Read Luke 19:11–27.

Useful quotations

The *New Dictionary of Christian Ethics and Pastoral Theology* (1995) suggests that credit and debt problems occur because people become '. . . *in some real financial and psychological ways, servants of their possessions and slaves to their creditors.*'

poor – to those in genuine hardship – but no interest charged, reflecting the love of God and compassion for their distress. Gambling has long been recognised as one of the major causes of debt, and religious ethicists are, in principle, opposed to it for many reasons. Although Aquinas permitted gambling as long as it was not motivated by greed, and some Christians find it acceptable on the grounds of the good results which it may generate, **William Temple** condemned it on four grounds: it glorifies chance; it disregards the principles of stewardship; it makes profit out of someone else's loss; and it appeals to covetousness.

Business ethics ●●●

The ethics of business are largely concerned with financial dealing, but can cover a wide range of issues including the rights and duties of the corporate world – whether businesses should have a responsibility towards public welfare, generating income for the community, and jobs in areas of low employment. Concerns may also focus on the relationship between employer and employee: sexual harassment, drug testing, rules about alcohol consumption and employee rights to privacy. Other areas of concern include the transferability of skills and ideas to others. More individuals and companies are supporting 'ethical consumerism' – refusing to buy products or raw material from companies with a poor record of human rights, or to borrow from investors who invest in unethical concerns. However, business is not just about providing for the needs of society, but doing so in order to create resources so that the needs of the owner and their employees may also be met. The profit motive is essentially self-interested, however, and for this reason ethicists tread carefully. Profit making has a strong ethical connotation, however, and the religious thinkers warn against obsession with the pursuit of profit.

However, as cautious as biblical teaching may be on the issue of profit making, it does not condemn it as the result of diligent endeavour, as exemplified by the woman of Proverbs 31: '*She considers a field and buys it; with the fruit of her hands she plants a vineyard. She girds her loins with strength and makes her arms strong. She perceives that her merchandise is profitable. Her lamp does not go out at night*' (31:16–18).

Useful quotations

In 1974 the Church's Council on Gambling defined it as '*an agreement between two parties whereby the transfer of something of value is made dependent upon an uncertain event, in such a way that one party will gain and the other will lose.*' (In David Atkinson and David Field (eds), *New Dictionary of Christian Ethics and Pastoral Theology* (1995)).

Background

The Islamic Bank of Britain has recently been established, which, working on the strictest Shariah principles, enables Muslims to do business with banks without incurring interest.

Example

An advertising executive moving to another company may be forbidden by contract to take any clients from his old company with him.

Checkpoint 2

Analyse this problem from the perspective of religious ethics:
Someone in sales is up against some very tough quarterly objectives, but she can make them by concealing from a customer that the product he's interested in will be made obsolete by a new line in six months. Should she do it?

Exam question   answer: page 178

Why is profit making in business an issue of ethical concern?   (30 mins)

Animal rights

The role of animals is often a difficult one for religious believers, since they have to find a balance between recognising animals as fellow creatures made by and loved by God, and maintaining the order of creation in which humans were placed above the rest of creation.

Do animals have rights?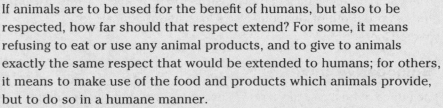

If animals are to be used for the benefit of humans, but also to be respected, how far should that respect extend? For some, it means refusing to eat or use any animal products, and to give to animals exactly the same respect that would be extended to humans; for others, it means to make use of the food and products which animals provide, but to do so in a humane manner.

If animals have rights, it means that humans also have responsibilities to protect those rights and to claim them on their behalf. We grant rights to many humans who are not able to express them or act on them themselves – children, the very old, and the mentally handicapped or incurably ill, for example. Having rights cannot therefore simply be a matter of being able to express them and, on these grounds alone, animals could be said to have rights. In the nineteenth century, **Jeremy Bentham** believed that the time would come when animals would be thought to have rights simply on the basis that they could feel pain. We believe that all humans have the right to be protected from pain because we know how it feels and that it is natural to avoid it. Why should the case not be the same for animals? In the twentieth century, the American philosopher **Peter Singer** used the term **speciesism**, to describe the attitude that humans are superior to animals, comparing it to racism, suggesting that it is just as wrong. If animals have rights then this must include the right to be recognised as intrinsically valuable in the same way.

However, some argue that only those who can make a choice can have rights, and since animals do not have choices in the moral sense of the term, they cannot have rights. Another argument is that while humans have reason – the ability to think, plan, look ahead, make judgements and assess the consequences of their actions – animals do not. Humans build sophisticated societies based on factors which go beyond the need to survive and seem to be uniquely capable of seeking a relationship with God and questioning their destiny beyond death. The crucial stage of human development, when homosapians developed a frontal lobe which enabled them to conjecture about the future, coincided with the development of a religious sense which enabled them to find hope and purpose in the midst of death and suffering. There is no evidence that this faculty also belongs to non-human animals.

Christians have traditionally taught that animals do not have the same rights as human beings. Humans were given 'dominion' (authority) over animals at creation and only humans have rights because they alone, not animals, were made in the image of God. Although farmers, scientists and those who care for animals should treat them kindly, it is legitimate to use them for the benefit of humans, particularly, as in the case of animal experimentation, when there is no alternative. **Augustine** argued that all commands concerning the welfare of animals were essentially for the benefit of humans. **Aquinas** claimed we have no duties to animals, and should only treat them with care so that cruel treatment does not carry over into cruel treatment of humans. **Descartes** regarded them as machines like clocks, which move and make sounds, but have no feelings.

Nevertheless, Jesus taught that God's care for animals and birds should reassure humans of his care for them and it is part of human calling to stewardship to care for animals, not to exploit them. Islam also teaches that animals are part of Allah's creation and as his Khalifahs, humans are required to respect them. The Qur'an allows the eating of halal animals for food, and the Shari'ah law permits the use of animals for experimentation. However, Islam forbids cruel farming methods such as battery farming, or force feeding animals to modify the flavour of their flesh or increase fat content. Most importantly, all animal products must be from animals which have been slaughtered sacrificially by a halal butcher.

Useful quotations

'God blessed them and said to them, "Be fruitful and multiply, and fill the earth and subdue it; and have dominion over the fish of the sea and over the birds of the air and over every living thing that moves upon the earth" ' (Genesis 1:28).

Checkpoint 2

Explain what is meant by this quotation: 'Food will not bring us close to God. We are no worse off if we do not eat, and no better off if we do. But take care that this liberty of yours does not somehow become a stumbling block to the weak' (1 Corinthians 8:8–9).

Useful quotations

'There is not a beast in the earth whose sustenance does not depend on Allah. He knows its dwelling and its resting place' (Surah 11:6).

Terminology

Khalifahs are stewards of Allah's creation.
Halal means permitted.

Exam question

answer: page 179

Consider the view that utilitarianism provides strong grounds to support animal experimentation. (30 mins)

Sexual ethics

Human sexuality is concerned not just with what people do, but who people actually are. It is at the heart of human behaviour and relationships and sexuality is an integral part of personality. The biblical emphasis is on man and woman united in marriage: *'For this reason a man will leave his father and mother and be united to his wife, and they will become one flesh'* (Genesis 2:24).

In the UK, the law regulates marriage relationships in a rather odd moral–legalistic way since sexual ethics are defined by morality rather than law, and yet although adultery is not illegal, it is grounds for a legal divorce.

Sex outside marriage

For Christians, the Bible states that sexual intercourse is for the marriage relationship only and that adultery and extra-marital relationships are forbidden. In the Ten Commandments it specifically states *'You shall not commit adultery'* (Exodus 20:14). Any behaviour that breaks the links between sex, personhood and relationship is sinful and should be avoided. However, many modern Christians believe this is too legalistic and sex should be seen in the context of loving, though not necessarily marital, relationships.

Marriage

Religious teaching defines marriage as an exclusive and lifelong binding relationship between a man and a woman that ends only with the death of one of the partners. For believers, the purpose of marriage is companionship, bodily union and the raising of children in a family setting.

Each partner has a specific role in the marriage. The man is the head of his wife, just as Christ is the head of the Church, while the wife is required to submit to her husband and to love and respect him.

Contraception

One of the most important purposes within Christian marriage is the procreation of children. The Roman Catholic Church has traditionally taken the view that every act of sexual intercourse must be open to the possibility of conception and that to use contraception is to prevent the transmission of a human life. However, today many Christian couples feel that contraception and family planning is the more responsible option.

Examiner's secrets

Avoid being judgemental in your discussion of sexual ethics. The exam is not the place to express personal opinions about such sensitive matters.

Checkpoint 1

Suggest another area of sexual morality which is not illegal, but may be considered wrong by some.

Useful quotations

'But among you there must not even be a hint of sexual immorality, nor any kind of impurity, or of greed, because these are improper for God's holy people' (Ephesians 5:3).
'The sexual act must take place exclusively within marriage. Outside marriage it always constitutes a grave sin' (Catechism of the Catholic Church).

Useful quotations

'Marriage is given, that husband and wife may comfort and help each other, living faithfully together in need and plenty, in sorrow and in joy . . . it is that they may have children and be blessed in caring for them and bringing them up in accordance with God's will' (The Church of England Service Book).

Divorce

A divorce is the legal termination of the marital relationship. The Bible teaches that divorce is contrary to God's wishes and that a marriage should be preserved as a holy relationship: '*To the married I give this command . . . A wife must not separate from her husband . . . And a husband must not divorce his wife*' (1 Corinthians 7:10–11). However, Matthew's Gospel suggests that divorce may be possible on the grounds of adultery: '*I tell you that anyone who divorces his wife, except for marital unfaithfulness, and marries another woman commits adultery*' (Matthew 19:9).

However, while agreeing that the marital relationship should ideally be lifelong, Christian groups are divided as to how strictly to interpret the biblical teaching on divorce and Christians will vary in how rigorously they apply biblical teaching. Many religious and secular ethicists argue that there are many ways in which human relationships of trust and commitment can be broken, and that it is unreasonable to refuse to allow a person to be divorced and released from a relationship that has ended.

Homosexuality

Some religious believers regard homosexuality as a sin and argue that homosexuals should not be welcomed into Christian fellowship, still less into the priesthood. For other Christians, however, homosexuals are just as much a part of God's creation as heterosexuals and should be just as welcome in the Church.

Whatever the origins of a homosexual orientation, religious believers are deeply divided over how to deal with it in the world and in the religious community. While the Lesbian and Gay Christian Movement argue that '*Human sexuality in all its richness is a gift from God gladly to be accepted, enjoyed and honoured . . .*' others claim that biblical teaching strictly forbids homosexual practice.

The 1998 Lambeth Conference of the Church of England established four perspectives on homosexuality:

→ Homosexuality is a disorder from which the Christian can seek deliverance.
→ Homosexual relationships should be celibate.
→ While exclusive homosexual relationships fall short of God's best for man, they are to be preferred over promiscuous ones.
→ The Church should fully accept homosexual partnerships and welcome homosexuals into the priesthood.

John Harris, in *The Value of Life*, maintains that homosexuality does not cause harm to society as a whole and, therefore, the individual's sexual relationships should be private and free from moral judgements.

Exam question   answer: page 179

Why is homosexuality such an important ethical issue for the Christian Church?   (30 mins)

Useful quotations

'*For the husband is the head of the wife as Christ is the head of the church. . . . Husbands, love your wives, just as Christ loved the church and gave himself up for her . . . husbands ought to love their wives as their own bodies. He who loves his wife loves himself*' (Ephesians 5:25, 28).
'*Now as the church submits to Christ, so also wives should submit to their husbands in everything . . . and the wife must respect her husband*' (Ephesians 5:24, 33).

Checkpoint 2

What, according to English law, are the ways in which it can be shown that a marriage has irretrievably broken down?

Action point

Find out how issues regarding homosexuality have become increasingly important in the Anglican Church over the last few years.

Useful quotations

'*If a man lies with a man as one lies with a woman, both of them have done what is detestable. They must be put to death, their blood will be on their own hands*' (Leviticus 20:13).
'*Neither the sexually immoral nor idolaters nor adulterers nor male prostitutes nor homosexual offenders . . . will inherit the kingdom of God*' (1 Corinthians 6:9–10).

War and peace

One of the most important functions of the state is to preserve the security of its citizens and the nation. In the religious context, going back to ancient times, people have expected God to protect them from their enemies. Yet in the Old Testament, God is frequently seen engaging in conflict against the enemies of his people – for instance, at the time of Moses, when God destroyed the Egyptian army by closing the Red Sea upon them.

Nonetheless, the biblical writers knew that the causes of war were rooted in human selfishness and greed. Wars are more likely to be caused by rivalry over land, wealth and international pride and status than over a genuine desire to fight evil with good. Thus, in the New Testament, Jesus refused to take the way of military power to achieve his goal, and challenged his disciples when they attempted to do so themselves. Jesus told his followers that they must expect to suffer injury and humiliation without resistance or anger. His concern was that his people should be prepared for the great spiritual battle between the people of God and the forces of evil.

The Bible does not answer clearly the central question of whether a religious believer should participate in warfare. The early Church adopted the general principles of non-retaliation and pacifism. However, one hundred years after Christianity had become the official religion of Rome the Emperor Constantine believed that the reluctance of Christians to fight was weakening Rome's defences and the Church was forced to say very clearly where exactly it stood. The solution was the Just War Theory.

The Just War Theory ●●●

Developed by Augustine, the Just War Theory proposed six conditions of going to war and three for conduct in war.

War must be in a just cause: to save life or protect human rights; to secure justice, remedy injustice; it must be defensive, not aggressive.

It must be declared by a competent authority: normally, this would be the government, who are the legitimate authority to declare war, although in the Islamic concept of *jihad*, the legitimate authority is that of a religious leader.

There must be comparison of justice on both sides: this is difficult to achieve, since both sides will claim that they are fighting a just cause.

There must be right intention: which must be as just as its cause, i.e. not undertaken in a spirit of hatred or revenge.

It must be a last resort: after all negotiation and non-military sanctions.

There should be a reasonable likelihood of success: there should be realistic prospects of its outcome resulting in a better state of affairs than would otherwise prevail.

Useful quotations

'Put your sword back into its place; for all who take the sword will perish by the sword' (Matthew 26:52).
'Do not resist one who is evil. But if anyone strikes you on the right cheek, turn to him the other also . . .' (Matthew 5:39).

Background

Paul wrote about the life of the believer in military terms: '. . . take up the shield of faith, with which you can extinguish all the flaming arrows of the evil one. Take the helmet of salvation and the sword of the Spirit, which is the word of God' (Ephesians 5:16–17).

Checkpoint 1

How did Jesus support pacifist principles on the Cross?

Terminology

The Jus ad Bellum rules govern going to war; the Jus in Bello rules govern conduct in war.

There should be a reasonable proportion between the injustice being fought and the suffering inflicted by war: the cause of justice must not be upheld by inflicting suffering on those the war was intending to protect.

Proportionality: the use of weapons must be proportional to the threat and only minimum force should be used.

Warfare must be discriminate: civilians must be protected as far as possible.

Pacifism ●●●

Absolute or **total pacifism** is the view that there should be no use of military force at all – whether or not the cause is just. Jesus did not rebel against the Romans and did not advocate rebellion or civil disobedience. In dealing with the world, Christians should meet their enemies not with hatred, but with kindness: '*Love your enemies and pray for those who persecute you*' (Matthew 5:44).

In Romans 13, Paul taught that the state should be respected as the bearer of God's authority to rule and that rebellion against the state is rebellion against God. Some pacifists take the view that violent struggle for justice is, sometimes, legitimate and may adopt **relative**, **selective** or **nuclear pacifism**. This is the view that innocent blood should not be shed and that civilians should not be killed in wars. Supporters claim that the role of the state is to protect civilians, not to kill them. The Church of England's report *The Church and the Bomb* declared: '*Such weapons cannot be used without harming non-combatants and could never be proportionate to the just cause and the aim of war.*'

In the Sermon on the Mount, Jesus promised God's blessing on peacemakers. Peacemaking is a divine activity which God's people are required to undertake, through prayer, public debate on issues of peace and war, and by making a positive stand for peace as a realistic and desirable goal.

Examiner's secrets

You should be able to evaluate each of these conditions for their strengths and weaknesses.

Useful quotations

'*True Christians use neither worldly sword nor engage in war, since among them taking human life has ceased entirely*' (Conrad Grebel in Peter Vardy and Paul Grosch, *The Puzzle of Ethics* (1994)).

Useful quotations

'*Consequently, he who rebels against the authority is rebelling against what God has instituted*' (Romans 13:2).

Checkpoint 2

Give an example of when this principle may be impossible for the religious believer to follow.

Useful quotations

'*Any act of war aimed indiscriminately at the destruction of entire cities or of extensive areas along with their population is a crime against God and man himself*' (Documents of Vatican 2).

Exam question answer: page 179

For what reasons has the Just War Theory been criticised? (30 mins)

Ethical language

The issues of ethical language (meta ethics) explore the problems raised by the use and function of ethical language, in particular examining the question of what is meant by the term 'good'. If it is impossible to arrive at a definitive understanding of this term, it may be that ethical statements are meaningless.

Normative ethics provides general theories about what is good and which attempt to offer guidance in specific situations while meta ethics analyses ethical language and examines in what sense, if any, moral statements convey truth. Cognitivism is the view that we can have moral knowledge and know descriptive moral facts and it is associated with moral realism, which asserts that moral attributes are properties that are a part of the physical world. As such ethical statements can be understood in the same way as other empirical (experience based) statements. Conversely, non-cognitivism supports the view that there is no moral knowledge, and moral statements cannot be said to be true or false because they are expressions of emotion or opinion. Moral statements prescribe what people should do, but do not describe facts.

The naturalistic fallacy or the is-ought gap ●●●

Naturalistic theories of ethics attempt to define good in terms of something which can be identified in the world or in human nature – for example, claiming that what is natural *is* good, or what makes us happy, fit or healthy. If we adopt this approach we effectively move to turn an *is* into an *ought*. **G.E. Moore** argued that we cannot identify morality with any other concept, such as happiness, because any attempt to do so will not be able to accommodate the full measure of that concept and so will always be inadequate. **David Hume** observed that there is nothing in a descriptive ('is') statement that allows us to proceed from what people *actually* do (a factual statement) to making a rule about what people *ought* to do (a value judgement) because they attempt to describe a situation which logically dictates what an individual is then obliged to do.

The naturalistic fallacy highlights the problem of the open-ended question: the view that statements are valid if they are not susceptible to the open question. For example, if goodness is pleasure, we might ask, 'Is it good to give people pleasure?' but since the answer to this could be yes or no, then goodness is not pleasure.

Intuitionism

G.E. Moore argued that 'good' can be defined no more successfully than 'yellow'. If we are asked to define yellow we can only define it in terms of something else which possesses what we consider to be the quality or characteristics of yellow. We give examples of yellow and yellow things, but we cannot define yellow itself. Instead, we have an intuition of yellow. In the same way, ethical values cannot therefore be defined, but are self-evident and can be known only directly by intuition. Certain attitudes or behavioural traits are perceived to be good, such as justice or love, but not because they are naturally so. Moore argued that goodness resists definition because people can have different moral opinions without logical contradiction, and yet there is a remarkable similarity in the way in which people reach moral conclusions and even in the conclusions they draw. An inner sense directs humans to know what is right or wrong but, as Moore argued, *'If I am asked, "What is good?" my answer is that good is good, and that is the end of the matter.'* (*Principia Ethica* (2004))

Emotivism

The emotive theory of ethics stems from the work of the Logical Positivists who sought to do away with all metaphysical language, which they deemed to be beyond empirical verification and thereby meaningless. It argues that if we make a claim such as 'Stealing is wrong' this is not to make a value judgement based on an objective point of reference, but rather we are simply saying 'I don't approve of stealing', or more colloquially, 'Stealing – boo!' **A.J. Ayer** reduced all moral talk to an expression of the speaker's feelings and maintained that to say, for example, 'Stealing is wrong' is an emotive, not a descriptive, statement. Ethical claims were not designed to make factual claims but to invoke certain emotional responses in the hearer and so what they mean is less important than what they accomplish. No matter how many reasons I may give for why I think stealing is wrong (or right) it is still fundamentally an expression of my opinion.

Checkpoint 2

What is Hume's Fork?

Useful quotations

Alastair MacIntyre observes: *'Emotivism rests upon a claim that every attempt, whether past or present, to provide a rational justification for an objective morality has in fact failed.'*

Background

A.J. Ayer developed emotivism in his book *Language, Truth and Logic*.

Exam question   answer: page 179

Examine and critically assess the view that there are no moral facts.

(45 mins)

Ethical concepts

An examination of ethical concepts can include many issues, at the heart of which is whether ethics is absolute or relative.

Absolutism or moral objectivity

Absolutism is commonly associated with **deontology**, a term which comes from the Greek *deontos* meaning 'duty'. Deontological ethical theories are concerned with examining the motivation for an act, not its consequences, and upon that basis establishing whether it is a morally right action. Deontological ethicists take the view that moral principles can be established *a priori* – that is, without experience. They are independent of experience because they are **inherently right**, irrespective of the outcome. A deontologist will maintain that there exists an **absolute** or **objective moral law** or code which can be discerned without reference to any hypothetical consequences, but which is always and intrinsically right. If something is absolute then it is right in all circumstances and for all people, irrespective of the likely outcome.

This is clearly quite different to a teleological approach to ethics, which adopts a more (although not exclusively) relativist approach and is concerned with **ends** rather than **means**. This view can also be termed hard universalism, which claims there is one universal moral code and does not acknowledge even the possibility of there being more than one set of morals. It is at the opposite end of the spectrum to **moral nihilism**, which claims that there are no moral truths. Taking an absolutist approach makes it possible to evaluate moral actions in a critical way, since if an individual or group is not conforming to the recognised absolute standard or law they can justifiably be condemned for it. However, this depends entirely on societies and individuals coming to an agreement as to what constitutes absolute morality, and that it is more than just a matter of personal preference or subjective opinion.

Relativism or moral subjectivity

Moral relativism argues that moral values are grounded in social custom. The principle holds that there are no absolute universal standards but that whether or not it is right for an individual to act in a certain way depends on, or is relative to, the society to which they belong. Moral judgements are therefore true or false relative to the particular moral framework of the speaker's community. Moral diversity

Checkpoint 1

Identify two absolutist moral claims and the basis for their supposed truth.

Background

Moral relativism should not be confused with ethical relativism, which holds that morality can be shared but only between closely-knit groups sharing a moral code and committed to a common action, e.g. an ethnic minority in a hostile situation.

is explained by the fact that moral beliefs are the product of different ways of life and are matters of opinion that vary from culture to culture (cultural relativism) or from person to person and in different situations (moral relativism). The view it reflects is rather that it is not possible or acceptable to judge the views or practices of any culture because there is no overriding standard against which it can be judged.

There are several key problems associated with relativism. There is no point to moral debate since opposing moral claims can be both true and false, relative to the culture from which they emerge, and it offers no room for social reform which would be seen to be posing a challenge to the norms of society. **J.L. Mackie** observed that the morality of individuals tends to be shaped by their society, not the other way round, and that although individuals are inclined to think that there is an objective standard of goodness, this reflects nothing more than a psychological need to find such a standard. *Moral subjectivism* is sometimes considered a sub-category of moral relativism, claiming that people are right in their own way. This is exceptionally tolerant but cannot solve moral conflicts since any individual moral stance is considered equally valid. Arguably, relativists fail to recognise the similarities between the morality of different cultures and place too much emphasis on the variations.

Moral descriptivism and prescriptivism ●●●

An example of *ethical descriptivism* is *naturalism*, which asserts that moral value is a real, objective property of the natural (physical) world – hence a moral judgement is either true or false, depending on the facts of the world as it exists. *Moral prescriptivism* describes the theory that moral utterances have no truth value but prescribe attitudes to others and express the conviction of the speaker.

Moral particularism claims that there are no defensible moral principles, and moral thought does not consist in the application of moral principles to cases. Rather, the perfect moral judge would need far more than a grasp on an appropriate range of principles and the ability to apply them. Moral principles are, at best, crutches that a morally sensitive person would not require and, in themselves, they may lead people to make errors in moral reasoning.

Checkpoint 2

Give two examples of moral situations which may be best judged relatively.

Action point

Identify a moral dilemma and suggest how it may be tackled by an absolutist and a relativist.

Examiner's secrets

These terms are crucial, because they identify the different ways in which people make moral decisions and judge the moral choices of others. They underline the reason why there is so much moral debate and disagreement.

Exam question   answer: page 180

Critically assess the view that ethical language is prescriptive.   (30 mins)

Answers
Religious ethics

God and morality

Checkpoints

1 Plato understood goodness as existing in its perfect and absolute form in the realm of the Forms. Aquinas similarly suggests that goodness originates in perfection, though he personalises the absolute Form in terms of God.
2 A categorical imperative is performed simply because the action is good and not because of the intended outcome. A hypothetical imperative is an action performed because of its likely consequences.

Exam question

If we argue that God is the source of moral law then behaving morally means obeying God's commands. However, there seem to be difficulties, even within religion, as to what constitutes morality – for instance, within the Christian community there is fierce debate over sexual ethics. Moreover, if God's commands determine what is morally right then actions which we would regard as morally wrong, e.g. killing homosexuals, could be seen to be right if God commanded them. In other words, the fact that God commands an action is not enough to make it morally right. However, if morality does not come from God, but from impersonal sources such as culture and the family, then our sense of right and wrong would appear to rest on nothing more than personal taste and social convention.

Utilitarianism

Checkpoints

1 Abolition of slavery, Factory Acts, introduction of free education, the postal service.
2 The majority have no authority to interfere with the freedom of the minority unless it is to prevent harm.

Exam question

Happiness is generally considered to be desirable and a goal which most humans strive after. An ethical theory such as utilitarianism is attractive because it places a high priority on human well-being and pleasure and it can be argued that an action which generates the most pleasure for the greatest number cannot be bad. Happiness generates other positive emotions and people are more likely to be inclined towards other good and beneficial actions when they are themselves experiencing happiness. However, happiness is often elusive and attempts to create happiness for the majority are not infallible. Furthermore, it may be argued that striving against adversity creates stronger moral characters than the pursuit of happiness. For those who support a morality rooted in religious teaching, the abandonment of divine rules and commands, which are arguably for the benefit of humankind, is a dangerous prospect. A version of strong rule utilitarianism would therefore be thought to be more acceptable.

Situation ethics

Checkpoints

1 Vietnam war, introduction of free and reliable contraception, sexual revolution, women established in the workplace, the invention of the teenager as a group with a clear identity and moral preferences.
2 Particularism, positivism, relativism and pragmatism.

Exam question

Situation ethics could be seen to have made a valuable contribution to late twentieth-century ethical debate, taking into account the political and social changes which had taken place since the Second World War. In a society in which sexual equality, sexual freedom and an increasing cosmopolitan atmosphere prevailed, the legalism of natural law and divine command theory was becoming increasingly oppressive. Social change was seen as positive and evolutionary and a new morality was necessary to accommodate this progression. However, situation ethics could also be seen as giving humans too much freedom to make subjective decisions without the guidance of rules and principles which have proved valuable over many generations. It requires people to make mature and responsible moral choices while providing only one criterion – that of *agape*. As the only intrinsic good it was presented as offering the best moral guidance in any situation. However, it is open to question whether people are capable of employing *agape* realistically and wisely.

Natural moral law

Checkpoints

1 Humanae Vitae (Human Life) 1968; Veritatis Splendor (Splendid Truth) 1993, Evangelium Vitae (Gospel of Life) 1995.
2 It is hypocritical and expedient as it attempts to justify what is essentially believed to be unjustifiable.

Exam question

Aqunias's theory of natural law, based on a strongly theistic foundation, depends on accepting a belief in the divine creation and ordering of the world, and of human beings within it. In a secular age, this has little appeal, and may be seen to be an unacceptable imposition on human freedom. Important choices such as whether to have children, to marry or to claim that the right to die is as important as the right to life could all be in conflict with principles of natural law. Furthermore, the advances made by scientific and medical research and the wider range of choices available to individuals mean that assumptions made in Aquinas's time are no longer necessarily applicable – that homosexuality is a deviation from the naturally 'correct' heterosexuality. However, natural law theory does identify codes which have universal appeal, such as the protection of life and human rights. Even if there may be occasional and acceptable exceptions, the principles still remain valid and important to a mature and stable society.

Kantian deontology

Checkpoints

1 For example, categorical imperative: 'Be kind to your friends'; hypothetical imperative: 'Be kind to your friends so they are generous to you'.
2 A statement of fact describes things which have objective truth in the real world. A statement of value ascribes moral value to those facts.

Exam question

Kant maintained that humans were torn between their desires and duty and only by living by rigorous principles of universalisability and the categorical imperative could they make the right moral choices. He believed that the Enlightenment offered the opportunity for humans to become more mature in their moral decision making, using reason alone without being guided by others – the Church, parents, superiors or the government. However, he feared the risks inherent in acting according to possible consequences, even lying to save a life since it was impossible to guarantee that the life would be saved. By contrast, James Rachels argued that to lie to save the life of an innocent person could not be considered an immoral action and that humans are likely to predict the consequences of our actions far more accurately than Kant feared. It is less likely that a person would *not* lie if they thought someone was placed in danger if they told the truth.

Authority, law and justice

Checkpoints

1 For example, societies which live under the Shariah law.
2 Society accepts the rule of law because it is ultimately beneficial.

Exam question

Natural law thinking maintains that reason should guide humans to what is right through their experience and observation of nature. Thus, human activities which fulfill the five purposes identified by Aquinas – to live, learn, reproduce, order society, and worship God – are permissible, while those which go against them are not. If natural law is

to be the principle on which social laws are based and enforced by the legitimate authority, they need to cohere with common reason and not infringe on the rights of human beings to exercise their freedom within reasonable bounds. Intuition may well lead us to support laws based on the right to life, the protection of the weak, and the encouragement of human potential through learning and social order. However, natural law thinking has been responsible for the persecution under the law of individuals whose natural predisposition may differ from the majority. Homosexuality, which may be genetically explained, was punishable under the law, and the savagery of punishments for relatively minor crimes against social order seems to go against our sense of what is just and humane – e.g. transportation for stealing a sheep.

Biblical ethics

Checkpoints

1 For example, debates about abortion, euthanasia, genetic engineering, living wills, medical treatment, capital punishment.
2 A covenant is a legal agreement that sets out the terms of a relationship between two parties.

Exam question

Ensure that you don't spend so long describing contemporary moral dilemmas that you don't get to grips with the application of biblical ethics to them. Select no more than three moral dilemmas which you can express very concisely and which focus on an issue that doesn't involve a lot of explaining. Every other candidate will be able to come up with moral dilemmas – only the good ones will be able to make clear links with biblical ethics and show knowledge of scholarship and text. Remember to allude to ethical theories which are rooted in biblical morality – natural law or situation ethics, for example – and avoid sweeping and inaccurate generalisations, such as 'Jesus taught people to ignore the law and just love everyone'.

Medical ethics (1)

Checkpoints

1 The continuation of the pregnancy would cause physical or emotional harm to the mother, her existing children or the foetus.
2 A utilitarian would examine the distribution of pleasure, goodness or happiness deriving from an abortion. A deontologist would work on an absolute principle which did not take circumstances into account.

Exam question

Make sure that you do not turn this question into a 'write all you know about abortion' question. The focus of the task is about the rights of the pregnant woman, and the best candidates will focus on that above all else. Once you have explained the thrust of the quotation – that the woman alone has authority to make decisions about her fertility and that no one else can criticise her choices – outline reasons why she may be thought to have an 'absolute right'. Comment on the term 'absolute' – it is an important technical term in ethics. What are the implications for others if the woman has this absolute right? Consider arguments from other perspectives too – who would take issue with this claim, and why? Come to a well balanced conclusion and aim to make reference to at least one or two secondary sources, such as Judith Jarvis Thompson.

Medical ethics (2)

Checkpoints

1 A living will is a document signed by the patient when in good health indicating that if they are ill or in an accident they do not want to be resuscitated or do not want extraordinary measures to be taken to extend their life.
2 Positive eugenics is when desirable characteristics are added to an embryo before implantation – good eyesight, intelligence or preferred physical features, for example. Negative eugenics is when undesirable features are removed from the embryo – predisposition to alcoholism, for example, or inherited diseases such as cystic fibrosis.

Exam question

Those who argue in favour of euthanasia often suggest that it is very expensive to provide medical care to those who are terminally ill or unlikely ever to recover. Given that money is limited, they say, it would be better to permit euthanasia and use the money that is saved to care for those who are less seriously ill. Similarly, the burden is lifted on families who may be obliged to go to great trouble and expense to care for dying relatives.

Those against, argue that this puts a monetary value on human life and that this is ethically wrong. Money should be channeled into hospices to enable the terminally sick to live out their days in comfort and dignity and to counsel them and their relatives to approach death positively. The view that euthanasia saves the health service money could be seen to be a very cynical way to approach life and death, which are under the control of God, not man.

Environmental ethics

Checkpoints

1 People need to be educated in recycling and ways in which to avoid environmental damage through dumping of waste and expenditure of energy. This requires that they lay aside convenience and are prepared to use time to protect the environment.
2 Because care for the environment and animals should not exceed care for human beings.

Exam question

Since most religions teach that the earth is precious and made by God out of his love and power, there seems to be no good reason for religious believers not putting concern for the environment high among their priorities. God's gifts in creation are for the benefit of humans, and not just for the present generation, so religious believers should consider it very important to ensure that future generations can look forward to an environment that is as beautiful and full of natural resources as we enjoy today. Already, it has been spoiled in many parts of the world, due to human greed and lack of understanding of how to care about the environment, but there is still a lot that religious believers can do to improve the state of the world and to preserve it for the future. However, some may argue that although care for the environment is a good and important thing, it should not be prioritised over and above other things. Some religious believers are concerned when they see people giving more care to environmental and animal rights campaigns than they think should be given, on the grounds that care for humans must always take precedence. Nevertheless, it is worth considering that unless we do take care of the environment, humans will suffer, so to make it a priority helps everyone either immediately or in the future and caring for the earth is, indirectly, caring for other human beings too.

Finance and business ethics

Checkpoints

1 Beneficence: goodness and generosity. The term is usually used to describe God's generosity towards humans. Stewardship: humans should take responsibility for and care for the resources God has provided. Tithing: the practice of giving 10% of gross income to the Church. Tithing is based on the instruction in Malachi 3:10 – 'Bring your tithes into the storehouse'. Jubilee: the principle that every 50 years all debts were cancelled, slaves were given the option of freedom and land was returned.
2 People should come before profit and an obsession with profit suggests a lack of dependence on God.

Exam question

Businesses argue that it is the responsibility of a business to make a profit for its owners and shareholders, and that it should do so in the most efficient commercial manner that it can. The problem is not about profit, but how the profit is made. Arguably, it becomes unethical when profit is made by exploiting workers and those in weak positions, such as farmers in developing countries who supply the rich companies of the West. It is also a matter of ethical concern if a company makes a profit through irresponsible use of resources and produces excessive waste and pollution. The profit motive can lead to people becoming greedy and ruthless and can hurt others as well as taking away their dependency on God.

Animal rights

Checkpoints

1 That which is due to an individual.
2 There is no moral value within Christianity about the eating or refraining from eating of any particular foods. Rather, the primary concern should be on not deliberately offending others if they have a moral objection to certain foods.

Exam question

A utilitarian perspective will consider whether animal experimentation contributes to the overall greater happiness of the majority and whether stopping it would reduce animal suffering at the expense of human well-being. Peter Singer, a utilitarian, claims that causing suffering to animals when an acceptable and practical alternative is possible is not morally justifiable and that when dealing with issues of suffering, animals should be treated as equal to humans. Eating meat, for example, is not necessary for human survival and the inconvenience caused to humans by ending the marketing of animals for food would be outweighed by the relief of suffering to animals. However, it is also possible to argue from the utilitarian perspective that animal experimentation is a necessary evil to prevent large-scale human suffering. Animals used to test cures for illnesses which can kill thousands of humans is always justified although this requires us to take a gamble. Some animals will still suffer in order to test cures which will not be used, but this is a risk worth taking.

Sexual ethics

Checkpoints

1 For example, homosexuality is considered morally wrong by some Christians and most Muslims, but is no longer illegal in the UK.
2 Desertion; adultery; unreasonable behaviour; separation for two (with mutual consent) or five years (one partner only can initiate divorce).

Exam question

The dilemma for the Christian Church is that the Bible seems to suggest that all homosexual acts are prohibited, and many religious believers feel that homosexuality is a sinful state. In particular, there are serious issues concerning whether or not homosexuals should be allowed to become priests. Other religious believers feel that homosexuals should be treated in the same way as heterosexuals because they are just as much made in the image of God. The Christian Church has attempted to compromise, for example, by allowing homosexuals to become priests in the Church of England as long as they are celibate. Some modern scholars, however, have suggested that a person's sexual relationships should be seen as a private matter anyway, and are not the business of the Church.

War and peace

Checkpoints

1 He forgave those who crucified him.
2 If the governing authorities are demanding morally wrong acts or supporting principles which violate Christian beliefs.

Exam question

The Just War Theory has been criticised because it seems to be impractical when faced with the harsh realities of conflict, and it can offer no guarantee of success. The realities are that wars are fuelled by emotions which cannot easily be controlled, and human error means that the innocent will always suffer despite best intentions. The theory offers no help in the case of nuclear war since the weaponry cannot be used proportionately or discriminately. On the purely ethical level, as a theory it can be applied to both sides engaged in conflict, with apparent equal validity. So, whose side is justice, and arguably God, on?

Examiner's secrets

Have some accurate and up-to-date facts about a contemporary conflict at hand ready to link relevantly to the Just War Theory.

Ethical language

Checkpoints

1 For example: utilitarianism – assumes that happiness equates with goodness; natural law assumes that what is natural and created by God is good; Kantian deontology assumes that *a priori* duties are the only intrinsic good. All move from an observation to a prescription.
2 He categorised language as being either analytic or synthetic. Analytic statements explain non-empirical relations of ideas, while synthetic statements explain matters of fact and are derived from empirical experience.

Exam question

This view may be expressed by an emotivist, on the grounds that ethical statements are nothing more than expressions of opinion or preference. Since they cannot be empirically verified they contain no factual basis and are meaningless if assumed to be assertions. Rather, ethical statements serve a different function, and may be intended to persuade or to influence. They belong to the form of life of the speaker and cohere with other, related beliefs which they hold. They are non-cognitive statements. However, an absolutist would argue that moral facts can be known and identified through use of reason or experience. These facts are universalisable and available to all. An intuitionist would also claim that we can know moral facts, although we intuit them rather than know them by definition. Hence, we cannot say 'Good is doing our duty', but we can intuit that acting dutifully is sometimes the right thing to do.

Ethical concepts

Checkpoints

1 For example, 'Abortion is always wrong because it violates the sanctity of life' or 'Faithfulness to a marriage partner is always right because marriage creates a supernatural bond created by God'.
2 For example, food laws, abortion, euthanasia, female circumcision.

Exam question

Prescriptive language involves commands which inform the hearer what the speaker expects them to do. Ethical language may be viewed as prescriptive even if it does not express a direct command. 'Abortion is wrong' effectively instructs the hearer, 'Do not have an abortion'. 'It is good to give to the poor' encourages the hearer to give. Kantian deontology works on the assumption that reason will guide all men to do their duty and act according to a categorical imperative motivated by a good will. While the emotivist argued that moral statements are expressions of feelings, R.M. Hare claimed that they are imperatives which work in the same way as other non-moral commands, such as 'Hurry up'. However, ethical terms are also descriptive. 'Good' or 'wrong' are used to describe the characteristics of a person or action, but they do not always serve as imperatives. 'The sea is good for swimming' does not prescribe a moral action. Furthermore, even if someone is described as having 'good' qualities, it does not necessarily mean that we are prescribing them for everyone else.

Revision checklist
Religious ethics

By the end of this chapter you should be able to:		
1 Have confirmed your knowledge and understanding of Utilitarianism.	Confident	Not confident. **Revise** pages 144–5
2 Be aware of the arguments for and against the relationship between God and Morality.	Confident	Not confident. **Revise** pages 146–7
3 Understand and evaluate the role of Situation Ethics as an ethical theory.	Confident	Not confident. **Revise** pages 148–9
4 Be clear about the key features of Natural Law.	Confident	Not confident. **Revise** pages 150–51
5 Have an understanding of Deontology as an approach to ethical decision making.	Confident	Not confident. **Revise** pages 152–3
6 Be able to discuss Justice, Law and Authority in relation to applied ethics.	Confident	Not confident. **Revise** pages 154–5
7 Have gained further knowledge of Biblical Ethics.	Confident	Not confident. **Revise** pages 156–7
8 Understand and evaluate the key issues raised by Medical Ethics.	Confident	Not confident. **Revise** pages 158–61
9 Have gained confidence in dealing with issues of Environmental Ethics.	Confident	Not confident. **Revise** pages 162–3
10 Understand the key areas of concern in Business Ethics.	Confident	Not confident. **Revise** pages 164–5
11 Know, understand and evaluate the ethical problems raised by Animal Rights.	Confident	Not confident. **Revise** pages 166–7
12 Be able to discuss debates within Sexual Ethics.	Confident	Not confident. **Revise** pages 168–9
13 Have a secure knowledge and understanding of the ethics of war and peace.	Confident	Not confident. **Revise** pages 170–71
14 Deal confidently with topics related to Ethical Language.	Confident	Not confident. **Revise** pages 172–3
15 Understand the fundamental Ethical Concepts underlying ethical debate.	Confident	Not confident. **Revise** pages 174–5

This chapter helps you to maximise your chances in the exam by developing key skills and techniques over the course of your studies. You need to take a long-term approach, not relying only on last minute cramming of basic facts. AS and A level exams demand more than that in order to fulfil all the assessment objectives which include evaluation as well as an understanding of basic information. Practise the equally important skills of processing and recalling information, applying it to questions and writing to time – all are necessary to achieve high grades.

Exam themes

You can obtain a copy of your exam specification and copies of past exam papers from the board's publications department or by downloading the specification from the board's website.

OCR (Oxford, Cambridge and Royal Society of Arts)
9 Hills Road, Cambridge, CB2 1PB – www.ocr.org.uk

AQA (Assessment and Qualifications Alliance)
Publications Department, Stag Hill House, Guildford,
Surrey, GU2 7XJ – www.aqa.org.uk

EDEXCEL
190 High Holborn, London, WC1V 7BH – www.edexcel.org.uk

Topic checklist

AS ○ A2 ●	OCR	AQA	EDEXCEL
The aims of AS and A2 Religious Studies qualifications	○●	○●	○●
Assessment objectives and trigger words	○●	○●	○●
Benefiting from your lessons	○●	○●	○●
The exam	○●	○●	○●

The aims of AS and A2 Religious Studies qualifications

Example

A synoptic question at A2 is designed to draw links together. The Edexcel specification describes its aim to *'draw together your knowledge and understanding of the connections between different modules from across your full Advanced GCE programme of study.'*

Examiner's secrets

If you follow the instructions you are given, are conscientious, thorough and communicate with your teacher, there is no reason why you – or anyone – should not do well.

Examiner's secrets

It's not just down to being clever. The skills you need in the exam are not just those the quick-thinking or opinionated students demonstrate in class. You need to be able to sustain developed arguments in writing and to have learnt the background material before expressing your opinion.

AS and A2 qualifications consist of three modules, which may include a coursework unit. Each module examines a specific discipline within Religious Studies and all specifications allow for a considerable diversity of options and at A2 you will be required to demonstrate your awareness of how the different topics interlink and overlap.

There are three main aims of the Religious Studies specifications.

Develop an interest in and an enthusiasm for a rigorous study of religion

If you are interested in and enthusiastic about your academic studies you will do better in the exam, but you will take away from this subject something that I don't think you can from many others. It has real 'value added' features, exploring aspects of human life and existence which are of perennial interest to virtually everyone who thinks about the world and our place in it. A rigorous study is one which involves being critical in the best possible sense of the word: analysing and evaluating the views of others and substantiating your own. If you are not prepared to have your own assumptions challenged in a safe and supportive environment, then Religious Studies is not for you! You may not come away from it with your views changed, but you will have had the opportunity to evaluate them against those of scholars past and present, and those of your teachers and classmates.

Treat the subject as an academic discipline by developing knowledge and understanding appropriate to a specialist study of religion

This should grow out of undertaking a rigorous study of religion. In the bad old days, folk thought that RE or Scripture was a safety net for those who were not very academic and who needed an easy option. Compulsory study of it in the earlier years at school did not always encourage students to see it as a valuable academic discipline to be pursued in the later stages of their school career. That has all changed! AS and A2 students will be more than aware of the academic rigour necessary to do well in this subject: knowledge of the contribution of scholars to the subject and an awareness of what enormous diversity there is in the range of views offered. The discipline is dependent on the skills developed in many others: language, history, philosophical debate in its wider context, and literature. No one would study the works of Shakespeare without recognising it as an 'academic discipline' so why should not this also apply to religious literature? The disciplined scholar relates everything to the question, alluding to narrative and text, rather than giving a blow-by-blow account of it in a way which may or may not be relevant, and their responses are ordered and structured and lead an argument to its logical conclusion.

Use an enquiring, critical and empathetic approach to the study of religion

The enquiring scholar seeks answers to questions of perennial importance, critically examining them before deciding which they believe to be the most convincing or effective, but not rejecting the views of others without recognising that they are of great importance to them. Religious and ethical views make a difference to the way in which people lead their lives and the scholar must therefore understand why they are held, even if they are not in agreement with them. We need to be aware of the historical, social and cultural influences on the way ideas have developed and of how the past leaves a legacy to the future. There are no 'right' conclusions to reach, but you will gain more credit for recognising the impossibility of definitiveness than for attempting to reach a dogmatic and unempathetic conclusion.

Don't forget that people are there to help you: you need never feel alone in your quest for a good A level grade. Every single member of staff at your school is on the same side as you, even if it doesn't always feel like it, but there are also other ways of getting help. Look out for revision courses and one-day or residential conferences, and encourage your teacher to attend exam board meetings. Everyone wants you to do well!

Watch out!

Narrative means storytelling and this is a particular risk when dealing with biblical material.

Action point

Make sure that you are aware of the contemporary setting of all the thinkers you refer to in your exam.

Assessment objectives and trigger words

Assessment objectives broadly fall into two categories:

AO1 – Knowledge and understanding.
AO2 – Critical argument and justification of a point of view.

Action point

Check past papers to make sure you can recognise AO1 and AO2 directed questions.

Terminology

Critical argument and justification of a point of view is evaluation. This is the most challenging skill in the exam, but the one which will ensure that you enter the higher grade bands.

More than 50% of assessment is concerned with the first objective, but you will not be able to move into the higher grade bands if you do not demonstrate your ability to fulfil the requirements of AO2. You will demonstrate that you have fulfilled the objectives by the acquisition of knowledge and the deployment of skills. Hence, you need to:

Acquire knowledge and understanding of:

→ key concepts within the chosen areas of study and how they are expressed in texts, writings and practices
→ the contribution of significant people, traditions and movements
→ religious language and terminology
→ major issues and questions arising
→ the relationship between the areas of study and other specified aspects of human experience.

Develop the following skills:

→ recall, select, and deploy knowledge
→ identify, investigate and analyse questions and issues arising from it
→ use appropriate and correct language and terminology
→ interpret and evaluate relevant concepts
→ communicate, using reasoned argument substantiated by evidence
→ make connections between areas of study and other aspects of experience.

As you move from AS to A2 you will be expected to demonstrate a wider range and depth of knowledge and understanding and a greater maturity of thought and expression, so the weighting of the objectives shifts as you move to A2 and more marks are proportionally credited to AO2 than AO1.

Trigger words

The use of trigger words in questions enables you to identify the particular skills you are required to deploy. AO1 trigger words invite you to demonstrate your knowledge and understanding, while AO2 trigger words invite you to evaluate that knowledge. Words you might expect to see in questions may include:

AO1 trigger words: describe; examine; identify; outline; select; what; how; illustrate; for what reasons; give an account of; in what ways; analyse; clarify; compare and contrast; differentiate; distinguish between; define; explain.

AO2 trigger words: comment on; consider; how far; to what extent; why; assess; discuss; consider critically; criticise; evaluate; interpret; justify.

You need to be aware of the difference between 'giving an account of' and 'considering critically'. To give an account you draw essentially on your knowledge, which you may then be required to evaluate through 'considering critically'. Considering critically, or assessing, or commenting on, involves drawing conclusions about the significance and value of what you have learnt. There are certain phrases which you may find useful to do this: 'This is important because'; 'The most significant is . . . because'; 'However . . .'; 'On the other hand . . .'; 'It is likely that . . . because'; Therefore . . .'; 'Nevertheless . . .'; 'The implications of this are . . .' As you work, keep asking yourself 'why is this relevant to my answer?' and 'what are the implications of this view/issue?' Don't go on to automatic pilot, otherwise you will simply narrate facts or, worse, story!

Action point

Practise writing evaluative sentences using the phrases suggested here.

Examiner's secrets

Although only a relatively low proportion of your marks are for AO2, it is impossible to obtain an A grade unless you score something for AO2.

Watch out!

Evaluation or AO2 is just as important in coursework and synoptic essays as in other parts of your exam.

Benefiting from your lessons

Example

Evaluative questioning includes questions such as:
'Am I right in thinking that you believe X to be right because of Y?'

Action point

Ask your teacher to explain to you the principles of marking as laid down by the exam board and how they would be applied to a homework essay you have completed.

However good your teacher may be, in the end, they cannot go into the exam for you. While they can give you information and guide you in the best practice for utilising it in the exam, you have to make sure you have learnt it and developed an effective examination technique.

Lessons

It is initially your teacher's responsibility to select the right information for your needs, but you need to take responsibility for the way you receive it and what you do with it after the class is over. So, develop good classroom habits. Ask questions about the material. Ask questions about the implications of the material the teacher is covering and about how it relates to other aspects of the syllabus. Your classes also give you the opportunity to practise the vital skill of evaluation. You will hear many views expressed that might be quite different from your own, which you can – in an empathetic (i.e. non-confrontational) way – evaluate. Be prepared in turn for your views to be evaluated by others, and to explain why you hold them: 'I think that Z is wrong because if you take Y into consideration, the conclusion cannot be X.'

Homework tasks

Because you have to write in the examination – indeed, the written word is the only vehicle you will have for assessment – you must use homework tasks as an essential tool for refining your written skills. Although they may take many forms, one of the most useful things you should be doing for homework is practising past questions which will enable you to be totally at home with the way your board and specification requires you to use the knowledge and understanding you have gained. Every homework exercise is an opportunity to learn the topic you're working on, so don't just stick it in the back of your file when it's marked!

Independent learning and consolidation

Even the best teacher is not going to cover absolutely everything in the class time available to them, although they will use that time to provide you with virtually everything you need to do well in the exam. However, it is the time you put in outside the classroom which will be decisive. You may read an article that no one else in your class has seen, watch a television programme, or simply just go over your class notes one more time and in so doing finally understand a difficult area. There is no doubt that the top grades usually go to candidates who are prepared to do something extra than attend class and do the work set.

Revision for the examination

It is never too early to start revision. From the moment the first topic has been completed in class you should be making concise revision notes, learning quotations and making essay plans. If you leave it until the exams are looming you will only have time to get it into your short-term memory, and you will feel far less able to deal with the unexpected or to spend time in the exam ensuring that your written style is the best you can offer on the day. Revision techniques do, and indeed should, vary. Everybody learns and remembers differently, so don't be led into thinking that you should be doing it exactly the same way as everybody else. Experiment with a range of strategies but make sure they are multi-sensory. This means that you should involve as many of the appropriate senses into the learning process as possible. If you are just reading through the notes in your file you are using only one method – reading – and therefore only one channel to receive and process that information. Reading, making fresh notes, applying them to a question, writing it out again, repeating it orally to a friend, all contribute to the cumulative process of learning and establish the material more firmly in your memory.

As you prepare for the examination, make sure that you are absolutely certain about key issues such as the day and time of the exam! You may think this is silly, but I have marked an exam paper on which a candidate had written 'Sorry about this, but I only just found out my exam was today'. This is not just a failure on the part of the school (if, indeed, they hadn't told her!) but also a failure on her part not to make sure she did know the right day and time. Knowing dates well in advance enables you to make a revision plan, allocating specific tasks to each day as the exam approaches, so that your revision is never random or unplanned.

The best candidate can achieve a disappointing result if they don't work to time, writing one or two long answers but resorting to a plan, notes or a side-long offering for the others. If you have an hour and a half to answer two questions, that means 45 minutes per question, not an hour on one and half an hour on the other.

Action point

Check the TV listings every week for programmes which relate to Religious Studies. There are many, especially on Channel Four. Look on their website and on the BBC religion and ethics site.

Action point

Ask your teacher to help you make a revision grid to plan your revision.

Action point

Revise with a friend. You can help each other by testing and learning, as you learn from correcting their mistakes as well as getting your answers correct!

Examiner's secrets

You must practise exam questions to time and not just under homework conditions.

Watch out!

It is a myth that working late at night with music on in the background is the best way to prepare for an exam. You need to be able to concentrate and to be wide awake the next day.

The exam

Don't believe that the exam is something you can't control. If you have done the right preparation, the exam will be straightforward.

It's not all over till the fat lady sings, and so you don't have to be fatalistic about the exam. Keep in control and, even if the questions are not the ones you hoped would come up, you can think calmly and carefully and use the material you have learnt to relevantly answer the questions that are there! Do what you are asked and nothing else! Don't panic and leave early, but think. Read what you have written and check it over for silly mistakes and misspellings. Ignore what everyone else is doing, even if they leave the room, faint or cry, and don't spend time in pointless post mortems after the exam. What's done is done at that stage, and you need to have peace of mind to prepare for your next paper!

Myths

There are many famous myths about exams. Let's dispel some of them here!

The examiner will not mark my script if my writing is untidy
All exam scripts have to be marked and although untidy or eccentric writing slows the process down, it will not stop it being marked. If it's really bad the script will be passed to different senior examiners until a mark can be established. However, you can make life easier for everyone if you write with a good pen, leave lines between paragraphs, underline scholars and start a new essay on a new page. If your writing is really troublesome, and if it actually slows down your thinking process as well, then investigate the possibility of having an amanuensis or using a computer.

It's good to come up with your own ideas in the exam
Please don't! Or don't unless you have carefully thought them out a long time in advance and discussed them with your teacher. I was horrified to read an example of a real-life religious experience in one student's essay: a woman travelling on a train saw an advert for Courage beer and interpreted it as a message from God. They took a whole paragraph to describe this and gained no credit whatsoever! Another student quoted Oprah Winfrey as an authority on an ethical issue! I can't believe that their teacher had seen and approved these in advance.

Ethics is all common sense: you don't have to learn anything in advance
And we wonder why students often do badly at AS Ethics! Ethics is a highly academic discipline and you must know as many scholars and have as many well-learned factual and critical comments at your

fingertips as for any other aspect of Religious Studies. Don't fall back on the same tedious old examples, or rely on so-called real-life illustrations which take pages to relate. Real-life examples are not found on *EastEnders, Casualty or Holby City* either, whether or not your teacher (like me!) refers to them in class. Use broadsheet newspapers for good material, which you could then follow up on the Internet, but again, learn some discretion. As we know, the Internet contains some excellent material, and a lot that is not!

Scholars are all dead

Teachers and students get unnecessarily worried about this aspect of answering questions. First of all, most examiners will agree that a scholar is someone who has published a mainstream or specialist work. This means not your vicar's editorial in the church newsletter (however learned it is) or a pamphlet handed out on the street. However, this leaves a lot of other options open. Some teachers are nervous about citing authors of specialist A level textbooks as scholars. There is no need for anxiety here. A level textbooks are specialist resources written by experts: use them freely. Sometimes teachers have their favourite scholars who may have written books that are less well known. These are also fine to use. In fact, it would be nice to see some less familiar names cited in students' essays. In your own research and reading you may find out about a scholar that no one in your class has heard of before. Show your teacher what you have found and, as long as it reflects a considered, academic response, it will no doubt be suitable. Use scholars as servants to help you produce a coherent, well-supported essay and all the credit will go to you!

Examiners take marks away for mistakes

The exam-marking process is a positive one. We don't take marks away, we give marks, but if you don't say something mark-worthy, we can't give them – it's as simple as that. If you make mistakes, they won't be penalised, but they can't gain anything. Similarly, marks are not taken away for bad spelling, style or presentation, but if we can't get to the heart of what you're saying because it's muddled then you will miss out on the marks we are genuinely keen to give to you.

Examiner's secrets

Often the best, most senior examiners are marking 1000s of papers. Because they are very experienced they will mark them very accurately, but they have to mark them quickly. They don't have time to read them several times so you have to make everything very clear to help them credit you appropriately.

Watch out!

When you are preparing for the exam don't just read through material. Very little goes in this way. You have to be writing all the time.

Watch out!

Don't use the exam as an opportunity to take risks. It's the last opportunity to get it right so do what you've been told and don't think you know better than your teacher or the examiner!

Watch out!

When scripts come back to us for remarking, the mark rarely changes. Examiners tend to get it right! There are usually very good reasons for the marks you get so trust the system. It is not against you.

Select glossary

A posteriori   On the basis of experience

A priori   Without, or prior to, experience

Aesthetic argument   The argument that beauty in the universe requires an explanation

Agnosticism   Literally, without knowledge

Analogy   Making a comparison between two objects or situations in order to emphasise the similarities between them

Analytic statement   A statement which contains its full meaning within the word or phrase

Anthropic principle   The reason and purpose of the universe is to support human life

Anthropocentric   Centred on the needs and interests of man

Anthropomorphism   Likening a non-human being to man

Anti-realist   Subjectively true

Aseity   Possessing the essence of existence within itself

Atheism   Literally, without God

Atonement   God is made at one with man through the death of Jesus

Authority   Reliable, orthodox and truthful; power bestowed through receiving a divine commission

Big Bang cosmology   The theory that an enormous explosion started the universe around 15 billion years ago

Bliks   Unverifiable, unfalsifiable ways of looking at the world

Categorical imperative   An action performed for its own sake, out of duty, and not for any other motive or outcome: e.g. 'Be kind'

Church   The body of believers set aside and made holy for God's purposes

Cognitive (realist) language   Assertions which make factual claims about an objective reality

Cognitive language   Claims which refer to matters of factual, objective truth

Conscience   'The inner aspect of the life of the individual where a sense of what is right and wrong is developed'

Contingent   Liable to decay; dependent

Conversion   An experience which brings about a change

Corporate   Experiences which are shared by a group, usually those who share a common religious belief

Covenant   An agreement ratified between two parties

Creed   Approved statements of belief

De dicto   Of words

De re   In the nature of things

Demythologise   Remove the miraculous or mythological elements from narratives

Doctrinal   The body of beliefs held by the Church

Dualism   The belief that mind and body are separate entities

Ecumenism   An attempt to break down denominational divisions

Epistemic distance   A distance of knowledge, dimension or awareness

Equivocal   Same word use with different meanings

Eschatological   Concerned with the end of time

Euthrypho Dilemma   Is something good because God commands it, or does God command that which is good?

Evolution by natural selection   The scientific theory that the individuals within a species that are best adapted to their environment will survive to produce offspring, passing on favourable hereditary characteristics. All organisms share common ancestors and the universe as a whole is evolving

Ex nihilo   'Out of nothing'. Used to refer to God's activity in creation

Faith   Assumptions and a way of life not based on certainty gained from empirical testing or scientifically provable testimony

Falsification   The means of proving a statement false

Grace   God's underserved favour to humankind

Hard determinism   The view that all freedom is illusory

Holy   Sanctified, set aside for God's purposes

Hypothetical imperative   An action performed in order to bring about a specific or general goal: e.g. 'If you want to be liked, be kind to your friends'

Immanent   God known in his activity within the world

Immortality of the soul   The belief that the soul belongs to the realm of the eternal and can therefore exist after the death of the contingent body

Immutable   Unchanging and unchangeable

In intellectu   In the mind

In re In reality

Incarnate Becoming flesh

Inconsistent triad The philosophical problem of evil posed as a logical impossibility. God cannot be both all powerful and all good, and evil exist

Induction The method of reasoning which leads us to draw conclusions about the future on the basis of what we know of the past

Infinite Without limitations of time, space, knowledge, freedom or power

Interventionist An act which intervenes in the regular or expected pattern of things

Logical impossibility Something which is impossible because it defies reason

Logical necessity Something which must be the case or must apply

Logical positivism A school of philosophy which argues that something which cannot be verified or falsified by the use of sense experience, maths or logic is meaningless

Materialism The belief that mind and body cannot be separated and that each influences the other

Metaphysical freedom Being responsible for one's choices

Mysticism An experience in which the ultimate reality is vividly encountered

Myth A symbolic, approximate expression of truth

Natural law That which happens regularly within nature

Necessarily existent Cannot not exist

Non-cognitive (anti-realist) Language which serves other functions which are made meaningful by their context and other statements within that context

Non-cognitive language Non-factual claims

Non-realism or anti-realism The truth of our assertions about the world is not independent of our relation to the world and whether our claims are true or false is connected with how we establish whether they are true or false

Numinous An experience of that which is wholly other

Objective Claims which refer to external facts or values

Objective moral laws Codes of morality which have an empirical or factual basis

Ockham's Razor The principle that the simplest explanation is the most likely

Ontological Concerned with being

Paradigm Prevailing way of interpreting the world

Post mortem existence A continued life after the death of the physical body

Practical freedom Freedom to do what one wishes

Predicate An attribute or characteristics belonging to the description of a thing

Principle of credulity We should believe what people say unless compelled to do otherwise

Principle of testimony That people generally tell the truth

Privation An absence or lack

Probability The relative frequency or likelihood of an event taking place, or of circumstances unfolding in a particular way

Proof Incontrovertible evidence that something is the case

Providential A universe in which God foresees and controls future events in order to care for his creation

Qualification Redefining the nature of God in order to avoid the implications of the problem of evil

Rational argument Argument based on empirical evidence or reason

Realist Objectively true

Redemption The price of redeeming humankind from the power of sin

Reductio ad absurdum To reduce to an absurdity

Religious ambiguity The view that the universe does not provide overwhelming evidence of God's direct involvement, so it can be interpreted religiously or non-religiously

Resurrection The recreation of the physical body

Revealed theology A system of theology based on God's revelation to humankind and not on what humans can deduce through logic and reason

Scepticism An attitude of philosophical doubt; questioning the nature of reality or of language claims

Scientific realism Science provides us with a true picture of an independently existing reality

Soft determinism The view that I am free to perform an action as long as I am not coerced into doing it or prevented from doing it

Subjective   Claims which are based on personal preference

Summum bonum   The perfect state of affairs; virtue crowned with happiness

Symbol   A pattern or object which points to an invisible or metaphysical reality and participates in it

Synthetic statements   Those which require further clarification or explanation

Teleological   Concerned with end or purpose

Theodicy   A defence of God that offers reasons why God should permit evil to exist while not qualifying his nature

Transcendent   'Being beyond'. In the context of God, it is used to describe his being beyond and outside the world

Trinity   The doctrine that God is known in three persons, Father, Son and Holy Spirit, all equally God, undivided, and yet distinct

Univocal   Same word used with the same meaning

Verification   The means by which the truth of a statement is proven

Via negativa   Assertions which emphasise what God is not rather than making positive claims about him

Index

A posteriori 104
A priori 106
Abortion 158
Absolutism 174
Aesthetic Argument 102
Agape 149
Allegory of the Cave 132
Analogy 124
Analytic 106
Animal Rights 166
Anthropic Principle 103
Anthropomorphism 103
Anti-Realism 122
Aristotle 133
Atheism 120
Atonement 12, 88
Authority 154

Banquet, Parable of 56, 58
Baptism 11
Big Bang 131
Birth Narrative, Luke 54
Birth Narrative, Matthew 54
Black Theology 15
Blik 109
Blind Man, The 91
Bread of Life, I am the 90
Business Ethics 156

Calming of the Storm, The 61, 63
Categorical Imperative 110
Category Mistake 119
Christology 6
Cleansing of the Temple 70, 72, 78
Cognitive Language 122
Conscience 145
Consumerism 164
Contingency 104
Contraception 168
Cosmological Argument 104
Council of Chalcedon 7
Covenant 22, 24, 29, 38, 40, 43, 52
Creation 130
Critique of Religion, Psychological 121
Critique of Religion, Sociological 121

De dicto 107
Debt 164
Deductive 106
Demythologisation 123
Deontology 110, 152
Descriptivism 175
Design Argument 102
Deterrence 155

Discipleship 64, 69, 94
Divine Command 144
Divorce 169
Docetism 6
Double Effect 151
Dualism 118

Embryo experimentation 161
Emotivism 173
Environmental ethics 162
Epistemic Distance 113
Equality 155
Equivocal Language 124
Eschatology 67
Eternal Life 82
Ethical Language 172
Evangelicals 17
Eucharist 10
Euthanasia 160
Euthyphro Dilemma 110
Ex Nihilo 4
Exodus 24, 29

Falsification Principle 129
Feeding of the Five Thousand 90
Feminist Theology 15
Festivals 52
Foetus, Status of 158
Forms, Theory of 132
Fourth Gospel, Authorship & Date of 78
Fourth Gospel, Greek Influence 81
Fourth Gospel, Jewish Influence 81
Fourth Gospel, Prologue 84
Fourth Gospel, Purpose of 82
Free Will 115
Freedom 154

Gambling 164
Gate for the Sheep, I am the 91
Gnosticism 4
God, Creator 134
God, Goodness of 135
Good Shepherd, I am the 91
Grace 12, 85

Harm Principle 147, 154
Hedonic Calculus 146
High Priestly Prayer 94
Historical Jesus, The 8
Holy Spirit 69, 86, 93
Homosexuality 169
Hypothetical Imperative 152

Immortality of the soul 118
Inconsistent Triad 112

Intuitionism 173
Irenaean Theodicy 113

Jesus, Arrest of 71, 73, 94
Jesus, Crucifixion 74, 76, 95
Jesus, Resurrection of 75, 77, 95
Jesus, Trial of 71, 73, 94
John the Baptist 66, 85
Jus ad bellum 170
Jus in bello 170
Just War 170
Justice 154
Justification 13

Laity 16
Language Game Theory 128
Last Supper 70, 72, 92
Law of Moses 25, 29, 64
Law 25, 29, 85, 154
Liberation Theology 14
Life After Death 118
Life, Sanctity of 158
Light of the World, I am the 90
Liturgical worship 10
Logical positivism 126
Logos 81, 84

Marriage 10, 168
Medical Ethics 158, 160
Messiah 40, 53, 66
Meta-Ethics 172
Miracles 60, 116
Moral Argument 110
Moral Evil 112
Myth 123

Natural Evil 112
Natural Law, Moral 150
Naturalistic Fallacy 172
Nature, Laws of 116
Near Death Experience 118
Nicodemus, Conversation with 88
Non-cognitive Language 122
Numinous 108

Objectivity 174
Ockham's Razor 104, 117
Omnipotence 4, 112, 114
Ontological Argument 106
Ordination 10, 16
Orthodoxy 17
Outcast, The 68

Pacifism 174
Parables 56, 68
Paraclete 86, 93
Paralysed Man, The 60, 62

Passion Narrative, Luke 72
Passion Narrative, Mark 70
Passion Narrative, Matthew 70
Personal Identity 118
Pharisees 53
Plato 132
Pneuma 86
Pontius Pilate, Trial before 71, 73
Poor, The 14, 55, 68
Praise 67
Prayer 11, 67
Prima Facie duties 153
Principle of Credulity 109, 117
Principle of Testimony 109
Principle of Utility 146
Privation 112
Probability 163
Problem of Evil 112, 114
Process Theodicy 114
Proof 103
Providence 103
Punishment 155

Rehabilitation 154
Relativism 174
Religious Experience, Argument from 108
Religious Experience, Biblical Accounts of 108

Religious Experience, Types of 108
Religious Language 122, 124, 126, 128
Replica Theory 119
Resurrection and the Life, I am the 92
Resurrection Narrative, Fourth Gospel 95
Resurrection Narrative, Gospel of Luke 76
Resurrection Narrative, Gospel of Mark 75
Resurrection Narrative, Gospel of Matthew 75
Resurrection of the body 119
Retribution 154
Rich, The 68
Rights 155

Sacraments 10
Sadducees 53
Saints 16
Salvation 42, 66
Science and religion 130
Sermon on the Mount 157
Sermon on the Plain 316–318
Sexual relationships 168
Sin 12

Situation Ethics 148
Social Contract 155
Spirituality 17
Stewardship 163
Subjectivity 174
Suffering 5, 41
Summum Bonum 110
Symbol 122

Theodicy 112
Trinity, Doctrine of 6
Triumphal Entry 70, 72, 92
True Vine, I am the 93

Universalisability 152
Universe, Origins of 130
Univocal Language 124
Utilitarianism 146
Utilitarianism, Rule 146

Verification Principle 127
Via Negativa 124

War and Peace 170
Way, Truth and Life, I am the 93
Women, New Testament Presentation of 68, 86
Worship 10